THE SECOND AMERICAN REVOLUTION

THE STEVEN AND JANICE BROSE
LECTURES IN THE CIVIL WAR ERA

William A. Blair, editor

The Steven and Janice Brose Lectures in the Civil War Era
are published by the University of North Carolina Press in
association with the George and Ann Richards Civil War Era
Center at Penn State University. The series features books
based on public lectures by a distinguished scholar, delivered over a three-day period each fall, as well as edited volumes developed from public symposia. These books chart
new directions for research in the field and offer scholars
and general readers fresh perspectives on the Civil War era.

THE SECOND AMERICAN REVOLUTION

THE CIVIL WAR-ERA STRUGGLE OVER CUBA AND THE REBIRTH OF THE AMERICAN REPUBLIC

GREGORY P. DOWNS

THE UNIVERSITY OF NORTH CAROLINA PRESS

CHAPEL HILL

Manufactured in the United States of America
Designed by April Leidig
Set in Arnhem Pro by Copperline Book Services, Inc.

The University of North Carolina Press has been a member of
the Green Press Initiative since 2003.

Cover illustration: *Garroting of the Cuban Patriot General Goicouria,
at Havana, May 7, 1870.* From The New York Public Library.

Library of Congress Cataloging-in-Publication Data
Names: Downs, Gregory P., author.
Title: The second American Revolution : the Civil War–era struggle over
Cuba and the rebirth of the American republic / Gregory P. Downs.
Other titles: Steven and Janice Brose lectures in the Civil War era.
Description: Chapel Hill : The University of North Carolina Press, 2019. |
Series: The Steven and Janice Brose lectures in the Civil War era |
Includes bibliographical references and index.
Identifiers: LCCN 2019022664 | ISBN 9781469652733 (cloth) |
ISBN 9781469652740 (ebook)
Subjects: LCSH: Imperialism—History—19th century. | United States—
History—Civil War, 1861–1865—Influence. | Cuba—History—1810–1899. |
Cuba—Politics and government—19th century. | Atlantic Ocean Region—Politics
and government—19th century. | United States—Foreign relations—Spain. |
United States—Foreign relations—Cuba. | Spain—Foreign relations—
United States. | Cuba—Foreign relations—United States.
Classification: LCC E661.7 .D68 2019 | DDC 973.7—dc23
LC record available at https://lccn.loc.gov/2019022664

For Sophia and Gabby,
something else you can share
that you don't particularly
want to share

CONTENTS

ILLUSTRATIONS

ACKNOWLEDGMENTS

First, and foremost, this book is a product of, and a tribute to, two unusually imaginative historians once affiliated with Penn State University. My friend the late Tony Kaye encouraged me to think about the Brose Lectures as a chance to range more widely than I had done in my two monographs. To take risks. To risk foolishness. He meant it as a compliment. The only goal of living is to grow. I am sure, although Tony never explicitly said so, that he lobbied our mutual friend Bill Blair to issue the invitation for me to deliver the lectures over three days in October 2016. Bill, in his wise way, hoped to save me from some of my foolishness but to preserve that sense of high-wire riskiness. And he was delighted when I turned a lecture series on the Civil War era toward a discussion of Cuba, Spain, Mexico, and the U.S. Constitution. I became friends with these two scholars through their shared project, the *Journal of the Civil War Era*, and their shared hope of fostering imaginative and historiographically rigorous work that broadened and redefined our understanding of the era. This work continues in a journal that is a tribute to the two of them, and to many others. I am proud to have been a part of it.

In my visit to the Richards Civil War Era Center at Penn State, I was fortunate to work with Barby Singer, Matt Isham, and the many other people who make that institution run. I also had the good fortune to talk about this project with Amy Greenberg, the preeminent historian of expansion and antebellum America, as well as with Zachary Morgan and many others. Steven and Janice Brose hosted a memorable gathering at the closing of the lecture series. And my friends Kate Masur and Gayle Rogers came in from Chicago and Pittsburgh to hear me.

At the University of North Carolina Press, Mark Simpson-Vos helped guide this work from lectures to a book, and he urged me to take even more chances, even as he also saved me from some bluster. And Anna Faison, Jessica Newman, Dino Battista, and Mary Carley Caviness worked hard to turn the mess of words into a book.

Many people helped me along as I stumbled toward improving my Spanish. Manuel Cuellar provided extraordinary tutoring and cheerleading, before he moved on to his own career in academia. Before that, Alexandra Castano and the fine teachers at El Taller Latino Americano and Robert Diamond helped me get started. My parents-in-law, Reinaldo and Phyllis Cardona, listened, mostly patiently, to my abhorrent accent. My wife, Diane Cardona Downs, spent a year talking to me almost exclusively in Spanish, to the immense frustration and occasional bemusement of our daughters. Gayle Rogers patiently fielded too many texted questions. The somewhat clunky translations in this manuscript, unless otherwise noted, are mine

In trips to Spain, Cuba, Mexico, and Great Britain, and in preparing for them, a number of people helped me learn the lay of the land. Particularly I thank the extraordinarily generous Eduardo González Calleja, Consuelo Naranjo Orovio, Luis Miguel García Mora, Juan Pro Ruiz, Juan Pan-Montojo, Romy Sánchez, Reinaldo Funes, Jane Landers, Elena Schneider, Ada Ferrer, Olga Portuondo, Adam Rothman, Erika Pani, María del Pilar Blanco, John and Natalia Walker, and friends at Cambridge, as well as the many archivists and librarians who aided me. Nakia D. Parker conducted research for me in Texas, and Kate Masur and Aaron Sheehan-Dean and Eduardo González Calleja shared research findings with me. The University of California, Davis, provided a series of grants and research support that made those research trips possible, and department chairs Kathy Olmsted and Edward Dickinson helped me gain entry into the libraries.

I appreciate the questions, critiques, and hospitality at talks at Colegio de México, the University of Wisconsin and Wisconsin Veterans Museum, the University of Chicago Politics of Emergency in American History symposium, Duke University Law School, the University of Texas Law School, the University of Pittsburgh, Clemson University, the Southern Intellectual History Circle at the University of Texas at Dallas, Georgetown University, Southern Methodist University, Dickinson College, Oakland Rotary, the Society of Civil War Historians, the American Historical Association, and the Comité Internationale des Sciences Historiques. Many of these ideas germinated in papers at University of Calgary and the Remaking Sovereignty conference, both hosted by Frank Towers and Jewel Spangler. History Department colleagues at University of California, Davis asked probing questions in a colloquium, particularly Andrés Reséndez, Rachel St. John, and José Juan Pérez Meléndez.

Several friends took time out from their own work to read the manuscript. Brian DeLay, Brian Schoen, Adam Rothman, Elena Schneider, Sandy Levinson, Steve Hahn, Ari Kelman, Niels Eichhorn, Corey Brooks, Luke Harlow, Caleb McDaniel, Steve Kantrowitz, Laura Edwards, Andrew Zimmerman, Mark Graber, and Brook Thomas, and, as always, Kate Masur saved me from numerous infelicities and logical fallacies, though surely not enough! Aaron Sheehan-Dean, Mike Vorenberg, and an anonymous reviewer provided extraordinarily helpful reports for UNC Press and shared their own work and ideas.

As I began this book, we moved across the country from New York to the East Bay of Northern California and discovered a new, wondrous life there. My thanks to neighbors, friends, Sunday night "elite" basketball players, bayside bikers, renegade Epworth Methodists, Albany Social and Economic Justice Commissioners, Green Day fanatics, Davis faculty and friends, fellow volleyball sufferers, Girl Scout parents, baristas, and bartenders who made us all feel welcome. And to Diane, as always, for always, for everything. I carry your heart with me (I carry it in my heart).

Since the publication of my last monograph, our two daughters, Sophia Marie and Gabriella Francesca, have lobbied me to dedicate my next book to one or the other of them. But not to both. I am disobeying (and disappointing) them by dedicating this book to the two of them. In ways they do not yet appreciate, they share not only an intimate history in our household and in our towns but also a broader history. They are products of the late nineteenth-century world, a world that tied together, ephemerally and unequally, the places their grandparents and great-grandparents and great-great-grandparents called home: Puerto Rico, Hawaii, the U.S. South, New York, and Italy. What mix of magic and chance brought us into each other's orbits, their parents, born a continent apart in San Francisco and Brooklyn? We look for the world they will make, the life of their world to come.

THE SECOND AMERICAN REVOLUTION

THE SECOND AMERICAN REVOLUTION?

Our confusion about the central event in United States history begins with the name: the Civil War. What can be confined within the words "civil" and "war" is only a fraction of what transpired. The Civil War was not merely civil—meaning national—and not solely a war, at least in the narrow sense that we sometimes use the term. Even though extraordinary military campaigns raged across the eastern third of the country, and smaller ones elsewhere, the struggle could not be restricted to battlefields or resolved by surrenders. The most famous battles were matched by dramatic, violent, and permanent transformations of the nation's economy, political order, and constitution. The war did not simply resolve contradictions in the U.S. governing structures; the war created a new political order through military-enacted revisions of the nation's founding document, the Constitution.

The war was not solely a war. When historians emphasize battlefields over the internal transformations that the war brought, we domesticate the Civil War, we turn it to a brothers' war, a restorative, even conservative war for Union. In the process we make the Civil War something less meaningful and unsettling than it actually was. And in the process, we allow the myth of the Civil War to confuse our sense of how the Constitution actually functions, how our political system came to be, how we might fix it.

And the conflict was not merely civil, meaning national. The war was, instead, part of an international crisis. The Civil War not only spilled across borders and affected other counties, as many wars do, but was fought, in part, over competing visions of the world's future. Would the world be shaped by free-labor republics? Or by some combination of slavery and monarchy? In response to the war, Great Britain, France, Spain, Mexico, and other Atlantic nations re-created their alliances, their expectations, and in some cases their futures. If it was not a world war, it was a war, in part, about the future of the world, or at least the future of the North Atlantic and the Gulf of Mexico. When we miss these aspects, when we domesticate the Civil War, we construct a politics narrower than its participants' imaginations and experiences. We lose sight of their own international vision, their own habit of looking beyond the nation's borders to understand their own nation's politics.

Modern vocabularies, cultural needs, and implicit comparisons hang like fog over the Civil War, making it hard to see the landscape clearly. But nineteenth-century Americans often called the conflict the Rebellion, or the War of '61, or the War of Secession, or the Insurrection.[1] Although the appellation "Civil War" seems neutral, even inevitable, the Civil War emerged as the default reference only early in the twentieth century, fifty years after the war, and as part of a broader effort to depoliticize the conflict and speed reunion with white Southerners.

Some even called it the "second American revolution." The *New York Herald* turned to that phrase on the drizzly morning of March 4, 1869, to capture the transformative impact of Ulysses S. Grant's upcoming presidential inauguration. Grant's oath would be not simply the normal turnover of office, the *Herald* wrote, but a division in time, "an initial boundary marker between the dead things of the past and the living things of the New Testament." Like the British Glorious Revolution, the French Revolution, and the assumption of Emperor Augustus, Grant's inaugural would designate a new way of demarcating the present. There was a before—the First Republic produced by the First American Revolution—and now there was an after—the product of the Second. Grant, "the great Union leader of the war of our second revolution," would now be the "pioneer of the new government resulting from our second revolution. . . . Grant accepts the revolution as its representative elect, and so it is fixed."[2]

For the *Herald*, the phrase "the second American revolution" captured two interconnected processes—one national, one international—that distinguished revolutions from normal political change. Domestically, the "new government resulting from our second revolution" was transformed by the "expurgation of the old constitution founded upon slavery." Not just slavery but the Constitution that protected slavery had been overturned. Grant would complete the work of making a new Constitution by forcing the last few rebel states to ratify the Fifteenth Amendment under threat of martial law. This was not simple reform but a violent, permanent remaking of the reunited nation's political system.[3] A violent, permanent, fundamental recreation: this is one way of defining revolution.

And internationally, the *Herald* also expected the new political regime to revolutionize the world, beginning with the island of Cuba, one of two remaining strongholds of slavery in the Americas. Five months earlier, Cuban insurgents had risen against the Spanish crown in a bid for independence that turned slowly to a war against slavery, a war that the *Herald* desperately wished to join. Grant's inaugural "will make a sensation in England and Spain" and the "insurrectionary island of Cuba," the *Herald* wrote. Now that Republicans had purged the Slave Power from U.S. government, the party would surely purge bondage from the globe and counter the Spanish and British and French monarchies that the *Herald*, somewhat inaccurately, blamed for the survival of slavery.[4] The first step to making a United States–led republican world order, the *Herald* believed, was to recognize the Cuban insurgents' rights as belligerents, a recognition that would make it legal for U.S. citizens to aid the Cubans openly. Cubans then would establish a U.S.-backed free-labor republic. The United States would help drive both slavery and monarchy from the Americas and extend the country's economic and political influence—and the republican form of government—across the Atlantic. An international crisis that fueled a wave of struggles in other countries that in turn upended geopolitical alliances, this too was a way of defining revolution.

Still, the word "revolution" seems jarring to many Americans. By 1861, the United States already had one Revolution that created a republic. If the Civil War simply preserved that republic, then it must not have been much of a revolution. *If* the Civil War simply preserved that republic. Many U.S. myths depend on casting the Civil War as the salvation of that first republic, that first revolution, that first Constitution. All too often, the Civil War becomes a restorative Union war, or a resolution of the Constitution's internal contradictions, a conflict generated from within the founding moment.

Yet, the *Herald* suggested, the Founders' Constitution failed at its basic task, to create a stable republic. Therefore, it had to be replaced. And it had to be replaced by irregular and revolutionary methods. The United States government in the 1860s used martial law, military governments, and Washington ultimatums to force states to transform the Constitution in ways unimaginable in the 1850s. Republicans passed a series of postwar amendments by military force, re-created property and labor relations in the South in one of the largest property seizures in world history, and engineered longer-lasting changes through occupation. The Civil War thus represented, not the fulfillment of the old Constitution, but its partial destruction or, as the *Herald* wrote, its abrogation. In any other circumstance, describing any other country, we would not hesitate to say what is plainly true: the constitutional changes of the Civil War were not normal, not legal, not even strictly constitutional.

In some ways the war represented not the salvation of the republic but its death. The years 1861 and 1870, respectively, marked the fall of the First American Republic and the rise of a Second Republic founded on a Second Constitution created in a Second American Revolution. The 1860s rebirth of the United States destroyed a good deal—more than we can perhaps bear to acknowledge—of the country and the norms that existed before. It required forcible, political change—change at the barrel of a gun—to create the Second American Republic, as it had required force and violence and irregular processes to create the First.

Yet U.S. politicians, editors, and historians frequently minimize the Civil War's disintegrations, camouflaging the nation's rupture in reassuring stories of continuity and stability. The Civil War, therefore, becomes what I call a whitewashed revolution, a revolution that dares not speak its name but clothes its transformations in lulling tales of reform. The Civil War is obscured, like England's Glorious Revolution, behind a curtain of comity. By turning away from the war's revolutionary processes, Americans overestimate the nation's constitutional continuity and naturalize the nation's stability. Oddly, this is true among both the nation's critics and its celebrants.[5]

By analyzing the Greater Civil War as a revolution, we can demythologize U.S. history and see the nation as if it were someone else's country and not our own.[6] To Cincinnati editor Murat Halstead, the bitterest lesson of the Civil War was that the "American people have no exemption from the ordinary fate of humanity."[7] That ordinary fate includes the enduring role of violence in U.S. history, not as exception but as norm. Brute, raw force did not just intrude into a stable legal order; violence created and re-created that legal order. The disappearance of force in stories of progressive change has created an oddly defanged U.S. political history, in which progress advances by law and peaceful protest, reaction by violence. This mode of history grew out of the peculiar conditions of the post-World War II United States, its power in the world, its veneer of consensualism, its interventionist Supreme Court, its relative domestic peace. This constrained political history cannot capture the messiness of United States history, and political history will only thrive again once it is as weird and as disturbing as the nation's past, once it operates beyond those guardrails and captures the full sweep of American politics, with its violent repressions, its violent possibilities, its coups, its revolutionary triumphs, its myths, its rumors, its dangers. The coerciveness of this constrained political history is never clearer than in the portrayals of the Civil War. To stuff the Civil War and its transformations into a consensual, progressive view of U.S. history, it is necessary to re-create a Civil War less violent *and* less transformative than it was.[8]

But Americans are not the only people to underestimate the revolutionary nature of the Civil War. Social scientists and historians of other regions almost never mention the Civil War when they recount revolutionary moments or analyze revolutionary situations. In part this is because of the way the study of revolution developed. For decades scholars studied a small cohort of world-changing revolutions: the French, the Soviet, the Chinese. Each of these great revolutions transformed the country's internal politics, global geopolitics, and—perhaps most important in this schema—political thought. Driven by what a recent scholar of the Russian Revolution terms "apocalyptic millenarians," these grand "political and social transformations" alter not just governments "but the nature of the sacred" and lead to what Edmund Burke called a "revolution of doctrine and theoretical dogma."[9] These "great revolutions" raised the hope (or fear) of a progressive march from, in Marxist terms, bourgeois to proletarian revolution. To the initial list, some historians added England's Glorious Revolution, the Haitian Revolution, and the Algerian Revolution as key moments in the development of limited monarchy, abolition, and decolonization. Revolutions were bloody and they were purposeful and they birthed a new world. By these lights the Civil War did not count. Nor, for that matter, did the American Revolution. Nor, with exceptions for Fidel Castro's Cuba and Toussaint-Louverture's Haiti, did any revolutions in the American hemisphere.

But great revolution paradigms collapsed over the past three decades as it became clear that history had not reached either a liberal or a Marxist endpoint. First, the Iranian Revolution suggested an entire category of religious motivations left aside in the first waves of revolutionary theory. Then the Soviet Union's collapse shattered both Marxist and anti-Marxist teleologies. During the Soviet disintegration, new, unpredictable revolutions broke out in the former Soviet Bloc. The subsequent "color revolutions" and Arab Spring revealed that the "great revolutions" model did not explain uprisings that lacked great revolutions' utopian qualities. In short, great revolutions explained the history of ideas better than the history of lived experience.[10]

Recently a "fourth wave" of revolutionary scholarship has expanded social scientists' definitions and their analysis. Concepts of revolutionary situations and revolutionary waves capture important aspects of these revolutions. Instead of emphasizing avant-garde revolutionaries, scholars now examine revolutionary situations that arise during crises, when competing political groups claim sovereign authority. In those moments previously moderate, establishment figures—often bureaucrats or minor politicians or military officials—intervene, at first to restore order or implement small reforms. As crises worsen, managers act boldly and comprehensively, transformed by

time into reluctant but real revolutionaries. History made revolutions as
much as revolutions made History. The U.S. Civil War was in some ways such
a reluctant, managerial revolution.[11]

The fruit of these republican revolutions is what I call bloody constitutionalism. In moments of bloody constitutionalism, managerial revolutionaries
temporarily turn to violence to implement new political systems, then try
to return to peace. Crucially, those new systems are meant to be endpoints,
not preludes to further utopian revolutionary change. Bloody constitutionalism is both transformative and temporary, transformative in its long-term
impact, temporary in its narrow definition of the window of revolutionary
time. Bloody constitutionalism differs from simple states of emergency in its
scope; new constitutions are intended to last forever, not simply manage a
crisis. Bloody constitutionalism differs from reform in its forcible methods.
Revolutions work by irregular processes, often military violence or threats,
not through elections or normal lawmaking. Those irregular processes in
turn re-create a nation's basic structures: the constitution that guides political conflict, the forms of property that create economic power, the terms of
labor and contract. But bloody constitutionalism differs from truly utopian
revolutions in its very constitutionalism, its search for stability. There is little
desire for a permanent revolution. Bloody constitutionalism therefore is defined by its curtailed vision of revolutionary time. Bloody constitutionalists
imagine a brief revolutionary window in which it becomes possible to accomplish seemingly impossible political transformations and then return to
banal, normal time.

To return to normal time, bloody constitutionalists often discredit the very
irregular processes they relied on, hoping to prevent those processes from
becoming naturalized. They create what I call a whitewashed revolution,
one that obscures its origins in order to naturalize its gains and to prevent
future revolutions. In revolutions inside a constitutional order (as opposed
to revolutions to *create* a constitutional order), these transformations are
often couched publicly as restorations, ways of fulfilling the true, often buried goals of the old order, whether an older monarchical regime (as in the
Glorious Revolution) or the First American Revolution and Constitution (as
in the Second American Revolution). But that restorative, reformist rhetoric
obscures the new foundations of the new republic.[12]

And revolutions are born from and aim to transform geopolitics. Revolutions are inherently international events, often part of a revolutionary wave
that carries from one location to another. Leaders aim to recast their nations'
place in a world order and, thus, to reshape the world order. Revolutionaries

in turn learn rhetoric, technologies, and strategies from insurgents in neighboring countries. A successful revolution provides hope, inspiration, and sometimes direct support to rebels in nearby countries, producing a revolutionary wave that seems to roll mysteriously until it stops. The color revolutions and the Arab Spring are particularly vivid examples of revolutionary waves, but scholars have discovered other lost waves in the past.[13]

These concepts of revolutionary situations, bloody constitutionalism, whitewashed revolutions, and revolutionary waves help us lift the fog from the U.S. Civil War and to see the conflict more clearly. The U.S. Civil War emerged from a revolutionary situation, when multiple groups claimed sovereign authority. Despite these roots, it became a transformative revolution that permanently, forcibly re-created the United States' political and social structure. Many of its leaders, although certainly not all, were bloody constitutionalists who aimed to restore normal political time once they had transformed the nation, and they from the beginning created a fiction of continuity, a whitewashed revolution, to try to defang and protect their revolutionary gains.

And the Civil War was part of a revolutionary wave born in Cuba and Mexico. This Gulf wave and the exiles who rode it radicalized the United States and revolutionized first pro-slavery Southerners and then, even more significantly, antislavery Northerners. And then the wave reverberated back to Cuba, Mexico, and Spain. This story is far less known, at least compared to the more familiar stories of U.S. influence on (and greed for) Cuba and Mexico. But many important influences flowed the other direction, from Cuba to the United States, and U.S. historians have much to learn by reversing their gaze.[14] As Cuban slaves rose in mass rebellions in 1843–44, and white Cuban creoles in smaller insurrections between 1848 and 1857, Spain exiled hundreds of revolutionaries, many of whom landed in New York and New Orleans. Cuban exiles convinced U.S. politicians and editors that Cuba was on the verge of revolution; some taught U.S. politicians the rhetoric of world revolution. White Cuban creoles inflamed U.S. politics, particularly during the tensions over the Kansas-Nebraska Act. And Cubans excited not only Southern planters but also Northern antislavery politicians, helping them embrace an antislavery expansionism, even antislavery imperialism, that made the conflict with the South a struggle over competing visions of the world. This antislavery imperialism, as much or more than the better-studied proslavery expansionism, became the revolutionary force in U.S. politics.

So, too, do the Civil War's consequences no longer seem solely domestic, once seen from the vantage of Cuba and of Cubans. As the revolutionary wave rolled back out of the United States, 1860s insurgents in both Cuba and Spain claimed to be the allies and heirs of U.S. Republicans. They cast republican uprisings in Cuba and Spain as a culmination of the U.S. Civil War. For a time, the domestic revolution of Reconstruction rose in tandem—and perhaps mutual dependence—with republican revolutions in Cuba and Spain, each following and, in some way, building on the other. After 1874, the three revolutions collapsed together.

Fortunately, historians do not have to build this new view of the Civil War from scratch. Three scholarly movements have prepared historians to ask broader questions about the Civil War era. Historians working transnationally explored aspects of the United States' story that cannot be contained by national boundaries.[15] Many other historians discovered Caribbean and European roots and consequences of the Civil War, especially in work on international abolition.[16] A number of historians have analyzed white Southerners' international ambitions and influences, drawing on older work on foreign policy history.[17] It has become increasingly obvious that we should not, indeed cannot, tell the story of the Civil War properly unless we look beyond the nation's borders. Nevertheless, it remains tricky to fulfill these goals. It is always tempting to internationalize U.S. history by showing the country's impact on the world, as Don Doyle's fine synthesis suggests. But such export-oriented analysis risks a Cold War inscription of national distinctiveness. So, too, do import models of the world entering U.S. history—that make the United States a container receiving the world's ideas and people and products—foreshorten our imagination. Truly transnational history employs multiple national archives and historiographies to capture international movements of people, ideas, and commodities as they shape different national efforts at domestic state-making. I draw on Cuban, Spanish, British, Mexican, and U.S. archives and, to a lesser degree, on histories produced in those places to attempt an international history of nation-state formation, a transnational history of domestic politics.[18]

Extraordinary Cuban and Spanish Empire historians have created new, rich narratives of nineteenth-century Spanish expansionism, Cuban insurgencies, and economic transformations that should, indeed must, lead U.S. historians to rethink our assumptions about the mid-nineteenth-century world. Nineteenth-century Spain now seems dynamic, creative, and potentially threatening to the United States. Cuban historians have reexamined the development of a "second slavery" in nineteenth-century Cuba, as planters imported slaves and industry to produce sugar.[19] Together, these works challenge U.S. historians to stop ushering Spain off-stage after the early 1800s Central and South American revolutions and to treat Cuba as a productive economic and political site on its own terms, not simply a location of United States' fantasies. Mexican historians have similarly deepened understandings of midcentury crises in that country.[20]

Last, legal scholars have asked probing questions about U.S. constitutionalism, how it works, and to what degree it actually structures U.S. governance. Bruce Ackerman has argued that the U.S. Constitution has been revolutionized three times in a series of popular movements that forced extraordinary changes through irregular means, rendering the original Constitution a symbol more than a limitation. In response, law professors and constitutional historians have debated the number, type, and relevance of these constitutional revolutions. These debates at times confirm political and social historians' suspicions of constitutionalism but, more important, provide a language for analyzing nineteenth-century constitutional transformations and disruptions, and they can help historians expand our sense of the boundaries of U.S. political history.[21]

Although my particular topics—Cuba and the Second Constitution—may be somewhat unusual, my phrasing is not. Leading historians have turned to that word "revolution" to try to convey the rupture the Civil War made in U.S. history. Looking backward to the American Revolution and forward to revolutions in France, China, and Russia, many of the most esteemed U.S. historians have invoked one form or another of revolution to describe the impact of the Civil War. Perhaps the most influential versions remain the Dunningite denunciations of the racial revolution of Reconstruction, the libertarian critique of a revolutionary expansion of the national government, W. E. B. Du Bois's proletarian revolution, Barrington Moore's bourgeois revolution, James M. McPherson's "second American revolution," and, especially, Eric Foner's "unfinished revolution."[22] Although these arguments differed in the type of revolution they diagnosed, and thus in their implications, they shared both a vocabulary and a sense of the period's revolutionary impact.

Nevertheless, neither the *Herald* nor generations of historians have had much luck convincing the public—or political scientists and sociologists, or even our own field. When U.S. historians invoke the idea of a second American revolution, contemporary audiences often seem surprised, social scientists dismissive. The U.S. Civil War almost never appears on lists of world revolutions or in the analyses of revolutionary scholars.[23] This represents a missed opportunity, a foreshortening of both United States' history and the social scientific study of revolutions. There are many reasons why this renaming has not quite stuck, some attributable to the particular frameworks individual scholars used. But, mostly, historians have struggled with the vagueness of revolution, a word that too often can be a synonym for transformative change.[24] But clearer definitions for revolutions and new information about the role of the military in shaping the Constitution and about the centrality of Cuba and Cubans give hope that scholars, at least, are ready for a reappraisal. Perhaps the public is, too, in this period of reflection about the impact of the Civil War and Reconstruction.

In a line so rich and true it has become a cliché, T. S. Eliot wrote in "Little Gidding" that "the end of all our exploring," far from the terra firma of home, "will be to arrive where we started / And know the place for the first time." Things "not known, because not looked for / But heard, half-heard, in the stillness between two waves of the sea."[25] From Havana, from Madrid, from London, from their archives and from their vistas, we can come back to the Civil War, and know it again and recognize the half-heard sounds, and see what we had not previously looked for. This book is less a finished argument about the outcome of those explorations than an argument for the importance of these explanations. Leaving the safe shore of terra firma, we might return to a Greater Civil War and see it and hear it again, and also as if for the first time.

CHAPTER 1

THE SECOND AMERICAN REPUBLIC

Ulysses S. Grant's inauguration in March 1869 did not complete the Second American Revolution, despite the *New York Herald*'s optimism. To add voting rights to the Constitution, Republicans needed approval from the states. So in April 1869, congressional Republicans demanded that Mississippi, Texas, and Virginia ratify the Fifteenth Amendment in order to return to a state of peace. But Kentucky senator Garrett Davis complained that it was "revolutionary" to make peace dependent on the permanent transformation of the Constitution. Congress was changing the nation's founding document under threat of "military government for an indefinite period of time." Here, Davis found a precise, usable meaning for "revolution": the forcible and permanent transformation of a political and social order. But Davis did not confine his remarks to the constitutional revolution. What he most dreaded was the racial revolution that black voting would bring. African American enfranchisement, Davis told the Senate, "dooms all the white people of most of the southern States" to the "barbarous, ignorant, despotic government" of black-majority Haiti because of the "general unfitness and incompetence of the negro race to take part in self-government."[1]

Throughout the Civil War and Reconstruction, Democrats conjured dual specters, conjoined revolutions: one racial and one political, each feeding the other. Overturning the Constitution was the only way, Democrats argued, to overturn the nation's racial order. During bitter 1867 debates about the enfranchisement of black men in rebel states, Ohio congressman William Mungen derided racial equality. "If the whites, the negroes, Indians, Chinese, and Esquimaux, are all alike . . . our Radical friends may with some degree of propriety and assurance call them 'men and brothers,'" Mungen said. "I admit their humanity, that they are all men and not monkeys; but I deny the 'brotherhood'; I deny the fraternity." For support, Mungen dredged up references from embryology, cranioscopy, physiology, and ethnology that demonstrated (to him) the folly of the political, social, and sexual "amalgamation of the races." Yet racial revolution could not be separated from political revolution, for Mungen or most Democrats. To create black equality, said Mungen, Republicans resorted to the "utter destruction of our system of government and the erection of a vast consolidated empire to be administered upon the maxims of military despotism." Since, Democrats believed, white supremacy was natural, even scientific, even biblical, only tyranny could destroy it.[2]

It is easy to take the Democrats' racism more seriously than their constitutional analysis. After all, Democrats seemed to give more thought to race than to the law. Mungen's racial analysis was broad and deep, if obviously inaccurate from our perspective; his political analysis was hurried and hysterical. Democrats developed arguments about political revolution to enrage, not enlighten. And they grossly exaggerated. Democratic congressmen compared Republicans to Emperor Augustus, Oliver Cromwell, Warren Hastings, Russian tsars, Habsburg emperors, and Napoleon; predicted that "the history of the Jacobins is to be rewritten and re[en]acted here in these United States"; and talked wildly of bayonet rule and guillotines. But in the former Confederate states, there were no guillotines, few executions, no emperors, and nothing like the Reign of Terror.[3] Republicans responded, much more convincingly, that they were neither revolutionaries nor racial egalitarians. Instead, many Republicans softened the era's transformations (and moderated their image) by treating the Civil War and emancipation as an extension of the nation's founding, a mere amendment to the Constitution, a culmination of the Constitution's promise, a resolution of its contradictions, a perfection of its vision, a crisis, not a new beginning, a reformation, not a revolution. And historians frequently take those Republicans at their words. Inverting Democrats' critiques, we now ask whether the Civil War was actually a revolution at all since it did not permanently overturn white supremacy.

Yet Democrats captured important truths about the *methods* of the Second American Revolution. To transform the Constitution, Republicans did rely on war powers, martial law, and threats of force. And quite a few Republicans, although probably never a majority, eventually agreed that they ran a revolution. The first to embrace revolutionary talk were the abolitionists, avantgarde antislavery leaders who turned the "second American revolution" into a compliment and who celebrated the opportunity to break the nation's constitutional logjam. "The excuse which was urged for the original compromises of the Constitution has clearly no weight in the present crisis," a *Liberator* correspondent wrote in December 1865. "Congress is not obliged to chaffer, but is able to dictate and bound to dictate." This second American revolution could go forward only with the "aid of the military."[4] Military force to create permanent constitutional change: this matched Garrett Davis's summary of revolution.

Many mainstream Republicans eventually made similar points. Seemingly moderate Republican senator John Sherman wrote in 1863 that the Civil War "may, like the French Revolution, travel in a large circle, destroying all that have taken part in it; still there is no way but to go ahead."[5] Conservative attorney George Templeton Strong wrote of Reconstruction, "We must not be too nice and scrupulous about the Constitution in dealing with these barbaric, half-subdued rebel communities, or we shall soon find that there is no Constitution left."[6] As James McPherson documented decades ago, future president James Garfield turned to Louis Adolphe Thiers's *History of the French Revolution* early in the Civil War and discovered the "remarkable analogy which the events of that day bear to our own rebellious times." In 1867, Garfield said, "We must remove the rubbish and rebuild from the bottom. . . . We must lay the heavy hand of military authority upon these Rebel communities, and . . . plant liberty on the ruins of slavery." Fiery Republican congressional leader Thaddeus Stevens called for a "radical revolution" to "revolutionize Southern institutions, habits, and manners." And Georges Clemenceau, writing from Washington for French newspapers, described the period as "one of the most radical revolutions known in history."[7] Many Southern freedpeople saw the sudden, violent end of slavery and the establishment of voting and civil rights as a truly revolutionary moment, one that could be compared to France or England or—even more radically—to the revolution in Haiti. We must be cautious, of course, about relying on Democrats to describe Republican beliefs; so, too, however, must we be cautious about taking moderate Republican claims of continuity at face value, especially since many moderates at the time acknowledged the revolutionary break.[8]

In the years after Confederate surrender, the Second American Revolution created a Second Constitution that birthed a Second American Republic in a Second Founding.[9] Republicans turned to military power—to force—in order to revolutionize Southern society by emancipating four million slaves, compelling states to abolish slavery, and imposing military-backed governments and legal systems. Then Republicans used military force to enact a constitutional revolution by coercing rebel states into ratifying new amendments that fundamentally transformed the Constitution. The Thirteenth, Fourteenth, and Fifteenth amendments all owe their inclusion in the Constitution to ratifications by states under military rule. This violent, extralegal authority over the Confederate states paralleled other oddities of the nation's governance in this crucial period, especially the permanent creation of entirely new states by peculiarly constituted congresses. By the time Republicans were finished in 1872, the nation's map, House, Senate, Supreme Court, and Constitution all were permanently different. And the changes depended in large part on a fractional, peculiarly constituted Congress's turn to military force. Reconstruction was both unconstitutional and absolutely necessary. Any thoughtful study of the Constitution and of the U.S. political system must wrestle with that apparent (but only seemingly apparent) contradiction.

To understand this transformation, we must begin with the words themselves. Revolutions are notoriously challenging to define, but I draw on recent claims that they are *"rapid, mass, forceful, systemic transformations of a society's principal institutions and organizations. . . . Revolutions seek to overturn a society's social, economic and political structures, and recast its international relations, all within a relatively short time-frame."*[10] Force, permanent transformation, and speed capture what distinguishes revolutions from other political moments. Revolutions rely on methods that are not available in normal political time; they depend on threats of violence. In a revolution from below, the massed forces of the people may constitute such a power; in a revolution partly steered from above, the military may constitute a revolutionary tool. In both cases normal politics and legal processes break down, as due process dissolves in the face of outside, potentially violent authority. Force separates revolutions from reform, which aims for large-scale changes through existing political systems. Yet force alone does not constitute a revolution; else, coups and revolutions would be indistinguishable. Revolutions aim for permanent, fundamental transformation of a society's basic political and economic order: its constitutions, its property relations. A coup may violently change who rules a system; a revolution violently changes the system itself.

We worry about revolutions, as distinct from insurgencies or coups, because they speak not only to political orders but to the way humans experience time. In revolutions, time accelerates. What might have taken generations becomes possible in days or months. Revolutions close when normal methods displace force, when governing orders solidify in place, when time slows to its normal, lulling state. But revolutions need not be complete or total, nor need they always pursue the most radical possible outcome. They simply must achieve forcible, permanent, fundamental transformation of a governing order.

Seeing the Civil War as a revolution is painful and disconcerting. It requires us to reexamine a myth precious to many Americans, the myth that the Civil War saved the Union, preserved its fundamental character. To acknowledge the birth of a Second Republic is to abandon the myth that the Constitution saved the United States. As we diminish the Constitution, we diminish the Founders, too. In endless debates about the Founders' moral limitations, we lose sight of the practical ones. They were fathers of a country that died. Perhaps Americans should look elsewhere for guidance and wisdom. But myths about the Civil War do more than reinforce veneration of the Founders. A just-so story of constitutional resilience anchors a hopeful, false vision of the future, a promise that having survived civil war in its past, the nation can survive its present. This optimistic view reassures us that American politics is meant to be safe and reliable, an ahistorical dreamtime free from the horrors that dissolve other nations.

Myths of U.S. stability reassure us that political problems can be solved within normal boundaries, that the Constitution provides reliable guardrails. Across the political spectrum, assumptions about continuity shape how people see the country and how scholars analyze its past. These assumptions constrain our political history and our political imagination. For moderates, continuity and safety is something to be cherished, the root of U.S. prosperity and endurance, the First Founders embraced as wise men who built a system. For radicals or reactionaries, continuity is something to be decried, a barrier to a different future, a system constructed by First Founders intent on stifling change. But only by remarkable leaps can Americans credit the very Founders who established the system that led to civil war for the nation's survival during that Civil War. The endurance of such illogic suggests the psychological need to fix the United States to a stable past as a way of avoiding facing a potentially unstable future. To abandon faith in the country's past is to challenge our faith in its present, to realize that nothing inherently prevents the nation from driving off the highway, that there is no guarantee of safe arrival.[11] To admit that belief is to ask disconcerting questions about how violence and chaos shaped the U.S. past, and the likelihood that they will mold the country's future. Fearful of looking too closely, many Americans close their eyes and assume that the rails will hold.

The Civil War challenges the U.S. myth of stability with its fierce bloodshed, its irregular governance, its glimpses of chaos. Americans therefore spend enormous energy defanging and domesticating the conflict. Stories about the Civil War brace those imagined guardrails. Instead of evidence of the weakness of the country, the Civil War becomes proof of its strength. Perversely the Civil War is, especially in popular culture, a bloody conflict which proves that the United States is safe from bloody conflicts. To avoid noticing the steep cliffside just beyond the highway, Americans turn the Civil War into a restoration, a resolution of paradoxes, a conservative war for Union, a rebellion and not a revolution. But the facts remain.[12]

||||||||||||||||||||||||||||||||||||||

It is difficult to see the Civil War as a revolution when the conflict did not at first appear revolutionary, nor did its leaders seem self-conscious revolutionaries. But many revolutions—like recent ones in Ukraine, Armenia, Georgia, Yemen, and other countries—emerge from unexpected domestic and international crises, rather than the actions of self-conscious revolutionaries. What made the Civil War a revolution, and what made the Arab Spring and color revolutions, were the methods and the moments: forcible and permanent transformations of the fundamental political order, transformations that emerged during revolutionary situations no one quite planned for or even comprehended. Crisis inspired otherwise cautious women and men to transform their sense of the possible in a sequential metamorphosis of common sense; revolutionary situations sparked revolutions.[13]

Mid-nineteenth-century Americans mostly avoided styling themselves as revolutionaries because the word "revolution" smelled of anarchy. Revolutionary served as an epithet, not a self-description. Between the nation's founding and the Civil War, two things transformed U.S. views of revolution. First, the United States endured and prospered, giving many white Americans a stake in its stability and a fear of losing their property and form of government. Therefore many white Americans celebrated the success of the First American Revolution by affirming that they had no need for a second; revolution was safely buried in a golden past. Beyond the nation's borders, the history of revolutions seemed either dangerous or depressing. The French Revolution raised the specter of violence, especially the guillotine and the Reign of Terror. Even more significant was the Haitian Revolution, the uprising that eventually became an anticolonial and antislavery rebellion. As the second independent American nation, Haiti might well have allied with the United States against European empires. But most U.S. slaveholders saw Haiti as a nightmare, a senseless massacring of white masters by animalistic Africans. And they derided black Haitian governments as farces, while ensuring that the U.S. government isolated the island diplomatically and economically. Not all Americans were so skeptical. African Americans and some white abolitionist allies turned Haiti into a symbol of freedom and Toussaint-Louverture to a black George Washington, but they were a slim minority.[14] The 1848 revolutions in Europe likewise inspired both fear and excitement in the United States. Although Americans (including Southern planters) often celebrated antimonarchical revolutionaries like Giuseppe Garibaldi and Lajos Kossuth, their failures suggested the futility of revolution. Meanwhile, the more radical revolution in 1848 Paris revived fears of attacks on property.[15] And Americans looked southward for evidence of the destabilizing effect of revolutions on republics. In Mexico, ongoing coups and pronunciamientos reinforced the association between revolutions and anarchy. Revolutions thus seemed glamorous when led by moderate white men fighting monarchical despotism but frightening when rebels attacked slavery, property, or existing republics.

As the Civil War approached, both Republican and Democratic politicians denounced their opponents as revolutionaries and cast themselves as the defenders of American tradition. Democrats savored trashing "Black" Republicans as racial and constitutional revolutionaries. In 1858 debates, Senator Stephen Douglas dismissed Lincoln and the Republicans as "revolutionary and destructive of the existence of this Government."[16] Douglas also charged Lincoln with overthrowing the nation's racial order. Lincoln "holds that the negro was born his equal and yours," Douglas charged. "Now, I do not believe that the Almighty ever intended the Negro to be the equal of the white man."[17] When the vanguard revolutionary John Brown launched an armed raid on the federal arsenal at Harpers Ferry, Virginia, the Democratic-leaning *New York Herald* angrily attacked the "fanatics" trying to create a "second revolution in American history, embracing civil war and the dissolution of the union."[18] At the contested Democratic convention in Charleston in April 1860, both Northern and Southern delegates endorsed resolutions that called Republicans "subversive of the Constitution, and revolutionary" in their resistance to the Fugitive Slave Act of 1850.[19] So it was no surprise when, in October 1860, the *Herald* termed Lincoln's campaign the "Second American Revolution" as a way of urging people to vote against it. The *Herald* might have been surprised to learn that its editors would use the same phrase "Second American Revolution" in praise eight and a half years later.[20] But the story of revolutions is the story of such inconsistencies.

To defang these attacks, Lincoln and the Republicans defined themselves as protectors of the Constitution, Democrats as the actual revolutionaries. Republicans faced graver obstacles than did Democrats, who after all had decades of proslavery constitutionalism to draw on. But Republican lawyers and abolitionists developed their own antislavery vision of the Constitution. Many antislavery constitutionalists emphasized the Constitution's refusal to acknowledge slavery directly, the Northwest Ordinance's ban on slavery in northern territories, and the eventual prohibition of the international slave

trade as evidence that the Founders hoped to limit slavery. At their most expansive, Republicans suggested that the Constitution itself was antislavery
and had been thwarted by a deep-seated conspiracy of planters and Northern allies they termed the Slave Power.[21] Stripping away the Slave Power and
replacing it with a Liberty Power would restore the Constitution's natural
tendency toward freedom, they argued.[22] In celebrating an inherently antislavery Constitution, 1850s Republicans assured antebellum Northerners
that they could have their cake and eat it too, reduce or even eliminate slavery without calling the American experiment into question. The Republican
Party stuck to "the identical old policy . . . which was adopted by our fathers
who framed the Government under which we live," Lincoln assured an audience in New Haven, Connecticut.[23] Democrats had repudiated the Constitution's antislavery tendencies in favor of the "perverting" "dogma" that "the
Constitution protects slavery as property in the Territories," an antislavery
newspaper wrote.[24] Not all antislavery thinkers were quite so untroubled.
Some rejected this rosy view of the nation's past and called for sweeping constitutional revolution or drew new constitutions or celebrated John Brown's
raid as the "echoing, earthquake tread of the impending Second American
Revolution."[25] African American editor and physician Martin Delany called
for slave revolutions in the United States and Cuba. But most Republicans
and many abolitionist independents believed that peaceful change was possible. Even Frederick Douglass argued that an unshackled Republican Party
would be able to triumph simply by executing "the declared provisions of the
Constitution . . . in favor of liberty."[26] What stood in the way of liberty was
not the Constitution but the politicians who thwarted it. Perhaps there is no
more prototypically American position: venerate the Constitution and hate
the politicians who work within it.

What broke this antirevolutionary consensus and what created the revolutionary situation was South Carolina's secession in December 1860. South
Carolina's rebels did not merely issue proclamations; they revealed the thinness of federal power and provoked a sovereignty crisis, a frequent opening
to a revolutionary situation. As U.S. forces around Charleston retreated from
Fort Moultrie to Fort Sumter, South Carolinians seized abandoned federal
buildings, refused to enforce federal customs laws, fired on a steamship
bringing supplies to the U.S. forces, and prepared cannons to attack Sumter.
And the United States could not make Charlestonians obey. Thus Carolinians exposed the government's weakness. Breaking the spell of government

power, secessionists created space for women and men to think boldly about possibilities that might have seemed ludicrous or undesirable even weeks earlier. Revolutionary situations first change people's imaginations, then their responses.

Yet even these secessionists denied that they were revolutionaries. South Carolina's delegates argued that they left the Union only to protect themselves from Lincoln and other Republicans, who would use the federal government to constrain and eventually abolish slavery. South Carolinians claimed that Republicans were the actual revolutionaries, the secessionists merely protectors of a now-threatened Constitution. Republicans in Northern states shattered the Constitution by promising to exclude slavery from territories and preventing the return of fugitive slaves. "Observing the *forms* of the Constitution, a sectional party has found . . . the means of subverting the Constitution itself." With Lincoln's election, "the guaranties of the Constitution will then no longer exist."[27] South Carolina's actions created crises in other Southern states. In fraught conflicts, six more states seceded by February 1. The remaining slave states teetered in the balance, measuring their options, waiting for Lincoln's inauguration, and hoping for a peaceful resolution.

Not many white Southerners considered themselves revolutionaries, yet they nevertheless launched a revolution. Even as secessionist delegates met in Montgomery, Alabama, to proclaim their new confederacy, Confederates presented themselves as conservators. "We are not revolutionists," leading Southern intellectual James D. B. DeBow wrote. "We are resisting revolution."[28] The Texas declaration of causes denounced "this abolition organization" for "the revolutionary doctrine that there is a 'higher law' than the constitution and laws of our Federal Union, and virtually that they will disregard their oaths and trample upon our rights."[29] Confederate envoy and brigadier general Albert Pike acknowledged that secession might "produce revolution and destroy the government" but that revolution would be "the consequence, not of [secession] but of the unconstitutional act which made it necessary."[30] In his inaugural address, Confederate president Jefferson Davis called it an "abuse of language" to term secession a "revolution."[31]

Perhaps the most notable white Southern revolutionary was a politician who had earlier resisted secession, Confederate vice president Alexander Stephens. In his "Corner Stone" speech, Stephens did not claim continuity between the original United States and the Confederacy. Instead he called the creation of the Confederacy "one of the greatest revolutions in the annals of the world," because the Confederacy partly rejected the nation's Declaration of Independence. While the Confederate Constitution secured "all the essentials of the old constitution," the Confederate version also included "great improvements upon the old." The most important "improvement" was on race. The Declaration "rested upon the assumption of the equality of the races" and treated slavery as an evil. "This was an error," Stephens said. "Our new government is founded upon exactly the opposite idea; its foundations are laid, its corner-stone rests, upon the great truth that the negro is not equal to the white man; that slavery subordination to the superior race is his natural and normal condition. This, our new government, is the first, in the history of the world, based upon this great physical, philosophical, and moral truth."[32] Despite Stephens's rhetoric, however, Jefferson Davis's was by far the more common position. Most Confederates did not think that they needed to displace the nation's constitutional past to save slavery. They believed that slavery was integral to the Constitution.

Republicans in turn denounced secession as revolution, Unionism as conservation. In his inaugural, Lincoln called secession "insurrectionary or revolutionary."[33] Southern states could break from the Union only "against law, and by revolution," he wrote in his message to Congress's special session. As the Confederacy lacked a just cause, revolution was simply a wicked exercise of power, not of right.[34] Here, Lincoln fought Jefferson Davis for control over the international narrative. According to European norms, nations should recognize revolutionary governments only if their causes seemed just and their chances of victory significant. Otherwise countries would constantly insert themselves into one another's domestic upheavals. By labeling the Confederacy revolutionary, Lincoln told European nations that it should not be treated as a full-fledged state unless it prevailed by force of arms and could exert sole sovereignty over its space. Until the Confederacy exercised that power, the Confederacy could be blockaded, its ministers ignored, its claims disregarded. Davis meanwhile avoided the term "revolution" for precisely the same reason; he hoped to ease the path to European recognition.

When South Carolina Confederates forced the issue in April by attacking Fort Sumter, they created a new situation for other Southern states and the United States. There was no obscuring the sovereignty crisis. This assault destroyed the federal strategy of waiting out the secessionists and hoping for calmer heads to prevail. When Lincoln responded by calling up thousands of volunteers, Upper South states confronted a choice many had hoped to avoid. Rather than send troops to the United States, Virginia, North Carolina, Arkansas, and Tennessee put aside their prior reservations and seceded. Kentucky, Missouri, Maryland, and Delaware did not. The Civil War had begun.

So who were the real revolutionaries? From our perspective, the question seems quaint. Secession seems self-evidently revolutionary. Yet the most significant study of secession's legal status after the Civil War argues that there was widespread (although certainly not universal) acceptance of the constitutionality of secession even in the postwar North. When Supreme Court Chief Justice Salmon P. Chase tried to close the constitutional issue in *Texas v. White,* Justice Robert Grier dissented. Secession had been decided as a *"political fact,* not as a *legal fiction."* The verdict of the battlefield, not of the courts, had resolved the question.[35]

Those abstract arguments did not matter, not in the face of competing governments claiming sovereignty over the same ground. Both the United States and the Confederacy were entering revolutionary periods that swept away caution and drew women and men to bolder actions than they had planned or perhaps hoped. Prior words, no matter how sincerely spoken, proved of little predictive value in the swirl of events. Revolutions made people, and people made revolutions. As authors tried to capture the peculiarity of revolutionary time, they grappled with the limits of human agency, the pitiful inability of mere humans to control or even comprehend the world. Events seemed propelled not by individual choice but by some mysterious power, or perhaps by anarchy. The Fayetteville, North Carolina, *Observer* turned to the stage to make the "second American Revolution" the general setting, Jefferson Davis and Abraham Lincoln mere "characters figuring in the drama."[36] The German revolutionary Carl Schurz in 1864 dismissed the romantic, individualistic view of revolution. "Revolutionary developments are never governed by the preconceived plans of individuals," he told a Brooklyn crowd.[37] Lincoln had described this phenomenon of revolutionary situations as a young congressman. If a *"minority"* revolutionized, the majority "may revolutionize" in response. "It is a quality of revolutions not to go by *old* lines, or *old* laws, but to break up both, and make new ones."[38] John Stuart Mill wrote early in the war that Republicans were constrained by their constitutional views, "but the parties in a protracted civil war almost always end by taking more extreme, not to say higher grounds of principle than they began with. Middle parties and friends of compromise are soon left behind."[39]

Confused by these transformations, Americans discerned mysterious forces that guided events. Confederate lieutenant general Richard Taylor turned to metaphors of movement to explain what transpired. As "travelers enter railway carriages, and are dragged up grades and through tunnels with utter loss of volition," so, too, did men enter revolutions, carried on by forces "far in advance and beyond their control."[40] Others turned to God. "I claim not to have controlled events, but confess plainly that events have controlled me," Lincoln wrote in 1864. "Now, at the end of three years' struggle the nation's condition is not what either party, or any man devised, or expected.

God alone can claim it."[41] From a more radical position, activist Lydia Maria Child wrote that "all great revolutions and reformations would look mean and meager, if examined in detail, as they occurred at the time. . . . Still more wonderful is it to observe what poor, mean cattle God yokes to the car of progress, and makes them draw in a direction they are striving to avoid."[42] In our disenchanted age, we no longer have recourse to those meta-explanations but turn to metaphors: waves from physics and oceanography, crises from medicine. The "events" that "controlled" Lincoln, the "car of progress" that turned Child's "mean and meager" actions to revolution—these were the revolutionary crises that created a revolutionary situation and made a reluctant revolutionary out of an otherwise moderate lawyer and a Second Constitution in a nation that revered the First.

llllllllllllllllllllllllllllllllll

And so the revolution came, even though most of its leaders claimed not to be revolutionaries. After the initial sovereignty crisis of secession, previously staid actors stepped outside of civilian law and relied on military force. At first Republican politicians hoped they could manage the crisis without making broad changes to the governing system, but over time the logic of events guided them toward permanent, fundamental transformations of the nation. These methods—the military—and this outcome—a new Constitution— would turn a revolutionary situation to revolutionary consequences. Eventually, it would conclude with what I call bloody constitutionalism, an effort to sustain the fruits of that revolution and also to foreclose future revolutions by embedding the changes in a new, seemingly normal constitutional order and calling an end to revolutionary time. All along, even from the beginning, its architects tried to save the revolution by covering its tracks, clothing the new regime in the vestigial legitimacy of the old; this was what I call a whitewashed revolution.

The next sovereignty crisis emerged in border state Maryland and forced Republican leaders to decide whether federal authority expanded beyond normal legal limits. Maryland was home to both a large, mostly wage-labor city in Baltimore and significant plantations on the Eastern Shore and at the southern edge of the state. And Maryland surrounded Washington, D.C., along with already seceded Virginia. If Maryland secessionists prevailed, the Lincoln administration would almost certainly have to flee, signaling the United States' weakness to Europe. Republicans had few natural allies in the state; only 2.5 percent voted for Lincoln. But the administration had some collaborators. The governor, aiming to forestall secession, refused to call the legislature into session in February 1861. But neither did the governor respond when Lincoln asked for troops after Fort Sumter. Then, on April 19, the Sixth Massachusetts Regiment reached Baltimore and encountered rioters who aimed to block their entrance. When soldiers fired into the mob, secessionists in the Baltimore government destroyed bridges to prevent more Northern troops from arriving. To squelch the secessionists, U.S. volunteers seized control of the city and restored quiet. In that calm, Unionists regathered their strength and eventually prevented the Maryland legislature from seceding. To tamp down Southern sentiment, army officials began to arrest Maryland secessionists on military authority, including a rich landowner named John Merryman, who participated in the April bridge burning.[43]

Merryman's arrest forced Lincoln to decide whether he answered to normal legal processes. Did the United States remain in a peacetime state of law—in which case the army should not arrest civilians—or in a wartime state of exception? To protect the army from civil courts, Lincoln authorized Lt. Gen. Winfield Scott to suspend the writ of habeas corpus along the Eastern Seaboard. This marked a turning point in the relation between military and civilian law. Normally, any official who arrests a subject must respond to a habeas corpus writ by either charging or releasing the inmate. Therefore, the writ of habeas corpus was "perhaps greater securit[y] to liberty and republicanism" than any other part of the Constitution, Alexander Hamilton wrote.[44] Supreme Court Chief Justice Roger Taney thus ordered the army to deliver Merryman to the federal court. When an army officer refused, Taney bitterly criticized the government's interposition over federal courts and normal civilian law. The army had "by force of arms, thrust aside the judicial authorities and officers. . . . The people of the United States are no longer living under a Government of laws, but every citizen holds life, liberty, and property at the will and pleasure of the army officer in whose military district he may happen to be found."[45] Lincoln simply ignored Taney's opinion, and the army arrested the Baltimore police chief, four police commissioners, and other Marylanders.[46] Maryland Unionist Reverdy Johnson critiqued this assertion of military power as proof "that our fathers fought during the Revolution in vain."[47] Confederate-sympathizing Maryland cartoonist Adalbert Volck sketched Lincoln literally trampling on the Constitution and on habeas corpus.[48] While scholars have largely accepted Lincoln's "doctrine of public necessity," New York governor Horatio Seymour called it "bloody and treasonable and revolutionary" in a speech at the New York Academy of Music.[49]

To defend his actions, Lincoln turned to the revolutionary situation. Time had changed his powers. Lincoln admitted that his actions "would not be

This sketch by Confederate sympathizer Adalbert Volck shows Abraham Lincoln pressing the Constitution under his left foot as he drafts the Emancipation Proclamation. Background images tie Lincoln's act to the Haitian Revolution and John Brown's attack in Kansas. Courtesy of the Library of Congress, LC-USZ62-100066.

constitutional, when, in absence of rebellion or invasion, the public safety does not require them." But these were not normal times. "Believing that certain proceedings are constitutional when, in cases of rebellion or Invasion, the public Safety requires them," he transgressed normal legal boundaries to preserve order and forestall worse revolutions. He did so by expanding his notion of "constitutional" to mean necessary and prudent.[50] But at first this was merely a wartime exception. Although transgressive, his acts would not be revolutionary because they would be neither permanent nor fundamental; they were an anomaly. Indeed, Lincoln tried to restore as much of civilian law as possible to Maryland in order to sustain support from wavering Unionists. This was one way to distinguish an emergency from a revolution; changes would be fleeting, not permanent, not fundamental. Saving the Constitution might require going beyond the Constitution, but not for long and not to create permanent change. Because Lincoln often foreswore the most radical options at his disposal and because he couched his acts in reasonable rheto-ric, scholars often praise his moderation.[51]

As U.S. forces moved into Virginia and other seceded states, they faced much thornier situations. Powerful white Unionists were few, and there was little sense of a functioning loyal government. In much of the Confederacy, secession carried the loyalty of judges, sheriffs, and magistrates, and thus the entire civilian legal system, to the rebels. Therefore, the United States could not temporarily assist loyal local officials, as in Maryland. The Confederacy seemed ruled either by rebels (if the seceding officials remained legitimate) or by anarchy (if they did not). The army became the most effective tool to combat disorder, and often a government in itself. The United States first worked out these arrangements in northern Virginia, often within sight of either the federal capital or Fortress Monroe. But victorious assaults on port cities along the Atlantic coast increased the United States' zone of governance dramatically. By early 1862, federal troops controlled Roanoke Island and New Bern, North Carolina, and Beaufort, South Carolina, as well as surrounding islands. Out west, Ulysses S. Grant's assault on Forts Donelson and Henry in February 1862 opened up U.S. occupation of Nashville, then northern Missis-sippi, then Memphis.

Every U.S. success expanded the army's responsibility for pacifying the population. The army's main tool was its power of arrest, but that depended on the suspension of habeas corpus. Without that suspension, the army could not create order; the military needed the ability to hold and even pun-ish civilians. In September 1862, Lincoln subjected all rebels to "martial law" and suspended the writ for anyone imprisoned by military authority. Soon military officers applied this to Northern Copperheads who discouraged en-listment, and overly aggressive officers arrested Ohio politician Clement Val-landigham and suppressed the *Chicago Times*. But by far the most significant use of martial law was in the rebel states. Over the next four years, military commissions tried more than three thousand individuals, most of them white Southern civilians.[52] Some of these commissions, especially those held in the North, would become spectacular causes célèbres; many others were small parts of the day-to-day friction of warfare.[53] But this friction at times displaced the laws of government for the laws of war.

Slaves who lived and worked near federal lines tested the United States' will. One key site was Fortress Monroe on the Chesapeake Bay. When U.S. troops marched through surrounding towns, enslaved Virginians decided to turn the sovereignty crisis to their advantage. In the process they expanded the scope and nature of the war. From Hampton, Virginia, Frank Baker,

Shepard Mallory, and James Townsend and perhaps some women and children rowed to U.S. forces at Fortress Monroe to avoid being sent south to
build fortifications for the Confederacy. Maj. Gen. Benjamin Butler elected
not to return them. Soon dozens, then hundreds of slaves fled to the U.S.
fort. Ex-slaves worked as laborers and washerwomen in nearby camps, pro-
viding key services in exchange for wages and upkeep. By the law of Virginia,
however, Baker, Mallory, Townsend, and the others remained slaves. Butler
refused to recognize the applicability of the Fugitive Slave Law to Virginia
now that the state had seceded. But this was merely a temporary solution.
Therefore, the army and the Lincoln administration looked to the vast powers of war to override local law and justify their emancipation. Drawing from
the international law theorist Emer de Vattel and American antislavery politician John Quincy Adams, the administration endorsed the idea that a nation
could free its opponent's slaves in wartime even if it could not permanently
seize other forms of property. In General Orders No. 100, drawn up by law
professor Francis Lieber, the army claimed that martial law over the Confederate states meant the "substitution of military rule and force" for "domestic
administration and government." Although the military should be "strictly
guided by the principles of justice, honor, and humanity," the army had enormous powers of necessity, including the power to free slaves permanently.
"To return such a person would amount to enslaving a free person," the code
claimed.[54] Once free, ex-slaves would always be free. As the army moved
deeper into Mississippi, Alabama, and other Southern states, the number of
slaves who reached federal lines expanded into the thousands, then the tens
and hundreds of thousands. The transformation of the South would not be
temporary; the transformation would be permanent, and it would depend on
military presence and military law.

Still, the Civil War was not a military-directed revolution, even though the
military carried out revolutionary acts. For legitimacy Lincoln and congressional Republicans looked to the democratic process and to enduring republican institutions. But the Congress was itself transformed by the war, with
a large chunk of its membership resigning and heading South. Republicans
thus faced both an opportunity and a dilemma. The resignation of Southern
legislators gave Republicans vast majorities. Yet their absence also raised
questions about Congress's legitimacy. Democrats argued that this "fraction" of a Congress possessed only the temporary power to steer the war effort. Congress, they contended, should simply guide the war to a successful
conclusion and leave permanent transformation until peace.[55] Neither the
Lincoln administration nor congressional Republicans were moved by this

argument. They considered Congress a normally constituted body, capable of making typical, permanent law. Relying on Congress's constitutional right to determine its own membership, the House and Senate moved forward with reduced ranks, and the Senate expelled fourteen members for absence, including four from loyal states. Because Congress continued to meet in the same buildings in the same city with the same committees, because exceptional cases like Andrew Johnson remained in their seats, and because Congress still numbers its sessions as if the war did not create a break, it is easy to lose track of the fictional, if necessary, nature of Congress's claim to continuity.

The most powerful argument for the continuity and legitimacy of the U.S. Congress is commonsensical and also in its way catastrophic. What else could Congress have done? To handcuff Congress or limit its scope or treat it as provisional would be to reward the Confederates for leaving. Yet it is exactly this commonsensical transgression of boundaries—not from fanaticism but from a will to survive—that defines revolutionary situations and explains why previously moderate people behave in radical ways.[56] To justify their actions, congressional Republicans looked for precedent in their own rules, becoming expert at defining quorums and defending their ability to determine their own membership. But as they enacted significant, permanent changes, they shifted to a different argument than the president's. Lincoln's actions, in his view, were acceptable because they did not set precedent, but Congress shed those qualms and began to remake the nation.

Republicans thus straddled two contradictory definitions of time. While the army operated in a temporary state of wartime, this strangely constituted Congress moved forward as if it remained in normal political time. Northern Republicans were in the enviable position of legislating in the absence of most of their opponents. Armed with newfound and massive majorities, congressional Republicans pushed through a slew of legislation, including the Homestead Act, which apportioned western land and remade the Great Plains, the Morrill Land-Grant Act to fund public universities, an antibigamy law, a bill creating the federal Department of Agriculture, and allocations of land to railroads. These were all normal acts, remarkable only because they had been passed by an extremely abnormal Congress, yet would be binding until repealed. Even more crucially, Congress enacted confiscation and militia acts that helped free hundreds of thousands of slaves and open the way for black enlistment in the army. After Congress abolished slavery in Washington, D.C., in April 1862, the *Times* of London celebrated "the reformers of the second revolution."[57]

In 1862, Confederates' successful repulsion of the Peninsula Campaign and the bloody fighting in the Southwest shattered hopes for a quick end to the conflict and stymied recruiting efforts. At the same time the United States' capture of New Orleans and surrounding plantation regions brought many thousands of previously enslaved people into U.S. lines. Emancipating slaves and permitting the enlistment of African American soldiers seemed to resolve the questions of both slavery and recruitment. After Congress empowered the president in the Second Confiscation Act, and after victory at Antietam, Lincoln used his wartime powers to permanently reconfigure the nation's labor and racial order in the Emancipation Proclamation. Once again Lincoln acted on wartime powers, but now he was not constrained to temporary measures. All slaves, with a few geographical exceptions, would be free on January 1, 1863, if they entered areas of U.S. control. Thus the proclamation is the point when, for some scholars, "war becomes revolution."[58] Famously, if to many scholars unpersuasively, Karl Marx called the Emancipation Proclamation the shift from the "constitutional waging of war" to the "revolutionary waging of war."[59] Once again Lincoln turned to time for justification. His actions were unusual, he acknowledged in 1864, but so, too, were conditions. "I felt that measures, otherwise unconstitutional, might become lawful, by becoming indispensable to the preservation of the constitution, through the preservation of the nation," he wrote.[60] No longer, however, could he claim that the consequences of the war would be as temporary as the state of emergency; now a temporary state empowered a permanent transformation.

Still, Lincoln seemed cautious compared to the alternatives. Some congressional Republicans claimed a permanent purview over state slavery laws or an expansive wartime power over conquered territories. Lincoln's reliance on wartime powers reassured some cautious Republicans, for he acknowledged that there would again be limits on federal powers over state law once peace returned. Kentucky abolitionist Cassius Clay wrote from his diplomatic post in Moscow that Lincoln aimed "to overthrow slavery by war measures, and legal means, in the general government and states," unlike the *revolutionary* goals of Radicals Charles Sumner or Thaddeus Stevens, who attacked the existence of rebel states altogether. "Believing that there is power enough of an unquestionable legal character to throttle the monster, without going into debatable ground—standing by the Constitution as it is," Clay divided Republicans into "ultra radicals" like Sumner, "Ultra conservatives" who resisted attacking slavery at all, and "pragmatic liberals" like Lincoln.[61] Lincoln's pragmatism was indeed common among Republicans; many did not hope to wreck the balance of powers between federal and state government. Nevertheless, we cannot judge Lincoln's pragmatic steps solely against more radical options. Relative to U.S. history or other revolutions, Lincoln's threat to more than three billion dollars in property still represented a massive transformation of a nation's economy, not to mention an even more sweeping liberation of individual lives.

Nonetheless, the Emancipation Proclamation could not permanently end slavery; only altering state laws or the federal Constitution could do that. It was not even clear how permanent freedom would be. Prominent legal thinker Richard Henry Dana argued that the proclamation could not "alter the legal status of one slave in America" because it was a temporary wartime measure that would expire with peace. Although lawyers believed that ex-slaves who reached U.S. lines were safe, the proclamation might not touch those slaves who did not reach those lines before the end of the conflict.[62] The army's occupation of large sections of Louisiana, Arkansas, Tennessee, and Virginia raised the possibility of ending slavery by state law. As the army helped govern these states, Lincoln looked toward a revitalization of their civil governments to pull the states from the Confederacy. This opportunity, however, placed Lincoln in the complex position of relying on his military authority to guide states. If rebel state politicians had to respond to military force, were they actually returning to self-governance? Lincoln's December 1863 proclamation of amnesty set a low population threshold for reconstituting loyal state governments, yet the same proclamation used Lincoln's war powers to move toward abolition. Lincoln promised to pardon rebels who swore to support his proclamations, including the Emancipation Proclamation. Beyond this Lincoln suggested, although he did not require, that the refashioned state governments end slavery. Democratic congressman Joseph Edgerton called it "oppressive and unconstitutional" to demand that voters swear allegiance to the Emancipation Proclamation and "change, or submit to the change at his dictation ... their State constitutions, local laws, and domestic institutions." Lincoln had transformed the war "from one to preserve, protect, and defend the Constitution of the United States as the supreme law of the land, to a revolutionary war against the constitutional rights and sovereignty of Federal States, and virtually subversive of the constitutional Government of the United States."[63]

Lincoln's efforts bore mixed fruit. Tennessee built a government under Andrew Johnson that ended slavery and ruled large sections of the state with military assistance; Louisiana Unionists likewise constructed a government that ruled some areas around New Orleans with military help. But experiments in Virginia and Arkansas failed, and Congress did not immediately recognize any of these as permanent, stable governments. Rebel states therefore could not be the vehicle for ending slavery.[64]

So Congress created new states. Again Congress's actions fit constitutional rules, but Congress applied those rules in contradictory and extraordinarily aggressive ways. Perhaps nothing reveals Republicans' revolutionary goals more clearly than the permanent alteration of the roster of states and the creation of West Virginia. The West Virginia movement began when Unionist counties in northwestern Virginia held a convention in June 1861 to create a new state. But West Virginia delegates faced a conundrum. The Constitution allowed for the creation of new state governments from territory in existing states only if the original state approved. Since the government of Virginia, now in the Confederacy, would never accept this internal secession, the northwestern delegates first created a new, mostly fictional Virginia state government. A small number of voters then called a constitutional convention to carve out a state of West Virginia, and Congress recognized them in June 1863. Even staunch Lincoln supporter Lyman Trumbull wondered at the mixture of normal and abnormal processes, and the specter of a partial, wartime Congress making such a sweeping change to the nation's permanent political order. "I do not think, in the present unsettled condition of the country, till we see how we are to come out of this struggle, we ought to be admitting another State," Trumbull told the Senate. "I question very much whether we should divide these old States and admit portions of them as new States until we can see the whole ground." But staunch Radical Ben Wade answered that "amidst that turbulence is the very time to organize [the new state]. . . . Now is the time for great events, when you see that a commotion within the land has brought it within the compass of your power to do a great and mighty good. . . . To treat the fact of that commotion as a reason why you should not do it, is the narrowest statesmanship in the world. . . . We are able to do it now. What time may bring forth we know not."[65]

Less controversially but just as consequentially, congressional Republicans created a state out of the territory of Nevada in 1864 (and tried unsuccessfully to make states of Colorado and Nebraska). In the November 1864 presidential elections, Nevada and West Virginia both cast Republican ballots and added to Republican congressional majorities. Republican James Ashley of Ohio stated frankly in 1866 that "my object" in pressing to try to create Nevada, Nebraska, and Colorado was "two-fold: one to establish a new principle in the admission of States into this Union, negativing, so far as I could in the enabling acts, the old idea of State rights; the other to assure the vote of three more States, in case the election of the President and Vice President in the year 1864 should come to the House of Representatives."[66]

|||||||||||||||||||||||||||||||||||||||

With the Thirteenth Amendment, Republicans became a revolutionary party. Because the Thirteenth Amendment followed forms laid out in the Constitution and because it now seems inseparable from American history, it is easy to forget that it rested on the combined work of a strangely constituted Congress—a "fraction of the constitutional representation" from only loyal states—and military-regulated Southern state governments. Democrats denied that such an odd Congress could permanently remake the Constitution. The amendment proved that Republicans all along desired a "revolutionary change in our Federal system," Congressman Edgerton said. "They do not believe in the Constitution of the United States as its framers made and interpreted it. . . . By force of arms and by force of revolutionary and unconstitutional legislation [they] would make a new nation, a regenerated Republic, as they are pleased to style it, without slavery."[67] Pennsylvania Democratic congressman Samuel Randall feared that the amendment was the "forerunner of other usurpations. . . . Let the Constitution alone. It is good enough."[68]

Republicans did not intend to let the Constitution alone, nor did they hope to revolutionize everything about the United States. Some Republicans saw these actions as completely legitimate on their own terms, not revolutionary at all. A much smaller number were true utopian revolutionaries. But many were bloody constitutionalists, revolutionaries willing to turn to force and irregular methods for a period, but not forever. They wished to rely on powers of necessity long enough to embed changes, then return to normal time before those changes could be undone. The "amendment goes deep into the soil, and upturns the roots of this poisonous plant," Republican senator Daniel Clark said. "It not only acts for the present, but it provides for the future."[69] The "America of the past is gone forever," Republican congressman Isaac Arnold proclaimed. "A new nation is to be born from the agony through which the people are now passing. This new nation is to be wholly free."[70] In February 1865, the *Chicago Tribune* celebrated "the second American Revolution resulting in Liberty throughout the land."[71] While Democrats ran on the platform of the Union as it was, the Constitution as it is, many people wanted a "Union better than it was," the *Army and Navy Journal* wrote in April.[72]

The amendment passed houses that lacked representation from eleven states and included senators from one state, West Virginia, created by an anomalous process and approved by a fractional Congress. The Senate voted 38–6 for the amendment, a seemingly massive majority, yet thirty-eight votes would not have been enough to meet the two-thirds constitutional requirement if the twenty-two senators from the Confederacy had been present. When Democrats protested, the vice president responded that the body properly followed its own rules: "a majority of all the Senators is a quorum, and two thirds of the number voting, provided a quorum votes, is sufficient." California Democrat James McDougall responded, "That is not the opinion I entertain." Then McDougall layered his constitutional judgment with typical Democratic racist hysteria. "It belongs to demonstrated science, that the African race and the Europeans are different. . . . Quadroons have few children; with octoroons reproduction is impossible."[73] Watching the Republican tactics, Kentucky congressman Aaron Harding argued that slavery was so deeply embedded in the Constitution that no amendment could erase it, since any such amendment would destroy, not repair, the document. "If you pass such an amendment as this, you do it by the arbitrary and wanton exercise of power, stripped of all constitutional justification, and palpably unjust and oppressive. . . . There is danger that the Constitution, after all that has been done and suffered to preserve it, may at last sink and perish by the hand of revolution in the North."[74] Brooklyn Democrat Martin Kalbfleisch argued that the amendment was "subversive of the entire spirit" of the Constitution and destructive of racial laws, dooming the United States "to become the land of a race of hybrids, and thus by degrees be blotted out of existence in accordance with the immutable laws of nature."[75]

Despite McDougall's and Kalbfleisch's despicable racial opinions, it is worth pondering the constitutional questions they raised. Would we today accept the legitimacy of an amendment that passed while nearly one-third of the senators were missing, by whatever circumstance? It is easy to suppose that the constitutional transformation was legitimate because it was morally and practically necessary. But this way of thinking is premised on the very assumption that the revolutionary framework asks us to rethink: the capacity of the Constitution to resolve difficult political problems. Seen from afar, it is hard to shake the sense that Republicans were altering the rules of the game in order to change the game. These aberrations need not raise doubts about the validity of ending slavery, but they should raise doubts about the viability of the first Constitution.

As Republicans sought state ratifications for their amendment, U. S. Grant and his army cornered Robert E. Lee's Army of Northern Virginia near Appomattox Court House. Paradoxically, U.S. success threatened Republicans' ability to gain ratifications from three-fourths of the states, necessary to embed the amendment in the Constitution. With the rebel states at war, Congress could arguably count solely the twenty-five loyal states and succeed with nineteen state approvals, thanks to the addition of West Virginia and Nevada. But if the rebels surrendered and peace was restored, there once again were thirty-six states, requiring twenty-seven ratifications. Even if every loyal state approved, the amendment would not carry. The great danger to the amendment, therefore, was peace.

So the United States refused to offer peace to the Confederacy. Although Confederate general Robert E. Lee asked for "peace" that would restore normal law in the rebel states, Ulysses S. Grant offered only "surrender."[76] This semantic difference shaped the United States' approach to the postwar period as the United States held onto its war powers after the Confederates stopped fighting; this became evident when the cabinet and new president Andrew Johnson rejected U.S. major general William T. Sherman's peace offer to surrendering Confederates in North Carolina. Sherman's peace agreement might have curtailed the military's authority to overrule local judges, free slaves, strike down oppressive state laws, arrest and try criminals, replace local officials, and press governments to ratify the Thirteenth Amendment. In discarding Sherman's agreement, President Johnson and the cabinet decided that peace had not come because the war had not ended. While an outraged Sherman predicted "pure anarchy" and rebellion,[77] a Boston Reconstruction meeting in June 1865 celebrated the ongoing state of war's role in continuing "this second revolution."[78]

Wartime justified the United States' reliance on force to remake the Confederacy. The state of war created a temporary extraconstitutional space where military officers could carry out orders to interfere in political, criminal, and economic issues that they had no jurisdiction over in peacetime. Wartime in the United States did not quite turn power over to the military, however. Because the military remained obedient to politicians' orders, wartime conferred unusual power on the secretary of war, the president, and Congress, who now could use the army in ways unknown in peacetime. In the spring and summer of 1865, military commanders continued to exert direct control over the rebel states, and the army declared that it recognized "no authority but its own."[79] The army began to spread over the South, moving from roughly 120 outposts in March 1865 to more than 630, covering not just cities but plantation district market towns and railroad crossings, including places like Gillisonville, Grahamville, Pocotaligo, and McPhersonville in South Carolina. From these outposts, the army established itself as a supervisory government. At times the military used this power to oppress freedpeople; the U.S. Army included many bitter racists who attacked, abused, raped, and even murdered former slaves. But in many areas, soldiers were shocked by the ongoing brutality of white Southerners and enraged by the Confederates' depredations. These feelings led even racist white Northerners to listen more carefully when ex-slaves relayed information about conditions on the ground. In response, soldiers rode onto plantations and read the Emancipation Proclamation and, crucially, provided access to government for ex-slaves seeking to claim their rights. Ex-slaves brought news of ongoing slavery, whippings, denial of wages, and other forms of mistreatment that taught officers—and through them Northern politicians—the depth of white Southern resistance.

The army's presence revolutionized the South even if the army did not include many self-conscious revolutionaries. Southern antebellum society depended on the continual reinforcement of planters' power over slaves and of white men's power over black men and most women. This authority was reinforced by county courts and sheriffs, as well as local customs. These formal and informal systems of control reminded slaves (and some poorer whites) of their place in society. After Confederate surrender, planters aimed to re-create as much of this system as possible. But the army disrupted those plans by its presence. Freedpeople could exit local power and appeal to officers who answered to Washington. In parts of the South, officers took control of all criminal matters that involved freedpeople, either through their own courts or through the Freedmen's Bureau. Although military and bureau courts never functioned completely fairly, they offered alternative visions of authority that broke planters' efforts to monopolize it. In the presence of an army clothed in wartime powers, local law no longer claimed hegemony.

In summer 1865, President Johnson used the army's power to force rebel states to transform the Constitution. Johnson and some Republican moderates walked a thin line by both asserting wartime authority over the states and proclaiming that the states had not died or been territorialized. Johnson ordered states to reconstitute themselves and then ratify the Thirteenth Amendment "without delay" or risk continuing military rule.[80] Although some ex-Confederates urged complete resistance, the Mobile *Daily Tribune* suggested acquiescence since the Southern states were "subjugated, or overpowered. . . . That amendment is one of the humiliations which the South must submit to."[81]

Backed by eight rebel states held under martial law, the Thirteenth Amendment became the law of the land in December 1865. Almost one-third of the twenty-seven ratifications came from states under military control. Other crucial votes came from West Virginia and Nevada, brought in as new states by the fractional wartime Congress. The white Southern leadership had not acquiesced to Northern changes; it had been forced to be the instrument of transformations that Northern states could not accomplish alone. By early 1866, twenty-three of twenty-five loyal states had ratified the amendment; if only loyal states counted, that was far more than the constitutionally required three-fourths, but this alone would not equal three-fourths of the total number of states. Even more confusingly, Secretary of State William Seward named the rebel states in his proclamation certifying the amendment's ratification, but Congress did not seat their representatives. Therefore, rebel states existed simultaneously as states, when their ratification was needed, and as states in suspended animation, when it came to their representation in Congress and subjection to military law.[82] Such was the necessity of the moment.

African Americans discovered cracks in planter power and dreamed of broader revolutions to come. Martin Delany in the 1850s doubted black people's future in the United States, toured Liberia and Britain, and fictionalized a combined revolt of Cuban and U.S. slaves. But by 1863, he saw a new world being born in the new regiments of African American soldiers. From a bitter critic of the United States, he became an armed defender. First, he petitioned Lincoln for greater black involvement in the war, then he was commissioned a major to recruit black troops. These soldiers were part of a broad rebellion against planter authority, one that began with strikes during the war, continued with spying, and culminated in armed resistance to the slave power. On Saint Helena Island near Beaufort, site of some of the first schools for freedpeople in the South, Delany told a group of five hundred ex-slaves at the Brick Baptist Church that they too were a revolutionary force. "We now have 200,000 of our men well drilled in arms and used to War fare and I tell you it is with you and them that slavery shall not come back again, if you are determined it will not return again."[83] On Saint Catherine's Island, Georgia, New York–born Tunis G. Campbell organized a self-governing society under the auspices of the Freedmen's Bureau. Across the South newly forming Union and Loyal Leagues, filled with ex-slaves and former army soldiers, organized themselves into parallel governmental structures. Unlike Campbell, most did not directly challenge the federal government but embraced Washington as their only forceful ally.

||||||||||||||||||||||||||||||||||||||

As rebel states ratified the Thirteenth Amendment, President Andrew Johnson hoped to close the revolution and declare peace. Johnson imagined that Congress would consider each representative elected by rebel states. Some, especially Tennessee's, would be seated, and thus the state of wartime would end there. Others—including Confederate vice president Alexander Stephens— would be rejected because of their personal actions during wartime. White Southern leaders would learn to elect more suitable men. In time, the entire issue would be settled and the United States would return to peace, transformed by the end of slavery but otherwise intact. At this moment a *Liberator* correspondent warned that the "second American revolution" depended on Congress's willingness to abandon the great national myth that the Constitution could by itself resolve the country's political crises.[84]

But congressional Republicans had no intention of ending military rule over the rebel states or of bringing the revolution to a close. Therefore they inaugurated the next stage of the revolution in the simplest way: by taking control of the roll call that inaugurated the new session of the House of Representatives. Instead of calling out the names of each representative and then counting votes, the Republican House clerk skipped over all the rebel state candidates. Democratic congressman James Brooks termed this action "revolutionary" since it amounted to a seizure of control of the House by bureaucratic maneuvering.[85] Thaddeus Stevens and other radical Republicans hoped to sustain military power—and avoid peacetime—long enough to bring about further constitutional transformation, perhaps even black suffrage. The House and Senate referred all rebel states to a Joint Committee on Reconstruction until the Republicans were ready to return to a state of peace. Secretary of the Navy Gideon Welles angrily dismissed the "revolutionary" joint committee, while Johnson compared the committee to a French Revolution "directory."[86] Surely that insult was overstated. Yet it also must surely be admitted that, as Woodrow Wilson later wrote, "as much as possible . . . the forms of the fundamental law had indeed been respected and observed; but where the law clogged or did not suffice, it had been laid aside and ignored." This combination of punctiliousness and boldness reminded Wilson of Parliament's acts in England's Glorious Revolution.[87]

Between 1865 and 1870, Congress was reduced to a "fragment" because it refused to seat the representatives who arrived and asked for entry. Republican control was based on the constitutional provision that Congress could set its own rules for membership, but the execution went far beyond anything in U.S. history. For justification Republicans invoked contradictory claims of the Constitution's guarantee of republican forms of government, the right of conquest, Congress's authority over war powers, and analogies with territorial law (although it never explicitly classed the occupied states as territories). The Joint Committee on Reconstruction called the precise status of the defeated states a "profitless" abstraction; Lincoln termed the question "pernicious."[88] Republicans wanted to do things the Constitution did not permit; they also wanted to believe that they were preserving the Constitution's essence. Like most people, they became adroit at rationalization.

Throughout the winter, this "fragment of a Congress" began to remake the South.[89] Republicans knew they could not rely on white Southern acquiescence. In the rebel states, convention delegates and legislators restricted ex-slaves' freedom through Black Codes that limited African Americans' rights to travel, own property, bargain for work, and testify in court. Therefore, Republicans passed a Freedmen's Bureau bill that extended federal assistance to freedpeople via military control over civilian courts and, as Congressman Ignatius Donnelly approvingly said, moved toward a "new birth of the nation. The Constitution will hereafter be read by the light of the rebellion." The war's convulsions were "mightier by far than the old Revolution, mightier than all the revolutions of the world."[90]

Congressional Republicans also passed a Civil Rights Act that aimed, as Congressman Martin Thayer said, to be the "just sequel" to emancipation. Emancipation had been a "revolutionary measure . . . initiated by the conflict of arms and rendered necessary as a measure of war against the public enemy," and the Civil Rights Act strove to "carry to its legitimate and just result the great and humane revolution."[91] While Republicans found precedent for the Civil Rights Act in both the Fugitive Slave Act and international doctrines of preemption, the Civil Rights Act was even more revolutionary than the Freedmen's Bureau Bill. The bureau possessed extraordinary power but for a limited period of time; its authority largely expired in 1868. The Civil Rights Act, however, permanently empowered the military to intervene to prevent violations of civil rights.[92] The Republicans had become, Democratic congressman Francis Le Blond complained, a "revolutionary party" that wished to use war powers to create "radical and permanent changes."[93] But Republican senator Lot Morrill challenged Democrats who said that "the proposition is revolutionary." "I admit that this species of legislation is absolutely revolutionary. But are we not in the midst of a revolution?" The Civil War was a "revolution grander and sublimer in its consequences than the world has witnessed hitherto." Since the Constitution provided methods for amendment, Morrill said, the Civil War was a "revolution radical" but not a "usurpation."[94] To extend their majority and safeguard their bills, Republicans united to expel a New Jersey Democratic senator. When Andrew Johnson vetoed both bills, Republicans used that expanded majority to override his vetoes.

Since laws and military orders could be overturned by courts or future congresses, permanent change required yet another constitutional amendment. Republicans settled on an omnibus Fourteenth Amendment that established, for the first time, national citizenship for all those born in the United States and protected their "privileges and immunities" from oppressive actions by state governments. The amendment guaranteed "due process of law" and "equal protection of the laws." It also prohibited the payment of rebel debts, safeguarded the U.S. debt, barred some Confederates from high office, and readjusted federal apportionment to avoid awarding additional seats to Southern states that disenfranchised ex-slaves. It is true that the Fourteenth Amendment did not accomplish all that radicals like Republican leader Thaddeus Stevens "had fondly dreamed" of.[95] But Democrats had few illusions about the amendment's moderation and denounced Republicans as a "revolutionary party" that wanted to use war to create "radical and permanent changes" even though the "insurrection is put down."[96] President Johnson raised questions about the "constitutional validity" of the amendment. Congress had excluded representatives from eleven of the thirty-six states, even though ten of those eleven had sent elected representatives.[97] Even Supreme Court Chief Justice Salmon P. Chase worried that the amendment would alarm those constitutionalists who opposed secession but regarded "the real rights of States as essential to the proper working of our complex system."[98]

To ratify the amendment, Congress retained its hold over the rebel states, requiring that they approve the Fourteenth Amendment before applying for readmission. By extending the extraconstitutional time of war, Congress recognized that, as the moderate *Army and Navy Journal* wrote, "the political revolution" that the Civil War provoked "has hardly yet been completed" even "though the Rebellion is ended."[99] Republicans hoped that white Southerners would embrace the amendment and end the conflict; Stevens and his allies, however, counted on Southern recalcitrance to hold open the revolutionary situation.[100] Rebel states, except for Tennessee, refused to ratify it. "Worse terms may be imposed by Congress," the defiant South Carolina governor Benjamin Perry wrote, "but they will be *imposed* & not *voluntarily accepted*."[101] President Johnson and some of his allies called a National Union Convention to protest Congress's actions as "revolutionary." The "overthrow" of state power "by the usurpation and centralization of power in Congress would be a revolution, dangerous to republican government and destructive of liberty." The exclusion of congressmen was "unjust and revolutionary."[102]

The amendment's outcome hinged on the midterm elections of fall 1866. That these elections proceeded normally, in the loyal states, reminds us that the Second American Revolution occurred inside an existing republic. Elections, at least in the North, shaped the revolution's outcomes repeatedly, and military officials remained subservient to civil authority, although army officers intervened in elections at the request of politicians.[103] The Republican revolution was a republican revolution; its leaders believed in democracy and in constitutional closure, not in dictatorship; they remained restrained by popular will. Senator William Fessenden, a moderate by temperament, fought alongside Radicals and against Johnson in the summer of 1866. "I do not intend to yield the fruits of war, unless the people overrule me," Fessenden wrote privately, "and I don't think they will." Republicans took their revolution "to the country" in the 1866 midterms.[104] The issue was largely the Fourteenth Amendment.

Yet politics could not be confined to the ballot box. Johnson's allies promised that they were prepared to march on the Capitol, evict an "illegal, unconstitutional, and revolutionary" Congress, and forcibly install Southern representatives. Against this danger, Grant moved arms from the South to Northern storehouses and refused Johnson's request that he travel to Mexico.[105] In these fraught moments we see common revolutionary apparitions rising: two Congresses, perhaps two army commanders. On the ground, minirevolutions exploded as state and local officials in Florida refused to recognize one another and army commanders struggled to keep the peace. In Tennessee, the Ku Klux Klan began to spread as an armed wing of the Democratic Party, launching campaigns against Republican officeholders and freedpeople. White mobs murdered African American veterans and raped black women in Memphis, and then slaughtered black and white participants at a constitutional convention in New Orleans. In Union Leagues, freedpeople and white Republicans mobilized to claim their power and to defend themselves and their vision of a remade world.

Northern voters sustained the revolution in the fall of 1866, expanding Republican congressional majorities and rejecting Andrew Johnson's appeals. "All is chaos now in Federal politics, and the revolution will go on," Democrat Thomas F. Bayard wrote glumly to his father.[106] Republicans had waited for the people's consent, once they defined who counted among the people, and now they plunged forward. Although approval mattered a great deal to them, the newly elected members did not. Congress returned for a lame-duck session in December 1866 ready to advance. First Congress expanded its own membership by once again passing enabling bills for Nebraska and Colorado. Senator Edgar Cowan complained about such a decision "in this disturbed state of the country when balances of power are beginning to be of the utmost importance everywhere." Cowan accused Republicans of simply seeking to cement a two-thirds majority, thereby paving the way for impeachment.[107] After Johnson vetoed both bills and Colorado's statehood bid ran into complications at home, Republicans overrode the Nebraska veto and added the new state's representatives to Congress.[108]

Republicans then used their powers to pass the Military Reconstruction Act. This legislation revived the occupation of ten rebel states, placed the Johnson-backed governments there under military supervision, divided them into five military districts, and ordered commanders to register black male voters for new constitutional conventions. These acts relied on the continued assertion of congressional control over war powers; none was conceivably constitutional in a time of peace. It was, one critic said, "nothing less" than a "declaration of war against ten States of this Union."[109] But Republicans split over a simple question: Would they promise an end to the war? Both William Fessenden and Thaddeus Stevens wanted to continue military occupation indefinitely, until the white South acquiesced.[110] But other Republicans in the House and Senate were determined to add a stopping point, to promise an end to the revolution. If Southern states held biracial elections, created new constitutions, and ratified the Fourteenth Amendment, the states could return in peace. The staid *Army and Navy Journal* acknowledged that the Military Reconstruction Act was "abnormal, revolutionary, and, we had almost said, so unconstitutional a measure," and yet still endorsed the legislation as the only plausible choice in the situation.[111] So, too, did conservative Maryland Senator Reverdy Johnson, who considered the act "revolutionary" but backed it as the only way to end war powers.[112]

Democrats denounced the bill as "tyrannical" and "revolutionary."[113] President Johnson pronounced the bill a double revolution, of black over white and of military force over law. The "absolute despotism" the act handed to military officers would be used, Johnson complained, for the "Africanizing" of the South.[114] When Congress called a special session to continue the work in March 1867, Navy Secretary Gideon Welles compared it to the "Rump Parliament." "We are living in a revolutionary period, and the character of the government is undergoing a strain which may transform it into a different character," Welles wrote in his diary.[115] By 1867, President Johnson habitually referred to his congressional opponents as the "revolutionary" party. "Who now talks of the Constitution with respect?" he asked.[116] In November 1867, Johnson wrote that "certain evil-disposed persons have formed a conspiracy" to depose him in a "revolution changing the whole organic system of our Government."[117]

Some Republicans began to acknowledge the revolutionary break. They operated under war powers and intended to transform the Constitution but denied that those powers were new: Congress simply continued the authority of war past surrender. "Possibly the people would not have inaugurated this revolution to correct the palpable incongruities and despotic provisions of the Constitution; but having it forced upon them, will they be so unwise as to suffer it to subside without erecting this nation into a perfect Republic?" Thaddeus Stevens asked.[118] Most civil progress "has been through bloody revolutions," Republican congressman Ulysses Mercur said. "It seems to require a violent upheaving of society to enable it to break loose from the errors of oppressions which encircle it. . . . We are passing through a great revolution; we have not yet reached the end."[119]

Like Mercur, Republicans who acknowledged the "bloody revolution" nevertheless looked toward its conclusion. The curtain had not yet come down, but it would fall soon. Even most explicitly revolutionary Republicans remained bloody constitutionalists. The constitutional revolution was real, but it was also, always, almost at its end. They could love a revolution only once it was almost safely finished. Although Democrats charged that "the destructive work of the revolutionists—the architects of ruin—must go on," Republicans were actually seeking an exit from the revolutionary situation.[120]

Why did they grapple toward an end? Republicans believed most revolutions had ended in failure. They dismissed the French Jacobins and Cromwell not just because they were too radical but because they were too unsuccessful. Jacobins and Cromwell's supporters had not found a safe place to terminate their revolutionary situations and thus had lost first control and then their republics. Republicans looked to the 1868 presidential election as an end to the revolution, a reflection of both their democratic impulses and their fears of Northern backlash.

On the ground, the army fought white Southern politicians to save the revolutionary gains. These struggles revealed the brute force behind Congress's statute. In North Carolina, Governor Jonathan Worth refused to turn over his office to the new governor. Since Worth believed that Congress was not legitimate but merely a "body claiming to be the Congress and excluding 10 States of the Union, as a Revolutionary body" and that the new state constitutional convention was "unconstitutional—revolutionary," Worth would recognize neither the state election nor his defeat.[121] The sole power Worth would bow to was force, "military duress." Only when the army prepared to evict him, and only when Worth had exposed the federal government's reliance on brute power, did he leave.[122] Former Confederate lieutenant general James Longstreet urged white Southerners to accept conditions as out of their hands. "It is too late to go back to look after our rights under the law and the Constitution. . . . the only available law is martial law, and the only right, power. The more we seek for law, when there is no law, the greater will be our confusion."[123]

Some U.S. Army generals turned into revolutionaries as they struggled to control the bitter resistance of Worth and other white Southern politicians. One of the most notable was the mercurial Daniel Sickles, an antebellum Democrat who killed his wife's lover while a sitting congressman and then lost his leg in a disastrous fight at Gettysburg's Peach Orchard. The war changed Sickles's politics; so, too, apparently did a mission to Central and South America, where he was impressed by Afro-Colombian jurists and soldiers. Returning to a post in South Carolina, he found an ongoing state of insurrection, with white vigilantes attacking freedpeople, veterans, and even on-duty U.S. Army soldiers. The Military Reconstruction Act empowered Sickles to remake that society, so he used it. Sickles ordered his men to register voters, remove elected officials, prohibit assemblies of Confederate veterans, bar the carrying of weapons on roads and streets, and block the sale of alcohol and the distillation of grain into whiskey. The general ordered all civil officials to report to post commanders or provost marshals, under threat of arrest and removal by a military tribunal. To protect freedpeople, Sickles revised the state's vagrancy and competency laws, based on his authority as military governor. "A few months residence in the South destroys many illusions," Sickles wrote. "If contact with Negroes cures Negro-phobia, intercourse with rebels makes radicals." When a federal judge issued writs for men Sickles had imprisoned, Sickles refused to honor the writs. "It is quite true that the military should in general be subordinate to civil authority," Sickles responded, but "a great revolution is going on. Order must be maintained."[124]

In Louisiana, Maj. Gen. Philip Sheridan went even farther, dismissing the city officials Sheridan blamed for the previous summer's New Orleans massacre. In May, Sheridan fired the state governor, the city police chief, and all the members of the board of aldermen. Sheridan also wrote laws with his military power, outlawing segregation on trolley cars and opening up juries to black men in both Louisiana and Texas.[125] Louisiana was, one of the removed officials complained, "at the mercy of a single person."[126] Behind these forceful actions, hundreds of thousands of freedmen organized in spectacular fashion, voting in constitutional convention elections, sending hundreds of black delegates to the ensuing conventions, and then helping rebuild new state governments with public school systems and protections for tenant farmers. Meanwhile, President Johnson tried to end the revolution by

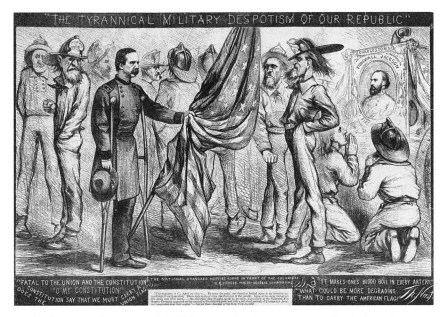

In this image, Maj. Gen. Daniel Sickles, portrayed on crutches and missing a leg, uses his authority as military governor of South Carolina to forcibly drape a U.S. flag over a Charleston fire engine company that wished to honor deceased Confederate Thomas "Stonewall" Jackson. Courtesy of the Library of Congress, LC-DIG-ds-09707.

changing its personnel, replacing both Sickles and Sheridan in August 1867. But, as Grant predicted, new men faced the same conditions and turned to the same tools. The revolution did not grow from the personnel; it grew from the conditions on the ground in the South.

When Southern politicians filed several legal challenges to military reconstruction, Congressional Republicans did not hesitate to defend their revolution against the Supreme Court. They had warned the Court early in the process that they did not intend to be bound by its rulings. During debates about Reconstruction, moderate Republican John Bingham derided fears of Supreme Court intervention. Congress's authority over the rebel states "has been settled and forever closed both by the sword and the ballot." If the Supreme Court declared that a fractional Congress could not remake the Constitution, Congress would simply "sweep away at once their appellate jurisdiction in all cases, and leave the tribunal without even color or appearance of authority." If the Court continued to intervene, Bingham proposed yet another constitutional amendment, for the "abolition of the tribunal itself."[127]

Congress had already remade the Supreme Court's personnel during the war, moving two circuits out of the South and freeing Lincoln to appoint free-state justices to replace slave-state jurists who resigned or retired. In 1863, Congress added a tenth, western seat to pack the court. When Johnson threatened Reconstruction in 1866, congressional Republicans reduced the Court's future size to seven so that Johnson could not fill vacancies.[128] After the Supreme Court ruled against the use of military tribunals in Northern states in *Ex parte Milligan*, Republicans worried about further cases in the South. "There never has existed, and there never is likely to exist, a nation which will allow constitutions or any form of any kind of paper to stand between it and such a change in policy as it deems necessary to its safety," the *Nation* wrote.[129]

In 1867, the Supreme Court accepted a plea for habeas corpus from William McCardle, a Vicksburg, Mississippi, newspaper editor imprisoned by the military for attacking Reconstruction in print. The Court also asked for a preliminary hearing on another case from Georgia. Immediately House Republicans passed a bill to require a two-thirds Court majority to strike down congressional legislation. To avoid permanently remaking the Court's jurisdiction, other congressional Republicans instead turned to a simpler solution: they stripped away the Court's jurisdiction over the case. Democrats complained that removing the Supreme Court's power was "revolutionary" and "Jacobinical" and substituted "force" for "law."[130] But Republicans were not swayed. "We established" the Court's jurisdiction, "and we may demolish it," one icily responded.[131] Andrew Johnson vetoed the bill as "not in harmony with the spirit and intention of the Constitution. . . . The Supreme Court of the United States has been viewed by the people as the true expounder of their Constitution."[132] But Congress overrode him. The next year the Supreme Court dismissed McCardle's case and accepted Congress's constitutional power to restrict its jurisdiction.

Unable to stymie Reconstruction by removing generals, President Johnson now tried to displace their boss, Secretary of War Edwin Stanton, a close ally of congressional Republicans. Republicans once more moved to protect the revolution from President Johnson. When Johnson appointed a new secretary of war, Stanton obeyed congressional instructions to hold his office. Stanton's replacement sat across the hall, a living emblem of dual governments and split sovereignty.[133] The House then impeached Johnson, on the grounds that he had violated the law by firing Stanton. Although the Senate failed by one vote to convict him, congressional oversight succeeded in neutering President Johnson and in sustaining war powers during the crucial period when several rebel states completed their constitutions, endorsed the Fourteenth Amendment, and returned to Congress. As Congress rushed the new biracial governments back to representation, Democrats complained that "if that be reconstruction, there have been no revolutionary, subversive, and treasonable measures ever contemplated" that "might not be called 'reconstruction.'"[134]

Black and white Republicans completed the reconstruction of North Carolina, South Carolina, Alabama, Louisiana, Florida, and Arkansas under military auspices and inaugurated the Second Republic with the ratification of the Fourteenth Amendment. Up to March 1867, twenty-one states (including Tennessee) had approved the amendment while thirteen (the other ten Confederate states plus three border states) had rejected it; others had not yet voted. Although Charles Sumner argued that Congress could accept the amendment if three-fourths of the loyal states ratified it, since Confederate states had committed suicide, many Republicans did not accept this logic. Military Reconstruction thus provided the margin for the amendment's ratification. Six of the necessary twenty-eight states that ratified the amendment had acted under military supervision. When Democratic legislative victories led two Northern states to rescind their ratification, two more states under military rule provided a broader margin for the amendment. Later, three states still under military rule added their ratification, but one more Northern state rescinded. In the nineteenth century, only twenty-two Northern states ratified the amendment, and three of those had rescinded ratification (with uncertain implications). Three of the nineteen consistent ratifiers had been created during the war by Congress: West Virginia, Nevada, and Nebraska.[135] The other votes were from states under military supervision. Without force to remake the states, the First Constitution would have remained intact. "You cannot find an instance where so great a revolution has been wrought" with "equal success," Alabama Republican senator Willard Warner crowed.[136]

The ratification of the Fourteenth Amendment in 1868 marks a birth of what some legal scholars call a "second American republic"[137] under a "second Constitution"[138] founded on "a new constitutional principle."[139] It was "an act of constitutional creation no less profound than the Founding itself," one leading scholar wrote.[140] Another called it a "major disruption in our constitutional history, which we try to camouflage as a single evolving constitution. . . . It is more illuminating to think of ourselves as having two constitutions: one the outgrowth of the American Revolution and the other the product of the war sometimes called the Second American Revolution—the Civil War."[141] Over the twentieth century, the Supreme Court used the

Fourteenth Amendment to transform the relationship between individuals and government, to protect individuals from state governments, and to justify federal power to enforce newly established rights. If the Thirteenth Amendment added ex-slaves to the national body politic created by the First Constitution, the Fourteenth Amendment eventually changed the terms of belonging. Since then the amendment has been the source of landmark rulings on school desegregation, gender discrimination, equal voting rights, and sexual privacy. No other amendment—no provision of the Constitution—affects jurisprudence and daily life so powerfully.[142]

But many of those transformations lay far in the future and were products of twentieth-century judicial opinions. Historians have carefully documented the Fourteenth Amendment's limited impact in the years after the Civil War. The *Slaughterhouse Cases* decision in 1873 emptied out the "privileges and immunities" clause, and later decisions vacated the amendment's enforcement clause, as the Court struck down civil rights laws, including in the 1883 *Civil Rights Cases*. By the end of the century, many of the amendment's guarantees seemed empty, although its protection of birthright citizenship remained in place. Beyond the Supreme Court's betrayal, the amendment itself was also limited. It did not, as some hoped, extinguish the states as sources of sovereignty. Instead, it put boundaries around state governments, allowing them room to maneuver—and thus the federal experiment to endure—as long as they did not cross certain thresholds.[143]

Republicans' satisfaction with the political system in the North and their wariness of utopian schemes explains the endurance of the federal system, the limits of revolutionary change. Republicans were bitter critics of the Southern states; many were not, however, bitter critics of the Northern ones. These Republicans meant to extend, by force, this Northern system over a South deformed by slavery. By staying within the forms of the Constitution, they hoped to find a peaceful exit that would permit them to solidify their gains and return to normal politics. Senator Carl Schurz celebrated the constitutional transformations. "We are charged with having revolutionized the Constitution of the country by the amendments recently ratified. . . . Well, sir, I do not deem it necessary to enter a plea of 'not guilty.' On the contrary, I acknowledge the fact." The Constitution "has been changed in some most essential points; that change does amount to a great revolution. . . . The revolution found the rights of the individual at the mercy of the States; it rescued them from their arbitrary disposition, and placed them under the shield of national protection." Still, Schurz acknowledged the limits. "The constitutional revolution has . . . indeed overthrown what I call State wrongs; but it was not designed to abolish what I would call the legitimate sphere of State rights."[144] Moderate, legalistic Republicans had worked from the beginning to empower Reconstruction without destroying the entirety of the constitutional system, and many oscillated between talk of revolution and talk of continuity. Lawyer Richard Henry Dana in 1865 both celebrated the federal government's power to demand transformation of the South while the Confederacy remained in the "grasp of war" *and* promised the same audience that "we have established a wise balance of forces. Let not that balance be destroyed. . . . Our system is a system of states, with central power, and in that system is our safety. State rights, I maintain; State sovereignty we have destroyed."[145] Reconstruction, then, had been legal, necessary, and forceful, but temporary. The revolution checked the states but did not destroy them.[146]

Ulysses S. Grant's election as president in November 1868 seemed to mark the triumph of the Second American Revolution, as the *New York Herald* wrote, but four states remained un-reconstructed, and the question of suffrage was still unresolved. In Virginia, Texas, Mississippi, and, debatably, Georgia, war powers continued to reshape not just life on the ground but the nation's structure of government. While those states were unrepresented, the revolutionary window remained open, and Congress aimed to use military force to remake the Constitution through the Fifteenth Amendment protecting the right to vote. Democrats again called constitutional transformation "unconstitutional and revolutionary."[147] Republicans argued that necessity overrode any constitutional qualms, at least during wartime. "I am for peace," Republican congressman Shelby Cullum said. "But, sir, let us not forget our duty, and that now is the time to strike at every element of wrong and oppression in the land that is in reach of governmental action, and that we can more easily eradicate any evil that may have crept into our system of Government now than we ever could before, or than we can in the future after the waves of revolution have all passed away."[148] To gain votes for the amendment, Republicans relied on the six states restored in 1868 plus Georgia, Virginia, and Mississippi, all still held under some form of military law. When New York rescinded its ratification, the amendment depended on Nebraska, added as a state by the fractional Congress, and military-governed Texas. Absent the four states still held under military rule in 1869, there is every reason to think that the amendment would not have carried. Without the six other states held under military rule as recently as 1868, the amendment would not have stood a chance. The Fifteenth Amendment was, Georgia legislator and preacher Henry McNeal Turner told a Macon celebration, "the finish of our national fabric; it is the head stone of the world's asylum; the crowning event of the nineteenth century."[149]

In this moment, almost everyone pondered further fundamental transformations of the Constitution. Between 1860 and the end of the March 1861 session of Congress, well over 210 amendments were proposed in Congress or to Congress by state legislatures. More than 90 were proposed between 1861 and March 1865, and almost 350 between December 1865 and March 1871. By contrast, only about 20 had been offered during the entire 1850s.[150] Even self-styled constitutionalist Andrew Johnson was pulled into the tide. In July 1868, he suggested amendments for the popular election of the president and the Senate, a new line of succession if both the president and the vice president left office, and term limits for federal judges. Although the Founders achieved "as near an approximation to perfection as was compatible with the fallibility of man," "time has developed imperfections and omissions in the Constitution," he wrote.[151] Johnson's amendments went nowhere, but they remind us that the Civil War era created a sense of possibility, a sense of the chance to perfect the republic, a sense many Americans have lost.

Revolutions raise hopes and then dash expectations. Feminist leaders had sought desperately to turn the Civil War to their advantage and to remake gender relations. But they would be disappointed bitterly when the Fifteenth Amendment did not reach them. Albert and Lucy Parsons and other radicals hoped to turn the revolution toward labor, pressing for eight-hour days and even the abolition of property. The revolution for freedmen did not portend a complete revolution for women or for gender roles or for labor. But the fact that a revolution meets limits does not mean that it was not a revolution; else no revolution would qualify.[152]

Revolutions do produce counterrevolutions, however. In 1868, vigilantes prevented tens of thousands of black voters in Georgia and Louisiana from participating in elections. Over 1870 and 1871, Ku Klux Klan chapters spread through the Carolinas, and other terrorists swept through the Mississippi Valley, slaughtering Republican leaders, raping women, and destroying African American homes. Republicans struggled to respond. They first used the anomalous case of Georgia. Georgia had expelled its black legislators, including Henry McNeal Turner and Tunis Campbell, in 1868 after having its representatives admitted to one—but not both—houses of Congress. When Congress returned Georgia to military authority, Democrats called this a "revolutionary class of legislation." "If this can be done in one instance it can be done in every State in the Union," Senator Daniel Voorhees said. "Indiana may be your next victim."[153]

Indeed, congressional Republicans seemed to be blurring wartime and peacetime. As Congress debated enforcement acts (including the Ku Klux Klan Act) between 1870 and 1875, members asked whether they had created permanent military authority over wayward states or simply a set of wartime powers that had expired with the end of the revolution.[154] But no one could quite define what normal powers were or who controlled the revolutionary situation. Would the United States be able to respond to pleas only from state governments or federal judges? Or could federal authorities intervene at will? After Grant suspended the writ of habeas corpus and sent the army to make hundreds of arrests in several South Carolina counties, the Ku Klux Klan faded. Some Republicans called for more interventions. "I reverence the Constitution," Senator Henry Wilson said, "but man is more than constitutions."[155] But Senator Matthew Carpenter, a moderate, warned them against going too far. "The Republicans of Wisconsin do not regard the Constitution as an evil."[156] Many Republicans, like Carl Schurz, now sought to close the revolution. Republicans could not "use the arm of national authority for the purpose of realizing by force what conception each of us may entertain of the 'ideal republic,'" Schurz said.[157] In 1872, Schurz and some other Republicans abandoned the party for a newly formed Liberal challenge that promised to clean up corruption but also to limit U.S. military intervention in the South.

A massive economic crash in 1873 and ensuing Democratic victories in the congressional races of 1874 stripped Republicans of power and brought the revolution to a close. The revolutionary party now could no longer govern at all. On the ground, Southern Democrats launched bold, violent counter-revolutions to reclaim their authority. Shedding their masks, white Southern Democrats held mass public rallies and launched blatant coups. Soon the South was filled with classic signs of a revolutionary situation: dual governments with two sets of legislatures or county officials claiming sovereignty. In the infamous massacre at Colfax, Louisiana, in 1873, white Democrats slaughtered surrendering African American Republicans. In 1874–75, Louisiana White Leagues defeated the New Orleans metropolitan police in the so-called Battle of Liberty Place and drove the governor from office. Only after the army forced Democrats to retreat did the governor resume power. In the winter, Democrats tried to claim the state legislature by physically seizing control of the meeting, expelling Republicans, and seating Democrats until the army again forced Republicans back into control. Insurgents in Alabama killed and wounded almost one hundred men in Eufaula, and mobs in Vicksburg, Mississippi, forcibly drove a black sheriff from office. Meanwhile in Arkansas a bewildering series of events allied a formerly Republican governor with Democratic legislators who sought to institute a new, reactionary constitution. Although African Americans continued to resist—led particularly by black women's organizing to defend a power that they believed belonged to the community—Democrats racked up victories across the South.

Democrats claimed that they had turned to force to beat back transformations enacted by force. They launched not a revolution but a redemption, they argued, a restorationist return to white supremacy and home rule. After Mississippi's paramilitary groups drove African Americans from the polls in 1875, Governor Adelbert Ames bitterly wrote to his wife, "Yes a *revolution* has taken place—by force of arms—and a race are disfranchised—they are to be returned to a condition of serfdom—an era of second slavery."[158] In 1877, after bloody campaigns in South Carolina and Louisiana, Southern Democrats completed their sweep of statehouses and began using their authority to strip away the local power that freedpeople had accumulated in the black belt. Over the 1880s and 1890s, Democrats passed laws to limit African American participation. Against the Republicans' bloody constitutionalism, Democrats turned first to bloodshed, then to constitutionalism of their own to justify their acts under the law. By the early 1900s, few African American men could vote in the former Confederate states. It was, Vice President Henry Wilson said, a "Counter-Revolution." In 1868, an African American in Savannah said that "a revolution gave us a right to vote, and it will take a revolution to get it away from us." His words proved prophetic.[159] Henry Adams, a former slave in Louisiana, surveyed the South for a safe spot but turned his eyes to Kansas.[160]

|||||||||||||||||||||||||||||||||||||

It is tempting to take the revolution's disappointments as evidence that Republicans were not real revolutionaries or that the Civil War era was not in fact a revolutionary moment. But the Second American Revolution did not fail; it succeeded, then was overthrown. The Civil War itself was a revolutionary period, even though it did not fulfill all revolutionary goals. If held to that standard, revolution would be by definition unattainable, its history blank page after blank page. The concept would be of no use in analyzing human society. On the firmer ground of this world, the Civil War remained a revolution even if partly overthrown by a counterrevolution. Some gains endured. Slavery, now destroyed, did not return. Abolition removed roughly three billion dollars of slave property. Freedpeople built legal families, churches, schools, businesses, farms, and futures. Despite the Supreme Court's limitations on the Fourteenth and Fifteenth Amendments, those clauses blocked state governments from explicitly racist statutes and forced disenfranchisers and segregators to turn to seemingly color-blind language to implement Jim Crow.[161]

Still, it remains difficult for Americans to think of the Civil War as a revolution. In part this is a tribute to the Republicans' efforts to whitewash their own role, the nation's own history. Like England's Glorious Revolution, the Civil War was defanged long before it was completed, in some ways even before it commenced. Republicans called their revolution a continuation both because the idea was useful and because some truly believed it so. There is no greater example of this whitewashing than the Gettysburg Address. There Lincoln reached backward "four score and seven years ago" when "our fathers brought forth, upon this continent, a new nation, conceived in liberty, and dedicated to the proposition that 'all men are created equal.'" The Civil War did not re-create that nation; the war saved the nation. "Now we are engaged in a great civil war, testing whether that nation, or any nation so conceived, and so dedicated, can long endure." Yet even in the Gettysburg Address, Lincoln closed with recognition of the transformation at work. Victory would mean that the "nation, shall have a new birth of freedom."[162] One cannot fault Lincoln for his evasiveness; he aimed to bind a nation together, not to delineate the past. And Lincoln knew that nothing could bind a nation so firmly as "the mystic chords of memory, stretching from every battlefield and patriot grave to every living heart and hearthstone," as he said in his first inaugural address.[163] But that was not Lincoln's last word. Four years later, in his second inaugural, Lincoln acknowledged both slavery and the nation's transformation. As the "war came," "each [side] looked for an easier triumph, and a result less fundamental and astounding."[164] At the Lincoln Memorial, the Gettysburg Address and the second inaugural face each other, across Lincoln's visage: the endurance of the republic facing the war's "fundamental and astounding" result. So, too, do two murals face each other. One, on Gettysburg's south wall is titled "Emancipation." The other, on the Second Inaugural's north wall is titled "Unity." The tension between those goals of emancipation and unity continues to shape the nation's remembrance of the Civil War.

In the aftermath of the war, Republicans increasingly aimed to whitewash their revolution, to naturalize the new nation by making it an extension of the old, to turn from Emancipation to Unity without abandoning the promise of emancipation. Republicans hoped—somewhat fruitlessly—to cast themselves as moderates, conservators of the true United States. They aimed to turn themselves from the party of war to the party that followed Grant's slogan, "Let Us Have Peace." Southern Democrats, mostly unimpressed, launched a counterrevolution against them. Yet this whitewashing campaign also worked. Democrats abandoned litigating the new amendments themselves and turned to exploiting their loopholes. The Supreme Court attempted to turn secession into a constitutional, not military question, in *Texas v. White* and other cases, recasting the Civil War as a struggle over interpretation rather than brute force. Nineteenth-century scholar John Codman Hurd remained skeptical of these constitutional claims, as did some Supreme Court justices. "When a revolution is recognized, there should be an end of all controversies based on an earlier history," Hurd wrote. "There is no question of constitutionality or unconstitutionality in a revolutionary change."[165] But it was easier and more reassuring to follow Chief Justice Chase and to defang the Civil War and cleanse the nation's political and legal history. Over the early twentieth century, Republicans acceded to Democrats' harsh racist views and often amplified them. The United States seemed to have survived the Civil War without fully revolutionizing either its Constitution or white supremacy, at least until the civil rights movement raised again the question of whether the nation's foundational racism could be expunged without transforming the interpretation of its foundational document.[166]

||||||||||||||||||||||||||||||||||||

Perhaps reckoning with the messiness and failures of the political system during the Civil War may help Americans think more imaginatively about politics today. Americans may have lost the sense of possibility that thrived during the Civil War and Reconstruction. In frustration or in relief, Americans tend to believe that the country's institutions are permanent. This permanence may be a source of celebration for moderates or of exasperation for radicals and reactionaries, but it is widely held. At times the contemporary American vision of politics seems to drift between complacency, reformism, and resignation.

Myths about the Civil War have helped to construct and support this complacency, as earlier myths about the American Revolution also obscure the nation's bloody, coercive, and undemocratic founding. The Civil War represents the gnawing challenge to American exceptionalism and to an American sense of stability. It is no wonder, then, that the Civil War has been the site of the most creative and significant efforts to wrestle this contradiction into submission, to turn the Civil War into proof of continuity. Unknotting that confusion—seeing clearly the failure of the Constitution and the political system—may be crucial for understanding how the American political and constitutional system does and does not work, arriving at a more mature sense of its dangers and a more robust sense of its possibilities, and writing bolder and more sweeping and weirder and thus more accurate political history.

To see the 1870s United States as a Second American Republic operating under a Second Constitution created by a Second American Revolution asks Americans to abandon their dreams of continuity and to develop a new, more vulnerable set of national understandings and also a new sense of the nation's possibilities. Thinking through the implications of the Second American Revolution might lead us to see the First Founders as less successful and less consequential than celebrators and critics have imagined. As architects of a country that failed, the First American Republic, the First Founders might shimmer as warnings or ideals but not as guides. Americans might have to shed the sense that the Founders possess answers to our current predicaments or blame for our situation. They might retain their glamor—like José Martí in Cuba, Miguel Hidalgo in Mexico, even Toussaint-Louverture in Haiti—as emblems of romantic struggles that do not quite speak to the present political conditions. We might see their work the way the French see the First, Second, Third, or Fourth Republics, as important preludes but also as relics who, having used up their magic, can safely be held and examined. Voices of the past, not oracles of the future.

The First Founders retain their force partly because their Constitution presumably constrains and empowers Americans. But in fact, seen aright, their Constitution is less meaningful and less constraining than Americans imagine. Many of the constitutional rights that Americans enjoy are derived from either the Second Constitution or the creative interpretations of twentieth-century jurists, and none are—or ever will be—self-enforcing; all still rely on the promise of enforcement, of force. They will always depend on political will and thus on reinterpretation of their contents.

Taking the Second American Revolution seriously would lead Americans to ponder new forms of public memory. Who among the Second Founders should be recognized on dollar bills, in statues, in city names? Beyond Lincoln and, arguably, Grant and Frederick Douglass, few of the Second Founders are well remembered, and none for their role in remaking, not saving, the Republic. The nation has outrageously neglected Thaddeus Stevens—one of the two or three most significant Second Founders—and is only beginning to come to terms with black Second Founders like Robert Smalls and Henry McNeal Turner and Charlotte Forten and Harriet Tubman. The nation might rethink its holy sites. Instead of Philadelphia and Boston, cradles of the First Republic, the birthplace of the Second American Republic might be at the

National Park Service sites in Beaufort or Natchez or New Orleans. More productive than raising new icons would be new debates. What would it mean to turn the congressional discussions over the Thirteenth, Fourteenth, and Fifteenth Amendments—including the extraordinary testimony from ex-slaves themselves and the petitions from women and men across the country— into the nation's founding texts, instead of the Federalist Papers?

A United States born from the bayonets of the 1860s and from the actions of terrified congressmen and generals may be a less appealing story. That narrative may even be a dangerous one. There is no shortage of fanatics ready to believe that the government can be changed only by violence and ready to turn that violence to bad ends. There may be good reason to forget the bloody and coercive roots of our rights and our freedoms. It may be safer to pretend that we live in a self-governing and perhaps self-correcting machine. Whitewashing has its purposes, even its pleasures. Liberals and leftists take shelter in a counteroriginalism that attempts to make equality an unimpeachable American value, despite all the evidence to the contrary.

But the past does not conform to our wishes. Nor does the future. Our hopes may not prepare us for the challenges Americans may face if their rights are attacked, if their legal system bends, if the nation's structures once again dissolve. A false belief in the functioning of our system may prevent us from debating the changes necessary to preserve the nation in moments of great stress, and may prevent us from imagining the kinds of bold actions it may take to save the republic or to save the rights of its citizens. Although history may not teach as many lessons as historians might wish, history in general—and the Civil War era in particular—reminds us that conflict and crisis are the common states of human society. All too often Americans, like the Casablanca police, seem shocked at crises and conflicts that appear routinely in other countries. Part of the burden of teaching and studying Civil War history is the call to prepare citizens for the normality of conflict, to help them face crises as they come and with all the tools at their command. Although those tools may not be sufficient to sustain a republic, they are more resilient than amnesia, more effective than wishful thinking.

CHAPTER 2

THE CIVIL WAR THE WORLD MADE

In November 1852, one African American writer prophesied "a general war" "instigated by slavery" and involving "all the leading nations of the world." The immediate trigger would be Franklin Pierce's election to the presidency, but the deeper cause was the ongoing struggle over slavery in Cuba. Pierce's support for the "annexation of Cuba," "H" predicted in a letter to Frederick Douglass, would spark a crisis in the Gulf of Mexico and draw France and Britain into a transatlantic war. The conflict would then spread across Canada, Mexico, and the Americas, ending either in the complete destruction of chattel slavery or in slavery's hemispheric triumph. "*Cuba* will be the point at which this almost universal conflict is to begin," "H" wrote. "Where it will end, the sagacity of man cannot foresee."[1] With hindsight, this writer's predictions seem perplexing. There was indeed a grand European war on the horizon, but it turned on Crimea, not Cuba. And of course, the United States never annexed the island, neither in 1852 nor in 1898.

But the letter was not as unusual as it seemed. Over 1851 and 1852, many mainstream U.S. editors and politicians believed that a crisis in Cuba would overturn both U.S. politics and world affairs. Antislavery politicians feared that Democrats would rush Cuba into the United States by force or payment and create two or three new slave states on the island. Proslavery politicians in turn believed that Northern opposition to annexation would "test" the "permanency" of the nation, as Florida's governor said.[2] Days before the election, the *New York Times* wrote that the "Cuban question is now the leading one of the time."[3]

A year and a half later, those hopes and fears indeed helped shatter U.S. politics. In early 1854, as Congress debated the Kansas-Nebraska Act, expansionist Democrats gathered a filibustering invasion force, a Spanish colonial governor seized the U.S.-owned vessel the *Black Warrior* in Havana harbor, U.S. diplomats cabled dire rumors that Spain would emancipate and arm Cuban slaves, Cuban insurgents prepared to rise against Spain, and Pierce's ministers attempted to force Spain to sell Cuba. In August 1854, abolitionist Wendell Phillips predicted glumly that "we shall have Cuba in a year or two, Mexico in five. . . . The future seems to unfold a vast slave Empire united with Brazil & darkening the whole West." Meanwhile, on June 2, 1854, federal troops marched fugitive Anthony Burns through an angry crowd of fifty thousand Bostonians en route to the harbor, where a ship would carry him back to slavery.[4]

Over May and June 1854, U.S. political parties indeed did dissolve under the pressure of three simultaneous, inextricably intertwined questions: Should the United States protect slavery in the West by permitting its expansion into Kansas Territory; should the United States protect slavery in the Upper South by using force to capture runaway slaves in Northern free states; and should the United States protect slavery outside the country by acquiring Cuba before Spain ended slavery there? In response, midwestern politicians created the first large-scale antislavery political party, the Republicans, to combat slavery both at home and abroad. Abraham Lincoln bound these internal and external struggles together in an October 1854 speech that attached the Republicans to "the liberal party throughout the world." Letting "slavery into Kansas and Nebraska" would allow it "to spread to every other part of the wide world," Lincoln said, and he quoted from a *London Daily News* article that castigated the United States for trying to steal Cuba.[5] Soon some Republicans would decide that the best response to Southern proslavery expansionism was to embrace antislavery expansionism, and to accept the Southern terms for a struggle over the future of the world. The stage was set for the Civil War in the first half of 1854, even though battlefield combat lay seven years in the future.[6] One way to understand the U.S. Civil War as a revolution is to examine its international and revolutionary causes. The Civil War was part of a set of interconnected rebellions that spread from Cuba and Spain to the United States over the 1850s, rebellions that emerged from common struggles over the role of slavery.

The Civil War was thus a part—and in some ways the product—of the "almost universal conflict" that Douglass's correspondent described. The Civil War was fought over the future of slavery inside *and* outside the United States. Global debates radicalized both anti- and proslavery politicians, injected revolutionary foreign actors into domestic debates, and eliminated grounds for compromise. Although the Civil War was not a world war, it was in part a war over the future of the world. It was a war between proslavery politicians who believed their system "the best in the world," producing "political freedom, combined with entire security, such as no other people ever enjoyed upon the face of the earth,"[7] and antislavery politicians like Senator

William Seward, who argued that "free labor" had "driven you [slave owners] back in California and in Kansas; it will invade you soon in Delaware, Maryland, Virginia, Missouri, and Texas. It will meet you in Arizona, in central America, and even in Cuba."[8]

Although fugitive slaves and Bleeding Kansas foretell the coming of the Civil War in most scholarly accounts, Cuban—and world—slavery is too often pressed to the margins. One way of draining the ideological content from the Civil War is to drain the global context; one way of domesticating the Civil War is to narrow its origins to the purely domestic, to make the fight about the limits of reform rather than the reach of world-changing ambitions. But fugitive slaves, slavery in the territories, and slavery in the Americas could not be disentangled; both anti- and proslavery politicians discovered this in the 1850s. The international stakes of domestic politics were high because the United States seemed uniquely poised either to destroy or to save global chattel slavery. Isolated by Haiti's rebellion and British and French imperial abolition, New World slavery was confined to the United States, Cuba, and Brazil by the 1850s. Slavery could not simply drift along; slavery would swell or it would shrink, and the U.S. government would help determine the path. Those existential stakes turned the Civil War from a struggle over reform to an externally oriented revolution. Once we see the United States within international events, it no longer looks moderate or restorative, in its leaders' intentions, in its methods, or in its effects. The full story of the relation between the antebellum United States and Cuba would fill volumes; this work aims to lay out one provocative line of approach in hopes of inspiring further work and additional arguments.

Cuba's role in the coming of the Civil War buttresses a growing historical literature on the Civil War the world made, on the international causes of the nation's most significant conflict. For many historians those causes are located in the transformation of the South into a militantly proslavery, expansionist region.[9] But this emphasis on Southern expansionism can become unbalanced. The acquisitive Slave Power described the fears of Northern abolitionists and the hopes of some Southern politicians, but it did not describe reality. Planters did not conquer the world; they did not even conquer the U.S. government. The limits of their power are visible on every political map of the hemisphere: the sum total of Southern annexationism after 1848 was the sliver of southwestern land in the Gadsden Purchase. Proslavery expansionism tells an important part of the coming of the Civil War, but only one part.

Just as important was the role of antislavery expansionism, a force that would eventually reshape the Cuban conflict. Many Northerners developed radicalized, international visions. To destroy slavery in the United States, they would need to destroy slavery in the world, and they could do so only by expanding U.S. power and turning it to good. Instead of an empire of slavery, they developed bold plans for an empire of liberty, plans that drew upon the settler colonialism that formed the backbone of the Republican Party, and then they applied that settler colonialism to the world. These international views form one part of the increasingly well-studied Northern, antislavery origins of the Civil War.[10] Many Republicans embraced antislavery expansionism, even antislavery imperialism, to steer the world away from slavery and help destroy it at home. Northern antislavery leaders fashioned a narrative of world affairs in which a Liberty Power fought against and often defeated the better-known Slave Power. By 1861, the force of the Liberty Power frightened Southern planters into the defensive response of secession.[11]

But it is important that we also see beyond the United States and analyze the self-conscious revolutionaries in Cuba who helped create crises on both the island and the mainland. The international roots of the Civil War began not in U.S. dreams of Cuba but in Cuba itself. Like other revolutions, the U.S. Civil War was created from an international crisis not of the United States' making. Cubans were agents, not just subjects, of the mid-nineteenth-century revolutionary transformations. Extraordinary work on the Spanish Empire, Cuban slavery, and Cuban exile populations provides new narratives for the midcentury Americas and reminds us that before the United States was a nation that remade the world, it was a nation made by the world.[12] In Cuba and in the United States, people have long noted that the island's future, like its past, depends a great deal on the United States. In the mid-nineteenth century, the converse was true as well. To many people, the future of the United States, and of Atlantic slavery, seemed to turn on Cuba. A revolutionary fever in Cuba could spread all too easily across the water to the United States.[13]

||||||||||||||||||||||||||||||||||||

While U.S. historians sometimes struggle to find self-conscious revolutionaries in the antebellum United States, revolutionaries were easy to spot a hundred miles away in Cuba. In 1851, some of the Cubans who would help destabilize the Gulf World began to torment Spanish authorities. These well-educated, young white Cuban creoles[14] near the eastern port city of Santiago de Cuba were angry about the August 1851 execution of four rebels in Puerto Príncipe (now Camagüey), and these *santiagueros* mocked the rituals of the Spanish imperial government and aimed to "destroy the monarchist customs of the population." Their rebellion began in dance halls, where they interrupted one reception, boycotted another, and unsettled a third by slic-ing a portrait of the queen. Outraged, the local governor first jailed and then banished the ringleaders, including a poet named Pedro Santacilia. Once inside the United States, Santacilia edited newspapers, founded revolution-ary clubs, raised funds for U.S. filibusters, lectured on Cuban history, sold weapons, lobbied Congress, published poems, and befriended exiled Mexi-can revolutionaries, including future Mexico president Benito Juárez.[15]

What originally marked Santacilia and these *santiagueros* as provocateurs rather than pranksters was an emblem that may help us reconstruct the revo-lutionary context of the mid-nineteenth-century Gulf: their blue and white ties, in some accounts white stars on a blue background. These seemingly innocent cravats revealed the young men as annexationists, Cubans who wished to attach the island to the United States as a method for separating Cuba from Spain. Their banners bound resistance to Spain to support for the United States in seemingly paradoxical slogans like "Independencia Cubano" and "Washington sí, [Queen] Isabel no."[16] Also woven into those emblems was a seemingly contradictory view of slavery. Many early 1850s Cuban-based annexationists wanted neither to end nor to empower slavery but to sustain and contain it; they feared both British efforts to abolish the institution and Spain's importation of vast new numbers of African slaves. In the blue and white stripes on their cravats, these white Cuban creoles tied together the struggles between slavery and free labor, between Europe and the Americas, and between republics and empires.[17]

Although the Santiago protests seem a world away from the Civil War, the road from Santiago to Fort Sumter, from cravats to cannon, reveals the politi-cal and ideological fractures in global affairs that turned isolated rebellions into interconnected revolutions, a general American crisis that disrupted the Gulf World and the surrounding Caribbean.[18] In the first decades of the nineteenth century, an older American system of governance and commerce had collapsed, and Americans—from the most powerful to the enslaved—struggled to define a new world being born.[19] The First American System, cre-ated in the sixteenth and seventeenth centuries, had tied hemispheric colo-nies to European imperial hubs that sought to dominate both trade and sov-ereignty. On Jamaica, Barbados, and Saint-Domingue, slaves generated more than three-quarters of the world's sugar production and produced fabulous wealth for British and French masters and empires; Indian slaves in Mexico and Peru did the same for Spain in silver mines. In 1750, as the First American System reached its apogee, the Gulf was governed by imperial strongholds in Havana and Veracruz and Mexico City and ringed by Spanish-controlled coasts in Florida and Texas, although the French in New Orleans and the ever-present British Royal Navy limited Spanish power.[20] Individual lands passed from one European country to another, especially during the ruinously expensive Seven Years' War, but the basic unit of power remained the empire, with imaginative claims of authority in Europe and purportedly tight regulation of trade. These empires were undermined (or perhaps sustained) by a wide variety of sovereignty claims by indigenous peoples, settlers, merchants, smugglers, planters, ship captains, priests, runaway slaves, and colonial governors.[21]

Between the 1760s and the 1820s, this First American System crumbled in a vast revolutionary wave that redefined the meaning of sovereignty and established the viability of New World republics. Settler colonists in British North America rebelled against taxes to pay off Seven Years' War debts. With French support, these British settlers won domestic sovereignty over what became the United States and thus the right to set their own rules on foreign trade.[22] French debt, some incurred in the American Revolution, sparked a republican revolution in France and then—just as momentously—a revolution in Saint-Domingue, where ex-slaves overthrew both slavery and empire and created the hemisphere's second republic in Haiti. As planters fled with industrial technology and some slaves, and as France cut trade with Haiti, the island's sugar exports fell by 99 percent between 1789 and 1795.[23] After Napoleon closed the French Revolution, the emperor invaded Spain and provoked, inadvertently, revolutions across Spanish colonies in the American hemisphere that eventually created numerous new (and mostly antislavery) republics. Indigenous rebellions in the Bajío meanwhile crippled Mexico's massive silver mining industry—cutting exports by half—precisely as the former colony gained independence. In the upheaval, Britain's navy, merchants, and nascent industries influenced what Americans grew and how they transported those goods to market.[24]

What would replace the First American System? In the struggle between different types of sovereignty, labor models, and trade regimes, the Gulf World and its surroundings produced new economic entanglements. After Haiti's abolition of slavery, French planters carried slaves and technology to new sugar plantations in Cuba and Louisiana, while Brazilian masters scrambled to meet European demand for sugar and coffee. In the rich Mississippi Delta above New Orleans, acquired from France after the Haitian Revolution, U.S. settlers displaced Indians to build enormous plantations that fed cotton to British and New England mills. To stock the Mississippi Valley with slaves, U.S. traders brokered the Second Middle Passage that forcibly moved a million slaves from the Atlantic coast; to feed the explosive sugar-based slavery in Cuba that provided roughly 30 percent of the world's production,

Spanish officials oversaw the importation of 630,000 African slaves to the island between 1791 and 1843. Thus, the Gulf region was home to the most expansive, capitalistic forms of what scholars call the second slavery in the sugar belt between Havana and Matanzas in Cuba and in the cotton belt along the Mississippi Delta. Over the 1820s, plantation agriculture began to spread along the Gulf coasts, as U.S. settlers transported slaves to Florida after the country acquired the region from Spain in 1821 and U.S. settlers carried large-scale cotton-based slavery to Mexican Texas.[25] Yet at the same time other parts of the Gulf World and its surroundings—especially Mexico, continental Latin America, and the northern United States—developed an increasingly distinct wage-labor system.

British and U.S. merchants bound the Gulf together in defiance of political maps or imperial sovereignty, creating networks of communications that could pass ideas as quickly as goods. Freed from British regulations, U.S. shippers traded promiscuously across the Gulf and the Caribbean, using their profits to invest in Cuban land, machinery, and, eventually, railroads. In 1826, 783 of the 964 ships that entered Havana harbor were from the United States.[26] By the 1850s, more ships entered and left U.S. ports from Cuba than anywhere else in the world except Canada, and Cuba became the United States' third most important trade partner. Cuba exported almost four times as much sugar to the United States as to Spain in 1850, and more than seven times in 1860. Mexico, meanwhile, remained marginal to both U.S. and British trade, struggled to replace silver as a source of revenue, and was subject to frequent threats of intervention by French, British, and Spanish creditors and their imperial governments.[27]

As the First American System collapsed, the Second American System emerged without either a single pole or a single ideological orientation, creating space for new political visions—both hopeful and apocalyptic. As long as these tensions seemed reconcilable, Gulf World people combined ideas promiscuously and—to our eyes—often contradictorily, reflecting the mixed economy, the deep rivalries for control, and the productive confusion about the future, a confusion by no means restricted to the United States. At any moment, Spain, Mexico, the United States, Britain, or France might loom large or fall into crisis, taking with them the vision of the future they seemed to represent. Constitutional republics rose directly alongside resurgent empires, and each created new, hybrid (and oddly similar) forms and tried to contain bitter struggles between centralizers and federalists.[28]

The Gulf and Caribbean were the site of an impressive imperial rejuvenation; empires did not seem to be fading in the face of republican triumph. In Cuba, Spain modernized its colonial bureaucracy, imposed martial law,

squashed an 1825 slave rebellion, stymied mainland efforts to invade the island, foiled 1820s plots to annex the island to the United States or Mexico,
and raised customs duties to give Spanish grain farmers special access to
Cuban markets.[29] An increasingly antislavery British Empire, freed from its
North American planters, ended the African slave trade in 1807, policed the
seas, and extended its influence over the Cuban and the African coasts under
the guise of protecting free labor. These Spanish and British Empires faced
two vast republics: the largest antislavery republic in the world in Mexico
and the largest proslavery republic in the United States. In the Gulf ports
of Havana, New Orleans, and Veracruz, as well as New York and Kingston,
Jamaica, merchants spread not only goods but rumors of political upheaval.
It was a chaotic, multipolar world, and also a generative one, in which people
combined republicanism and monarchism, slavery and freedom, liberalism
and reaction, in unexpected ways. The Second American System collapsed in
the 1890s, as the United States increasingly sought to impose a new imperial
regime over the hemisphere, but the Second System was more than an inter-
ruption, and its politics had meaning other than as prelude.[30]

ıııııııııııııııııııııııııııııı

In the 1830s nearly concurrent slave rebellions in the United States and Jamaica split the Second American System into pro- and antislavery camps. The
United States' Nat Turner rebellion and the Jamaican Baptist War prompted
grave reconsiderations of the future of slavery and different paths for the
United States and Britain. In the United States, two competing systems
emerged. Southern slave owners consolidated power and purged antislavery
from their region; Northern abolitionists roused the public, at first slowly,
against the institution. But Britain moved to abolish slavery in its American
empire in 1833 legislation and then pressured Spanish and French governments to follow suit. Meanwhile Spain and Mexico struggled with their own
crises. In Spain Fernando VII's death in 1833 sparked hopes for a constitutional monarchy. And revolutionaries in Texas overthrew Mexican rule and
started a proslavery republic.

Cuba became a battleground between these contradictory visions of the
future. Cubans around Santiago rose in 1836 against the decade-old regime
of martial law, a creole rebellion for individual rights (though not against
slavery). For what one Spanish official called "eighty days of anarchy," this
"scandalous" regime—whose backers included famed poet Porfirio Valiente
and Santacilia's father, Don Joaquín—held sway, as Cubans imagined a new,
equal role within the Spanish Empire.[31] But the Santiago rebels had misread

politics back on the Iberian peninsula. Even as reformers in Spain moved toward a constitutional monarchy for Spaniards in Europe, they ordered the Spanish military governor in Havana, Miguel Tacón, to crush the Santiago movement. Tacón exiled the leaders, including Santacilia's father, for inciting "anarchy and civil war." In Madrid, the Cortes refused to seat José Antonio Saco, a Cuban delegate who lobbied to end the slave trade in order to sustain a white majority on the island. The new 1837 Spanish constitution indeed expanded rights for Spanish citizens, but only for those born in Spain; the constitution placed colonials under special laws, almost a form of ongoing martial law. Spanish politicians barred Cuban representatives from the Cortes, and continued to ban white creoles from high military or civil offices. Then Spanish governors overwhelmed white Cuban creoles by importing 150,000 African slaves between 1835 and 1840. Slaves soon outnumbered both whites and free people of color in parts of Havana-Matanzas, while whites retained a bare plurality in the east around Santiago.[32] Meanwhile, indefatigable British consul David Turnbull encouraged both slaves and antislavery advocates in Cuba to expect British help. Other white Cubans feared that Britain would seize Cuba under the "pretext of the abolition of slavery."[33]

Cuba's central role in the global fight over slavery was obvious after an 1843 rising by newly arrived Africans. Although planters like Domingo del Monte encouraged the early discussion of rebellion, it became almost entirely a strike by enslaved Cubans and free people of color. Although scholars continue to debate how many enslaved people participated in the events known as La Escalera, Spanish officials responded as if the survival of slavery was at stake. Capt. Gen. Leopoldo O'Donnell ordered the execution of more than seventy enslaved and free Cubans and the exile, imprisonment, or torture of thousands of others. O'Donnell aimed both to crush the slaves' uprising and to teach white Cuban creoles to depend on Spain for their survival. In these tense times, the young Santacilia and his parents returned to Cuba from their Spanish exile.[34] The Cuba they came back to seemed ever farther from home rule. New Spanish *moderado* governments between 1844 and 1860 rebuilt the empire's finances and its navy to solidify its control of its most productive remaining colony. Spanish officials even contemplated expanding the empire in North Africa and the Americas.[35]

In the heightened politics of the 1840s, no slave revolt could be contained to Cuba. News of La Escalera sped across the Gulf, raising anxieties and hopes about slavery's future. For the U.S. consul, Spain's response was a heartening sign of slavery's survival. "No punishment can be too severe" in order to maintain the "salutary institution" of slavery, he wrote.[36] And some planters used the Cuban uprisings to paint U.S. slavery as particularly mild, Cuba's as particularly cruel. But other stories of La Escalera inspired some U.S. antislavery activists to embrace revolution. The executed poet Gabriel de la Concepción Valdés, a free black man better known as Plácido, became an emblem of global antislavery, written into poems by John Greenleaf Whittier and into journalism by William Lloyd Garrison.[37] African American newspaperman and physician Martin Delany, moved by Plácido's poetry and life, began to compose long letters on Cuban affairs for Frederick Douglass's publications, letters that simultaneously denounced U.S. expansionism and the cruelty of Spanish rule. "The instant of annexation of Cuba to these United States . . . should be the signal for simultaneous rebellion of all the slaves in the Southern States, and throughout that island," Delany wrote.[38] In a later article, Delany said, "Whenever you are ready, hoist the flag and draw the sword of revolution."[39] If Cuban slavery depended on the support of U.S. diplomacy, antislavery activists asked, then would reshaping U.S. diplomacy lead to the downfall of slavery on Cuba? Slavery made domestic questions international.

||||||||||||||||||||||||||||||||||||||

But planters saw the same harbingers and took revolutionary strikes to save slavery in Texas. Texas annexation represented both the triumph of the slave owners and a desperate maneuver to save slavery. Since Texas settlers' defeat of Mexico in 1836, many white Texans and Southern Democrats were eager for annexation, but Northern opposition made it impossible to gain the supermajority necessary to ratify a treaty. But La Escalera and Britain's diplomatic lobbying against slavery taught white Southerners that slavery faced a global crisis; the time to act was now. Therefore, President John Tyler and Southern senators moved quickly, and unconstitutionally, in order to save slavery and permanently alter the United States' internal balance of power. After Democrats elected ardent expansionist James Polk as president in 1844, Tyler's allies passed a joint resolution instead of a treaty. Democrats thus swept Texas inside the United States by a simple majority in a lame-duck session. Acquisition by joint resolution was a desperate act, but Southern planters believed that these were desperate times. Congressmen added proslavery senators and representatives, three hundred miles of Gulf coastline, and a border with northern Mexico. United States troops soon crossed that border and instigated an eighteen-month war with Mexico. After U.S. forces occupied Veracruz in March 1847 and Mexico City in September 1847, the United States extracted vast concessions from the Mexican government, including a territory as large as western Europe that encompassed California and New Mexico and the extended border of Texas.[40]

Victory over Mexico raised hopes and fears in both the United States and Cuba that the island would be next. Some white Cuban creoles saw the United States' victory as proof that there was now a force as strong as Britain in the Gulf. "The sympathies and feelings of the Creoles have been with us," the U.S. consul in Havana wrote in 1846, "but they have feared . . . the power of England."[41] By 1847, the same consul wrote, "The steadfastness and firmness of our new troops have filled all military men here with surprise, and astonishment, and some perhaps with alarm."[42] Rumors swirled that U.S. soldiers returning from Mexico would stop in Havana to aid a prospective rebellion. Still, many Cuban fantasies did not extend to independence, for the simple reason that Cubans remained fearful of British power. An independent Cuban republic would not be able to defend Havana against British bombardment, or the island's estates against a slave uprising. "They feel they have not strength enough to effect their liberation alone + therefore that they have no alternative but to seek the annexation" to the United States, the British consul wrote.[43] Meanwhile Cubans whispered that Britain would pressure the Spaniards to end slavery before the United States struck.[44] Nothing seemed predictable; everything seemed possible.

On the island, Cuban annexationism was not a product of U.S. manipulation but a homegrown revolutionary movement and one that elites embraced in many regions of Latin America.[45] In 1847 and 1848, Venezuela-born military officer and Cuban official Narciso López plotted a rebellion that attracted support from young white Cuban creoles, including many students. This Mina de la Rosa conspiracy linked López with annexationist Havana Club members like author Cirilo Villaverde, poet Juan Clemente Zenea, and professor Miguel Teurbe Tolón and his many students. But when Spanish authorities arrested one of López's followers, López fled to the United States for safety.[46] Although U.S. scholars sometimes portray López as a product of U.S. backing, Spanish authorities saw him as a "grave danger" with "very general" support among Cuban creoles, and the British consul described an "extensive" conspiracy in 1847–48.[47] Spain launched significant internal investigations, examining more than 50 Cubans in 1848 for supporting different uprisings, then more than 100 in 1850 and 200 in 1851, for a total of more than 750 between 1848 and 1855.[48] In these investigations, Spanish officials uncovered revolutionary networks of information and gossip that convinced them that the "greater part" of the creoles opposed the "domination" of Spain.[49] Spanish officials reported at least three potentially disruptive forces on the island. Planters in the Havana-Matanzas region, including some *peninsulares*, sought access to U.S. protection and commerce; many feared that Spain would eventually undermine slavery on the island under British and French pressure, and many hoped to buy grain and materials cheaply from U.S. merchants without the burden of Spanish duties. White Cuban creoles in the ranching and farming east meanwhile feared that Spain would import more slaves, and they long resented Spain's exclusion of creoles from high offices. And many slaves and free people of color saw Spain as a reactionary empire and sought antislavery support from France and Britain.

The 1848 revolutionary uprisings in Hungary, Italy, and France inspired revolutionary hopes on the island and beyond. "The revolutions in Europe have communicated new vigour to the cause of annexation in this quarter of the globe," a New Orleans newspaper wrote.[50] When the French 1848 rebellion ended slavery in Martinique and Guadeloupe, black Cubans (and a few whites) saw portents of a global collapse of slavery. In Santiago, black Cubans openly talked about British or French backing for a slave rebellion.[51] In this tense ideological struggle, rebellious students like Pedro Santacilia, drawn into the López insurgencies, connected Cuban rebellions to nationalist struggles in Poland and Italy and to earlier Latin American revolutions and to the U.S. revolution. It was no longer time to protest; it was now "necessary to die or triumph," Santacilia wrote.[52]

The revolutionary situation in Cuba could not be contained, for white Cuban creoles manipulated U.S. public opinion in hope of finding an ally for their struggle against Spain. Perhaps the most famous of these encounters occurred in 1848, when planter Cristóbal Mádan invited visiting U.S. journalist John O'Sullivan to gatherings of the anticolonial Havana Club. O'Sullivan, in Havana on honeymoon, was an ardent U.S. expansionist, the crafter of the phrase "Manifest Destiny," and a supporter of many 1848 European revolutions. At Madán's gatherings, O'Sullivan heard elite Cuban planters describe an island ready to rebel. The connections they made were deep; eventually Madán married O'Sullivan's sister. Back in the United States, Madán and O'Sullivan lobbied President James Polk to acquire Cuba and later (and more surprisingly) collaborated with abolitionist James McCune Smith to assist a U.S. freeman who had been kidnapped into slavery in Cuba.[53]

Also passing through Cuba were two other important hubs in the midcentury revolutionary network. One was the remarkable Jane McManus Storm Cazneau, already famous under her pen name of Cora Montgomery. Daughter of a U.S. congressman and allegedly the mistress of an aging Aaron Burr, Montgomery in the 1830s had touted U.S. settler colonization in

Mexican-controlled Texas and then raised funds for the Texas Revolution. During the U.S.-Mexican War, Montgomery traveled behind enemy lines to file stories for the *New York Sun*.[54] On the way home from Mexico, Montgomery and her *Sun* editor Moses Beach stopped in Havana and heard many tales of Cuban rebelliousness, and they repeated those tales in the *Sun* once they returned to the United States. "The possession of Cuba will complete our chain of territory, and give us the North American continent," the *Sun* trumpeted. "It is the garden of the world, the key to the Gulf, and the richest spot of its size on the face of the earth. . . . The Cubans are waiting for us."[55] With Beach's backing, Montgomery founded *La Verdad*, a bilingual Cuban exile newspaper that published Madán, rebel poet Porfirio Valiente, and soon Santacilia, too. These Cuban plotters and U.S. writers worked hard to spread word of an imminent Cuban revolution. By June 1848, Secretary of State James Buchanan officially invoked the "deep-rooted hostility to Spanish dominion" among the "Creoles of Cuba" as he tried to purchase Cuba from Spain.[56]

||||||||||||||||||||||||||||||||||||||

News of the Cuban crises reached the United States as mainland politicians struggled to resolve the problems created by the U.S.-Mexican War. Texas annexation and the United States' invasion of Mexico convinced many U.S. politicians that the fight over slavery was an existential one, a struggle over the survival of the institution and of the nation. On the floor of the House of Representatives, Congressman David Wilmot introduced a proviso blocking the expansion of slavery into new territory. The proviso became a referendum on slavery not just in the Mexican cession but in Cuba. Wilmot defended the proviso as the best way to block the future acquisition of Cuba, and Southern politicians denounced the proviso for its impact on Cuban annexation. When the Northern-dominated House passed the Wilmot Proviso and the Senate rejected it, Washington froze.[57] Although both political parties aimed to minimize the slave issue in the 1848 presidential election, a new Free Soil Party split from the Democrats, nominated former president Martin Van Buren on a platform opposing the expansion of slavery, and won 10 percent of the national vote. With Van Buren siphoning votes from Democrats, Whig Zachary Taylor won the White House. Although Taylor was a slave owner and a leading general in the U.S.-Mexican War, he aimed to restrain the expansion of slavery, particularly in California.

Narciso López and his U.S. supporters decided the time was ripe to force the United States to act by launching an invasion of their own. The Havana

Club dispatched José Ambrosio Gonzales, a well-educated Matanzas native, to the United States to aid López. After unsuccessfully offering one hundred thousand dollars to U.S. military leaders (including Robert E. Lee), the two men began recruiting large numbers of U.S. fighters in July 1849. López's own politics—and the overall politics of the filibuster movement—drew on many of the era's contradictory strains. At times López fought for independence, at times for defense of his reputation, at times for annexation to the United States, at times for money. For the moment, López and other Cuban filibusters deferred any final resolution of the island's future or simply dissembled, particularly as the movement grew. Although U.S. historians sometimes associate López solely with slave owners, he recruited across the eastern United States, drawing volunteers not only from Mobile, Baltimore, and New Orleans but also from Boston, New York, and Philadelphia, and he hoped to launch one invading force from New Orleans and another from New York.[58]

But López and his followers could not turn the U.S. government to their side. When López's U.S. aides transferred roughly three hundred men from New Orleans to Round Island, Mississippi, the Taylor administration informed the Spanish minister in the United States and then dispatched the navy to blockade the Round Island rebels. In New York City, U.S. marshals likewise seized steamers, and President Taylor issued a proclamation against piracy. Across the South politicians and editors protested. A month later, Mississippi voters elected inflammatory expansionist John Quitman governor. Although this and later filibustering expeditions would be remembered as U.S.-directed adventures, Mexico's consul in New Orleans believed that "great numbers of Cubans" helped plan the movement but withdrew when Taylor's proclamation convinced them that participation would cost them U.S. protection.[59]

Inside the United States, the struggle over slavery in California threatened to dissolve national politics. Army commanders there called a constitutional convention at which delegates banned slavery in the state. As white Southerners fumed, Senator Henry Clay sought accommodations to appease the South. But the Senate rejected Clay's compromise, and Taylor dug in his heels in support of a free-state California. In June 1850, Southern delegates met in Nashville to debate secession. But in July 1850, Taylor died, turning over the presidency to compromise supporter Millard Fillmore. Senator Stephen Douglas then divided Clay's plan into five separate bills that admitted California as a free state, banned the slave trade (but not slavery) in Washington, D.C., settled border issues between Texas and New Mexico, permitted Utah and New Mexico settlers to decide the future of slavery in those territories, and vastly expanded federal power in a new Fugitive Slave Law. Neither side was appeased. South Carolina senator John Calhoun talked of secession unless Northerners acquiesced explicitly to the expansion of slavery, while Ralph Waldo Emerson predicted that war with Mexico would poison the United States.[60]

Although the Compromise of 1850 seemed to favor the South, the North in some ways won the settlement.[61] The Fugitive Slave Act proved difficult to enforce, as several prominent Southern politicians had predicted, and only 150 cases were prosecuted in 1850 and 1851, although thousands of African Americans fled to Canada and many thousands more established mutual defense societies.[62] Meanwhile, Northerners won two key concessions: California and time. The *Charleston Daily Mercury* later complained that "the battle of Southern rights and Southern equality in the Union was fought in 1850. The balance of power was lost. The South was overcome by exclusion from California in her unrighteous admission into the Union. The North then gained the inevitable majority in the Senate. With the power of limitless expansion, the control of Government was won."[63] Never again would slave states match free states in the Senate, even though California at times elected Southern sympathizers. California was therefore the site of the "second American Revolution," a Wisconsin politician said, a victory in the war between "Despotism and Freedom."[64] Northerners also gained time; between 1850 and 1860, almost two million European immigrants entered the United States, settling disproportionately in the North and giving that region a consequential demographic and economic advantage.

The Compromise of 1850 was not much of a compromise, but the acts did momentarily quiet the political crisis. In 1851 and 1852, politicians repaired many of the breaches. By 1852, the Free Soil vote fell by half, as many antislavery Democrats returned home. Even the bedraggled Whigs fielded a credible, competitive candidate in 1852. The key institutional collapses that led to the Civil War—the dissolution of the Whigs, the regional fracture of the Democrats, and the creation of a powerful Northern antislavery party—still lay in the future.[65] The U.S.-Mexican War heightened political divisions over slavery and sparked fights over western territory, but the return of relative political peace in 1851 suggests that historians of the coming of the Civil War should be careful not to let the U.S.-Mexican War's narrative utility overwhelm their analysis of its significance.[66]

What broke the armistice, in part, was the prospect of acquiring Cuba. White Cuban creoles worked desperately to draw attention to the conflict on the island and in the process helped reinvigorate battles within U.S. politics.

They operated from newspapers and clubs in the key port cities that connected the United States to Cuba, especially New York and New Orleans but
also Baltimore, Savannah, Augusta, Charleston, Philadelphia, Key West, and
Mobile. In Spanish-language papers like *La Verdad* (based for a time in New
York and for a time in New Orleans) and *El Filibustero* and *El Guao*, Cubans
(and Cazneau under her pen name) worked to foster a revolutionary spirit in
bitter denunciations of "the tyrannical dispositions of Spanish power"[67] and
"its despotic institutions."[68] These writers freely mixed anti-Spanish anti-
imperialism with U.S. expansionism, casting the United States as a protec-
tor of colonized people and an emblem of republican self-rule even as they
raised the possibility that Cuba might be absorbed into the United States.[69]
Among the key people in this phase of Cuban exile writing were arms dealer
and Cuban Junta and Havana Club leader Domingo de Goicuría,[70] Valiente,
Francisco de Armas, Santiago Bombalier, Manuel Hidalgo Ramírez, Fernando Betancourt, Salvador Cisneros, Luis Hernández, Bienvenido Hernández, Melchor Silva, and Zenea.[71] In newspapers like the *New York Sun*, *New
York Herald*, and New Orleans *Daily Delta*, U.S. editors republished Cuban
opinions to prove that the island was on the verge of revolution.

Cuban exiles also helped normalize revolutionary talk inside the United
States. While many U.S. politicians remained wary of revolutions, Cuban exiles had no such caution. In both Spanish and English, they celebrated revolution and revolutionaries. Pedro Santacilia looked to Hungary and Italy and
Poland for examples of the striving for "independence, progress, and liberty"
but saw the greatest model in a United States that "has offered to a surprised
humanity the imposing spectacle" of republics.[72] There was "no other remedy
than revolution," Valiente wrote.[73]

World events were reshaping U.S. politics, nowhere more obviously than
in the white Cubans' closest allies, the expansionists affiliated with the
Young America movement. Their ranks included not only U.S. adventurers
and Cuban exiles but also the French-born politician Pierre Soulé and the
German financier August Belmont. Young Americans patterned themselves,
in part, after Kossuth, Garibaldi, and the exiled 1848 European revolutionaries who were "arriving to this Republic in swarms," a concerned Spanish
minister wrote.[74] Horrified by the monarchical resurgence in Europe, and
critical of the United States' unwillingness to support rebellions in Italy and
Hungary, Young Americans hoped to reinvigorate the United States from
within and then to revolutionize the Atlantic World.[75] O'Sullivan, Montgomery, Beach, Soulé, Belmont, Daniel Sickles, and the politicians who allied with
them helped white Cuban exiles blur the line between internal and external
politics.

Since Young Americans undermined the armistice of 1850, it is easy to as-sume that they followed a narrow, sectional, proslavery agenda. But many Young Americans were more committed to expansion than to slavery, and many hoped to annex Canada as well. Like the Cuban creoles, many held seemingly contradictory views of slavery or simply did not consider the issue as pressing as expansion or national rejuvenation. To Cora Montgomery, "union preserving" annexationists aimed to cut through the "great sectional struggle" and wave away "the mist and smoke of sectional prejudice."[76] As long as the United States also kept expanding northward and westward, "who could be so weak as to fear the addition of one, two, or three Slave states?" she asked.[77] As late as 1855, Montgomery celebrated her "great work" "in the paci-fication of these terrible disputes which are endangering the Union."[78] When slave owners provided the most logical path to expansion, Young Americans appeared to be tools of the South. But later in the decade, some were drawn to Northern free-labor expansionism, and during the Civil War, some switched their views on slavery and backed the Union as War Democrats.

Together, white Cuban exiles and Young Americans raised money and men for revolutionary strikes against Cuba in 1850 and 1851. Backed by Mis-sissippi governor John Quitman, López launched an invasion in May 1850 that reached Cuba, where they unfurled a newly designed Cuban flag. When local Cubans did not join the movement, López fled. In 1851, López gathered another force, backed by the nephew of the U.S. attorney general, among others. This time, Spanish soldiers captured the filibusters near Las Pozas and executed López and most of his followers. Because López failed to gain Cuban support on the island, and because many adventurers and proslavery enthusiasts joined his expeditions, historians sometimes underestimate his Cuban following. But leading Cubans like Madán, Gaspar de Betancourt y Cisneros, and Juan Manuel Macias, among others, were charged with sup-porting the movement.[79] And other revolutionary risings were afoot in Cuba. In summer 1851, not long before López's invasion, there were uprisings in Puerto Príncipe, and soon after the cravat protests in Santiago that led to Santacilia's banishment.[80] British consuls believed that strategic and logisti-cal problems, not a lack of general support, doomed López. "Had General López met with any success" in his 1850 expedition, there would have been an allied uprising in Havana supported "by a great number of the Troops stationed on the island," a British official wrote.[81] Despite the defeats, Santa-cilia, Zenea, and other Cuban exiles defended filibusters, including in the newspaper El Filibustero. Although the Spanish called the invaders "pirates," Santacilia compared them to the revolutionaries who founded the United States and the Spanish American republics.[82]

What thwarted filibustering was not Cuban creole diffidence but Spanish resilience and U.S. resistance. On the island, the Spanish government cracked down on rebels through sweeping arrests, executions, and expulsions that caused "universal panic" among white creoles, the U.S. consul wrote. Spain was in the midst of revamping its overseas empire, having reclaimed the west-central African island of Fernando Po in 1844. Spanish leaders dreamed of further expansion in Morocco and Santo Domingo.[83]

Spanish entrenchment in Cuba was matched by surprisingly consistent U.S. restraint. Despite abolitionist complaints that slave owners dominated U.S. foreign policy, their Slave Power thesis—the idea that slaveholders conspired to turn the federal government to slaveholders' ends—worked better as propaganda than as historical analysis.[84] Young Americans were repeatedly frustrated by their inability to gain governmental support or even acquiescence. After the 1850 expedition, federal grand juries indicted López and Quitman, forcing Quitman to resign as governor of Mississippi, although no leading filibusters were convicted. A Madrid official wrote in praise of the U.S. government's "good faith" and desire to be in "harmony with us" even as he noted the weakness of the government in the face of "the clamors of public opinion."[85] Although the U.S. government always had "pretensions" of taking Cuba, Capt. Gen. Leopoldo O'Donnell wrote, "these are sublimated to the probability of success." [86] Skeptical Spanish officials depended not on the United States' intentions but on the United States' interests. As Spain expanded its navy in the late 1840s, Southern politicians worried increasingly about the prospect of Spanish gunboats shelling Savannah and Charleston and Mobile and about the political fallout of a conflict with Spain.[87]

||||||||||||||||||||||||||||||||||

The failure to seize Cuba inspired Young Americans to redouble their efforts to control U.S. politics, in hopes of steering the country toward annexation. In 1852, Young Americans helped Franklin Pierce reintegrate Northern and Southern wings of the Democratic Party around the promise of expansion.[88] Haplessly the Whig Party embraced caution in its pledge never to "stand upon foreign ground. . . . Our mission as a republic is not to propagate our opinion, or impose on other countries our form of government by artifice or force."[89] Within days of Pierce's victory, U.S. consul William Sharkey saw "signs of revolution" in Havana because of the expected support from the new administration.[90] Pierce at his inaugural promised not to be "controlled by any timid forebodings of evil from expansion. . . . Our attitude as a nation and our position on the globe render the acquisition of certain possessions

In this section of a lithograph titled *Invasion of Cuba*, the artist celebrates
the filibustering attack on Cuba and bitterly critiques the United States for
abandoning Narciso López and his followers. In the image, Capt. Gen. José
Gutiérrez de la Concha grinds Cuba under his feet from his throne as he greets
the kneeling U.S. consul while Secretary of State Daniel Webster brandishes
an alleged secret treaty with Spain. At the top, Cuban firing squads execute
kneeling U.S. filibusters and an Afro-Cuban garrotes López.
Courtesy of the Library of Congress, LC-USZ62-89602.

not within our jurisdiction eminently important for our protection."[91] Everyone knew he was speaking of Cuba. Pierce's election "gives the strongest assurance to the rapacious and slavery propagating spirits of the country, that
the time has come to attempt extreme and audacious measures," Frederick
Douglass's newspaper complained, not long after it published the letter from
"H" predicting a world war over Cuban slavery.[92]

The battle over slavery expanded from an internal struggle to an external one, from an allocation of authority within the nation to the use of the nation to remake the Gulf World. In the process the slavery debate shifted from constitutionally limited congressional acts to wider ideological struggles. Even before the inauguration, the outgoing Congress tried to suspend neutrality laws that blocked citizens from aiding Cuban insurrections. Antislavery congressmen fought back ferociously, developing a global critique of slavery that tied its survival in Cuba to its persistence in the United States. In the House, abolitionist Joshua Giddings described scenes of armed Cuban slaves fighting off U.S. invaders and then sparking a massive slave insurrection in Florida and other Southern states. "The world is moving in favor of liberty," Giddings said. "I trust it will come in peace," but—quoting John Quincy Adams—"if it must come in *blood*, yet I say, LET IT COME."[93] What was needed, abolitionist newspapers wrote, was "the overthrow of the Slave Power" so that "foreign policy should be controlled by National, not Sectional ideas."[94] A correspondent wrote to Frederick Douglass in December 1852, "We are inclined to think that this Cuban question will serve to form parties and inflame the passions of the country."[95]

Pierce's victory immediately reshaped foreign policy, the one area where presidents exerted significant control in the nineteenth century. Expansionists filled his foreign ranks: James Buchanan to London with New York politico Daniel Sickles as his aide; John O'Sullivan to Portugal; August Belmont to the Netherlands; John Mason to France; and to Spain, Pierre Soulé, "the most brilliant and, perhaps, most respectable of the leaders of 'Young America.'"[96] In Madrid, Soulé defended "privately, and with great assiduity, those maxims of independence, and principles of Government, which it is his Mission on Earth, as he states to promulgate," according to the British ambassador. In London, Sickles offended British public sentiment by deliberately disrespecting the queen.[97] These would-be revolutionaries turned foreign policy toward a desperate hunt for Cuba.

Other international crises gave these Young Americans reason for hope. Britain was distracted by its contest with Russia for control of the Middle East, a contest that would soon lead to the Crimean War. Meanwhile the Spanish government suffered extraordinary financial crises, in part because of the profligate corruption of the queen mother, in part because of droughts, bad harvests, and the increased cost of grain. With tax revenues weak and the royal family in desperate need of funds, Soulé saw his chance. Purchasing Cuba could in fell swoop end monarchical rule on the island, save the Spanish treasury, expand U.S. borders, and preserve slavery. New Yorkers Sickles and Belmont, sure of the sale and eager for the commissions, competed with each other to draw up the projected one-hundred-million-dollar bond to buy Cuba.[98] But Spanish ministers had long told U.S. diplomats that "no Spaniard would ever dare to put his signature to any treaty" of sale. "Spain might indeed lose the Island, but sell it never!"[99]

Boxed in by financial crises, British lobbying, and U.S. pressure, Spanish leaders seized on a bold counterstrategy, unimaginable in normal times: they pondered ending slavery to forestall U.S. expansion. Reformist captain general José González de la Pezuela began to undermine slavery on the island. "It is said that he is strongly opposed to slavery, if not an abolitionist, and that he is the very man to carry out the views of our English brethren," the U.S. consul warned.[100] To draw British support, Pezuela opened the door to legal importation of nominally free African laborers and apprentices, as well as Mayans fleeing the Yucatán War and Chinese "coolies." By rumor Pezuela held a royal letter authorizing the emancipation of all slaves on the island. Pezuela then armed black militias in Cuba and prepared for war.[101] "The greatest activity is displayed in the enlistment of the blacks," the U.S. consul in Havana warned. "Emissaries are in every quarter, stirring them up with the positive assurance that the Americans are coming here to prevent the liberation of the slaves, and to enslave those already free."[102] Spain moved warships to Cuba to prepare to fight against the United States, while the U.S. consul asked for a proclamation of war.[103] By December 1853, the U.S. consul warned that "the friends of freedom, i.e., of Cuban independence, are very nearly crushed."[104]

The vision of armed black militiamen in Cuba inspired dreams of armed black men revolutionizing the continent. Martin Delany moved to free-soil Canada and later began composing *Blake; or the Huts of America*, a prediction that a cousin of Cuban poet-rebel Plácido would lead a bloody revolution to end slavery in both the United States and Cuba. Amid rumors that Britain conspired to end slavery in Cuba, a black Canadian contrasted the two countries. "The mission of Great Britain is to extend freedom to all men; but that of the American Republic to extend it to only a part, while the rest is to be kept in the most degrading bondage." The author pondered what would happen if Britain were "to land a few thousand of her Black troops in the South of the States" and "distribute a few hundred thousand muskets and rifles among their slaves, and that fire for freedom, which is now smothering within, would then burst out and burn to the nethermost parts of the Slaveholding Union."[105]

Fearing that slave revolution was contagious, U.S. planters and their political allies desperately struggled to block the "Africanization" of the island and the Southern United States.[106] The *New Orleans Times Picayune* warned that a Cuban slave uprising "would entail upon us a struggle with the negro communities upon our Southern borders, resulting, perhaps, in a war of extermination against four millions of free blacks."[107] In August 1854, John Quitman wrote that "the great question of our age" was "whether American or European policy shall prevail on this continent. Of this great question, Cuba is the battleground. . . . The European policy is to establish near us negro or mongrel states. Such a result would be fatal to us. Our destiny is intertwined with that of Cuba. If slave institutions perish there, they will perish here."[108] From Havana, the U.S. consul urged the United States to intervene quickly to prevent "a war of races + extermination" like Haiti, and in Madrid, the U.S. minister pressed the Spanish government to remove Pezuela.[109] Meanwhile around New Orleans, former Mississippi governor Quitman raised forces for yet another filibuster invasion of the island while Cuban exiles predicted a white "revolution" on the island inspired by creoles' and *peninsulares*' shared "fear of the blacks."[110]

Then a coup in Spain shifted the international context again. Not for the last time, politics in Spain turned (and perhaps turned on) the situation in Cuba. Beginning in the summer of 1854, a group of generals rose against the government in the Vicalvarada rebellion. Former military commanders with interests in Cuba were at the center of the uprising, especially O'Donnell, who had overseen the expansion of slavery in Cuba and crushed La Escalera; José Gutiérrez de la Concha, who had governed the island harshly during López's later expeditions; and Juan Prim y Prats, a former governor of Puerto Rico. Some Spaniards saw the work of a Cuban Slave Lobby in the revolution, as rumors spread of massive bribes and weapon purchases by Madrid families that owned plantations and slaves on the island. The coup plotters were backed, at least by rumor, by a small band of extraordinarily wealthy, mostly Spanish-born, planters in the Havana-Matanzas region who resisted U.S. annexation for fear it would undermine their special favors from the Spanish crown. During the so-called *bienio progresista*, these generals steered Cuban policy back toward slavery. Pezuela and his seeming antislavery ties were out; in was Gutiérrez de la Concha himself for a second tenure as captain general.[111] Newspapers reported that the revolution "caused a paralyzation of Mr. Soulé's intrigues for the acquisition of Cuba."[112] But the Spanish revolutionary spirit could not be neatly contained; popular uprisings on the streets of Zaragoza and impassioned cries for democracy from young Madrid professor Emilio Castelar laid the groundwork for rebellions in the next decade.[113]

Desperate to sustain their revolutionary momentum before the international context faded, Young Americans and their allies threatened war. The

Spanish seizure of the ship the *Black Warrior* for customs violations gave them a pretense. In Ostend, Belgium, Soulé, Buchanan, and Mason drafted a manifesto declaring that "Cuba is as necessary to the North American republic as any of its present members, and that it belongs naturally to that great family of States." Since Cuba endangered "our internal peace and the existence of our cherished Union," the United States would be "justified in wresting it from Spain" in order to prevent Cuba from becoming "Africanized and become a second Santo Domingo [Haiti], with all its attendant horrors to the white race."[114] These diplomats believed they had world affairs on their side. Britain and France were distracted by the Crimean War and annoyed by Spain's unwillingness to join. But these U.S. diplomats had misread the political situation back home in the United States.

||||||||||||||||||||||||||||||||||||

Over 1854, the Cuba crisis intersected with the domestic crisis over slavery in Kansas in ways that doomed both Cuban annexation and the spread of slavery to Kansas. By 1855, it was no longer quite so easy for anyone—young Americans or white creoles or Northern politicians—to waffle on the issue of slavery. Cuba, Kansas, and fugitive slaves had redefined politics and forced people to choose between contradictory views of the future. Although often separated, Kansas, fugitive slaves, and Cuba together radicalized both North and South. The Kansas crisis began in January 1854, when Senator Stephen Douglas, an ally of the Young Americans, tried to organize Nebraska into a territory to expedite the construction of a transcontinental railroad. But Southern senators demanded that the territory allow slavery. In a desperate effort to placate them, Douglas convinced Pierce to support repealing the Missouri Compromise to permit the now separated territories of Kansas and Nebraska to vote on the spread of slavery. When Southern and Northern Whigs divided on the issue, that party collapsed, and the Republican Party grew quickly out of the remnants of Northern Whigs and Northern antislavery Democrats. Meanwhile the federal government deployed armed forces to carry runaway Anthony Burns through the streets of Boston to ships waiting to return him to slavery in Virginia.[115]

The fight over Kansas was simultaneously a fight over Cuba. Antebellum Americans connected the two through the Kansas-Nebraska Act's recasting of federal policy in the territories, the ongoing Spanish threat of emancipation, and the belief that Southern senators intended to use the threat of Kansas as a trading piece for the richer- and more-useful acquisition of Cuba.[116] The Kansas act did not solely overturn the Missouri Compromise's ban on slavery in northern territories; it also affirmed the power of territories to determine the status of slavery for themselves from the beginning of their organization. While every new state had a right to legalize slavery, Congress had previously exerted greater authority over territories before statehood. The wording of the Kansas act explicitly cleared the way for every new territory to judge slavery for itself.

For Northerners skeptical that slavery would ever prevail in Kansas, this provision of the Kansas act seemed to be a response to a potential Spanish emancipation. If Spain ended slavery on Cuba before the U.S. annexed the island, the U.S. government would face the legal and political problem of reimposing, rather than sustaining, slavery. This presented significant legal and international challenges, since Northern antislavery lawyers and British diplomats had long rejected what they called reenslavement. Once a person was free, the national government could not reenslave them.[117] The Kansas act's embrace of a territorial power to choose slavery therefore opened a new path to reimpose the institution on the island of Cuba. If white Cubans upon acquisition enacted territorial laws for enslavement, then those local elites—not the U.S. government—would bear responsibility for the reimposition of slavery. Then, the United States could simply receive the Cuban slaves into the country. One antislavery newspaper wrote that although slavery was unlikely to move into Nebraska or Kansas, "the principle that Congress cannot interfere with the Territories, in the matter of Slavery" would lead directly to the acquisition of Cuba and other slave regions.[118] An anti-Nebraska convention called the Missouri Compromise repeal and Gadsden Purchase "utterly worthless except as a basis for the operations of millions upon millions more in the re-establishment of Slavery in Cuba."[119]

Many Northerners also believed that Kansas was simply a bargaining chip to be traded for Cuba in a future negotiation. Confident that northern settlers would eventually gain the majority in Kansas, or that cotton and other slave crops would not grow, they looked for ulterior motives for what seemed to be a fruitless effort by Southern politicians. They found their answer in the Southern senators' love of political horse-trading. What if Kansas was merely a chit? If Southern politicians could put Kansas's future in doubt, perhaps Northern states would be willing to trade Cuba's status for Kansas's future.[120] "It seems plain to us that, fatal as the [Kansas-Nebraska] measure is in these aspects, it is only a cover for broader propagandism of Slavery in the future," a group of antislavery congressmen wrote. "The object of the Administration, and of many who represent the slave States, is to prepare the way for annexing Cuba, at whatever cost, and a like annexation of half a dozen of the States of Mexico."[121]

The Kansas-Nebraska Act, the military's use against Burns, and the Ostend Manifesto represented high-water marks of Southern grasping, but not of Southern power. Once again, the administration retreated from proslavery plans and disappointed slavery expansionists. Riven by domestic conflict, the Pierce administration could not afford a foreign war; the government recalled Soulé, backed away from the Ostend message, and restored normal relations with Spain. When the Pierce administration prevented a ship of filibusters from departing in 1855, the Spanish government spoke "in very laudatory terms of the conduct of the United States," the British minister reported.[122] The planters' bid had lost. Still, the Kansas question would remain tied to Cuba for the rest of the decade, as antislavery newspapers and politicians continued to warn that Southern planters intended to trade their acquiescence to a free Kansas for the addition of Cuba as a slave state, just as a free California had been traded for the Fugitive Slave Act.[123]

These crises inflamed Northern public opinion against slavery and burned away much of the ground previously occupied by Southern-sympathizing Northerners, or doughfaces. With Kansas, Nebraska, Cuba, and the Burns case as prime issues, Northern Democrats suffered a crushing defeat in the fall 1854 midterms, losing more than a dozen seats each in New York and Ohio. The new Anti-Nebraska Party won thirty-seven and helped elect ardent antislavery expansionist Nathaniel Banks as Speaker of the House. In turn, Pierce did not mention Cuba in his annual address. "The reason of this silence, this obvious timidity is understood by every member," antislavery congressman Joshua Giddings said. "The condemnation" of Pierce's policy toward Cuba "by the people, at our recent elections, is seen and read of all men. It is written on the tablet of the moral Universe. It came to the president like the voice of the Almighty to the rich men."[124] In early 1855, U.S.-allied Cuban creoles launched another effort at revolution, conspiring to assassinate Capt. Gen. Gutiérrez de la Concha and draw the aid of U.S. filibusters. But Gutiérrez de la Concha cracked down brutally on the rebellion, jailing numerous Cubans and executing leading planter Ramón Pintó.[125] As Spain's new ships protected the island, Cuba seemed farther and farther away from joining the United States as a slave state.

This triumph inspired some antislavery Northerners to embrace an expansionist, antislavery Liberty Power. Many antislavery Northern politicians had long supported expansion—especially in Canada—until the 1845–54 crises made expansion and slavery synonymous. After 1854, Republicans felt increasingly free to once again embrace expansion, even empire, in the name of freedom. Republicans, born in a commitment to expanding their wage labor system across lands then held by Indians, found it easy to extend their settler colonialism across broader and broader landscapes, once slave owners' weakness became clear. Only our ahistorical association of slavery and expansion and our resistance to grappling with the settler colonialism at the heart of the Republican project prevent us from seeing the alternative that antislavery expansionists offered. The "majority of the Northern people," Senator John Hale said, "are proud of their free institutions, they seek their extension. . . . But they believe the Constitution was formed to protect and extend *Liberty*."[126] Antislavery politicians also helped defend themselves against long-standing charges that they were pro-British or even tools of the British Empire.[127] While earlier abolitionists celebrated "the extension of the English empire" and its "free institutions," antislavery politicians now championed the United States as the defender of freedom.[128] Congressman Gerrit Smith went so far as to support adding Cuba even with slavery, on the grounds that the United States would reform Cuban slavery and eventually eliminate it. And Smith derided abolitionist Wendell Phillips as a monarchist apologist for the British.[129] Denigrating anti-imperialism as essentially "Pro-Slavery Conservatism" the antislavery *National Era* declared, "We are for the extension of American Empire. . . . We want Cuba, Canada, the Sandwich Islands, and as much more of the American continent as may be had honestly," but only without slavery.[130]

This struggle between increasingly elaborated worldviews, differing visions of empire, turned domestic politics into something that resembled combat, even before Congressman Preston Brooks caned Senator Charles Sumner on the floor of the Senate in May 1856.[131] Some politicians made antislavery into a crusade, one that brooked no compromise.[132] Antislavery politicians and abolitionist editors amplified apocalyptic and revolutionary talk about an "inevitable final struggle in which victory or death must perforce be the motto of the opposing hosts for Liberty or Slavery."[133] In the process they brushed past a great deal of nuance, especially those Southern politicians like John Calhoun who feared that annexation would bring more nonwhites into the republic and those Northerners who doubted that Catholics, especially mixed-race Cubans or Mexicans, could govern themselves. Among the key disseminators of antislavery expansionism were abolitionist editors at the *National Anti-Slavery Standard*—the official publication of the American Anti-Slavery Society—William Lloyd Garrison's *Liberator,* Frederick Douglass's newspapers, and especially the Washington-based *National Era*, the most widely circulated antislavery newspaper and a hub of year-round antislavery lobbying in the capital.[134] Although these editors did not reflect Northern public opinion, they broadcast shockingly bold statements by Southern politicians and in other ways shifted the window of discourse, opening space for moderate Northerners to disagree with Southern politicians even if they held back from embracing antislavery. Like most political movements, Northern antislavery was clearer in its shared enemies than in its shared cause.

Antislavery newspapers at times embraced the necessity of revolution. Musing over the "trump card of Cuba," the *National Anti-Slavery Standard* wrote, "It seems to us that all these great changes involve revolutions, the shaking of dynasties, the entire reorganization of political systems. Come then . . . the wholesome storms that shall chase away the deadly malaria of oppression and injustice, and the keen and vindictive lightnings that may scathe the tall trees and perhaps strike down many human lives, but that shall purify the common air and bring life and health to myriads unborn!"[135] Another newspaper declared, "We are approaching the crisis which will decide whether Slavery or Freedom is to mould the destinies of America."[136] Antislavery writers tied the Slave Power to other forms of aristocracy, including monarchy, and cast the world struggle between republicanism and monarchy as part of the struggle between slavery and freedom. Thus they made the global fight against slavery part of the United States' championing of republics against thrones. Antislavery in the United States was moving toward a revolutionary position, but for the moment its success against Cuban acquisition softened any impetus to strike. Regular politics still seemed too promising.

||||||||||||||||||||||||||||||||||||||

After the failure of the Ostend Manifesto, white Cuban exiles found themselves adrift, their Southern allies helpless, Northern ones not yet ready for an embrace. As questions of monarchy and republic, of empire and colony, faded in the glare of slavery, white Cuban creoles could not quite find their footing. They struggled to address the central dilemma of U.S. politics—Where do you stand on slavery?— because of both their own complex views of the institution and their understanding that any answer would cost them half their potential support. By 1854, Santacilia was in despair about "our unfortunate Cuba," "in the middle of these indescribable flights of contrary emotions that sadden me and sicken me" and made him "lose reason" as he worried incessantly about a free black rebellion against the creoles. There was no point in politics "without enthusiasm," for despair made "patriotism sterile and unproductive." Wildly, he suggested trying to return to Cuba to negotiate with the captain general, a distant cousin. Santacilia, now editing *La Verdad* in New York, surveyed the bleak state of the movement and saw hope only in the constant provocation of Spanish tyranny. Plaintively, in what he called the "filibuster style," he wrote in *La Verdad*, "the Cuban revolution has not died."[137]

But these white Cuban creoles would not be stuck between slavery and antislavery forever. A series of other revolutions helped lead Cuban creoles toward antislavery. One was the Nicaraguan civil war, a conflict that Goicuría aimed to turn into a springboard to free Cuba. Filibuster William Walker's invasion of Nicaragua gave many Cubans another chance to gain an international foothold and, eventually, a grave learning experience about slavery and U.S. politics. Although Walker, too, is remembered as a tool of proslavery politicians, his own life confounds simple analysis. The leading recent scholarly portrayal calls him an emblem of "liberal imperialism" whose followers "not only opposed the expansion of slavery but also sought to uplift the native masses and free them from allegedly despotic elites." As an editor in New Orleans, Walker opposed filibustering invasions and was denounced as a "Yankee" for his caution. On moving to California, Walker backed the antislavery faction in the state Democratic Party and was again denounced as a tool of abolitionists. Even as he plotted invasions of northern Mexico and other regions, Walker avoided the issue of slavery and gained entry to New York antislavery circles through women's rights activist Elizabeth Oakes Smith. A civil war in Nicaragua gave this adventurer a new opening, and Walker joined the liberal side of an ongoing struggle for control. In this he was backed by many abolitionists, including Sarah Pellet, the first woman to apply to Harvard, as well as by numerous Cuban exiles of varying skin tones and political persuasions, including antiracist Francisco Agüero Estrada, a fan of Martin Delany's.[138]

With Goicuría as a key lieutenant, Walker landed an expeditionary force in Nicaragua, accepted an invitation to help direct a liberal government, and began a program of land reform. At first Franklin Pierce's government recognized Walker as legitimate, to the shock of British diplomats. But Walker had intruded into one of the great speculative regions of the world, as shipping magnate Cornelius Vanderbilt tried to corner the market in trade across Lake Nicaragua. When Walker voided Vanderbilt's concessions, Vanderbilt aimed to destroy him. Scrambling to sustain himself, desperate for more U.S. support, and under pressure from visiting proslavery expansionists Pierre Soulé and Cora Montgomery, Walker issued an order that seemed to impose slavery in September 1856. That order made Walker a hero in the South, but at the cost of turning the U.S. government against him; soon U.S. gunboats captured Walker and brought him to the United States for trial. These events provided sharp lessons for already observant Cubans. Goicuría and most Cubans withdrew from Walker's mission when he broke with Vanderbilt and seemed to embrace slavery. For Goicuría and the other Cubans, the lesson was simple: proslavery could not carry the government of the United States, much less the world. While Goicuría promised that he had no "pseudo-philanthropy" toward black people, he thought it "preposterously stupid" to impose slavery on Nicaragua. If Cubans wanted effective U.S. support, they would need to look beyond proslavery politicians.[139]

The Cubans also learned from the revolution under way in Mexico. There liberal politicians struggled against both Antonio López de Santa Anna and threats of Spanish intervention.[140] White Cuban creoles and Mexican Liberals allied together in the revolutionary world of New Orleans. Mexican Liberals, including regional governor Benito Juárez, Melchor Ocampo, José María Mata, and others settled there in late 1853 after fleeing Santa Anna's repressive rule in Mexico, and they befriended (and purchased weapons from) Cuban exiles like Goicuría, José Agustín Quintero, and Santacilia. Inspired by their common hatred of Spain, Mexican and Cuban exiles placed their individual battles into Atlantic World terms: revolutionary democratic Americas against reactionary, monarchical Europe. Together these two exile groups spread talk of revolution and violence, and over time Juárez's resolutely antislavery circle may have helped reinforce white Cuban creoles' slow turn against the institution. In 1855, Juárez and other Liberal politicians moved back south, aiming to overthrow the conservative government. As he accompanied his friend (and future father-in-law) to the dock, Santacilia bade Juárez farewell. By legend, in response, Juárez pledged that they would meet again in "México libre, o en la eternidad."[141] Eventually white Cuban creoles like Miguel Aldama, Carlos Manuel de Céspedes, Manuel and Rafael Quesada de Loynaz, Goicuría, and Santacilia participated directly in Mexico's ongoing civil war. Cubans had found revolutions but not yet one grand enough to threaten Spain.

Inside the United States, these international struggles helped turn the 1856 presidential election into a fight over the future of the world. The Whig Party all but disappeared, taking much political caution with it. In its place the Northern Republican Party flowered into antislavery imperialists. They nominated one of the nation's most famous champions of settler colonialism, John Frémont, explorer, military man, and California conqueror. The Republican platform explicitly tied the Kansas struggle to Cuba as examples of the "highway's man's plea that 'might makes right,' embodied in the

Ostend Circular."[142] Democrats meanwhile nominated an architect of the Ostend Manifesto and a Young American ally, James Buchanan. "Questions connected with the foreign policy of this country" were "inferior to no domestic question whatever," the Democratic platform promised. For Cuba, the platform pledged "every proper effort" to "insure our ascendancy in the Gulf of Mexico."[143] Two visions of settler colonialism struggled for supremacy, one embracing slave labor, the other wage labor, and their canvas was not just Kansas but the world. On the eve of the election, Lydia Maria Child celebrated this revolutionary fervor. "The battle with the overgrown slave power is verily the great battle of Armageddon."[144] In apocalyptic terms, abolitionist newspapers and orators made the election a struggle for the future: "Freedom for Kansas and peace with all [the] world, on the one hand; and on the other, Slavery in Kansas, and the acquisition of Cuba," one newspaper wrote.[145] The *National Era* stated, "Freedom must triumph, or else."[146]

James Buchanan's victory ushered in new U.S. efforts to acquire Cuba. His inaugural address celebrated U.S. expansionism, promised that any new territories would be added rightfully and for "self-preservation," and warned other nations not to "interfere."[147] Two days after the inauguration, the Supreme Court published the *Dred Scott* decision. Although the decision did not mention Cuba, Chief Justice Roger Taney found the Missouri Compromise an unconstitutional regulation of slavery in the territories, and Northerners interpreted this as a bar against congressional intervention against slavery in Cuba, if the island were annexed.[148] Antislavery speakers in turn used the Cuba crisis against the ongoing Kansas crisis, arguing that Buchanan defended Kansas's proslavery government solely to "clear the checkerboard" and "bring Cuba and Central America and the revival of the slave trade on the board."[149] But behind the scenes, Buchanan behaved cautiously. Spooked by Republican gains in New England and the mid-Atlantic and frightened of the economic crash in 1857, Democratic congressmen—including Southerners—feared the political and financial impact of acquisition. Even Jefferson Davis and James Henry Hammond termed annexation unlikely in 1857, prompting an antislavery newspaper to write that "slavery is growing timid. . . . Southerners feel the truth of Mr. Seward's declaration, that the contest is over, and that the victory rests with the North."[150] Cubans, too, saw little hope in the president. "Do you hope for something of Buchanan?" Porfirio Valiente asked. "I do not."[151]

But international affairs kept complicating domestic politics. In 1858, tensions between Britain and Spain once again thrust Cuba into domestic debates. As Britain signaled its distance from the Spanish government and

This 1856 campaign sketch denounces the Democratic ticket, and presidential nominee James Buchanan, for backing two forms of tyranny: slave masters' claims over Kansas (while the town of Lawrence burns in the background) and their lust for acquiring Cuba (as a Cuban town burns behind). This association between Bleeding Kansas and Cuba was common in 1854–56 and helped internationalize the domestic conflict over slavery. Courtesy of the Library of Congress, LC-USZ62-13211.

Buchanan scrambled to sustain Southern support, the president replaced the moderate minister to Spain with Kentuckian William Preston and asked Congress to fund a purchase offer. Senator John Slidell attempted to suspend neutrality laws that punished U.S. citizens for trying to overthrow foreign governments. These maneuverings prompted both Hammond's "Cotton Is King" speech and Seward's celebration of free labor's triumph. This argument set the context for Cuba's role in the 1858 Lincoln-Douglas debates. Seeing Cuba as a winning issue and a way to deflect from Northern critiques of the Kansas act, Stephen Douglas championed an expansionist vision of "one grand ocean-bound republic" in the Jonesboro, Illinois, debate. "The time may come, indeed has now come, when our interests would be advanced by the acquisition of the island of Cuba. When we get Cuba we must take it as we find it, leaving the people to decide the question of slavery for themselves." In reply, Lincoln argued for readopting "the policy of the fathers by restricting it [slavery] to the limits it has already covered—restricting it from the new Territories."[152]

Buchanan's December 1858 State of the Union address again raised the possibility of Cuban acquisition, and Southern congressmen quickly introduced legislation that would empower the president to act. Buchanan's "entire message constitutes an argument for extending the curse of human bondage" in Cuba, Mexico, and Central America, antislavery congressman Joshua Giddings complained.[153] At a March 1859 mass meeting in New York, Mississippi senator Albert Gallatin Brown predicted that Cuba would be the issue to reunite Southern and Northern Democrats. "We want Cuba to extend the commerce of Boston, Philadelphia, Baltimore, and New Orleans, as well as that of New York," Brown said. "I want Cuba for the extension of slavery."[154] Stephen Douglas, desperately trying to hold together a fraying Democratic Party, urged Democratic senators to authorize the president to act belligerently, hoping to force a war over expansion.

But the Slave Power dominated rhetoric more than policy. Despite Buchanan's assertive claims, the president feared provoking Spain or the North. And Southern Democrats rejected Douglas's proposal to empower the president to force a war, concerned that Spain might respond by shelling Southern coasts and issuing emancipation orders.[155] Over 1859, Buchanan's diplomatic efforts—and yet another filibustering attempt—came to naught. In despair, the *Charleston Mercury* wrote, "The North won" the battle for national supremacy. "Two parties, and two only, arise in the Union—a party of the North and a party of the South. The one to rule, the other to defend."[156] For New York newspaperman Henry Raymond, the "rising tide of Northern power" in the 1850s taught white Southerners a "keen sense of the growing superiority of the North," a superiority proven by the North's defeat of the "straws at which the slaveholding section has clutched" in Cuba and Kansas.[157] Despite James Henry Hammond's assertions, cotton was not in fact king of the world economy or even of domestic politics. The world economy—and even the economy of the United States—was too vast to be dictated by one crop or one region.[158]

White Cuban creoles like Goicuría then turned to Northern antislavery politicians for support. This concluded a decade-long journey from proslavery to conditional support for emancipation. As early as 1854, a small number of Cuban exiles—including Zenea—began publishing the explicitly abolitionist *El Mulato* in New York City, aiming to attack not just slavery but racial caste on the island. *El Mulato* celebrated the Afro-Cuban poet Plácido, lambasted slavery as a "monster," and sought alliance with Northern and European abolitionists, but the paper was attacked by most of the Cuban exile community. Over the next years, however, attitudes shifted.[159] Goicuría's journey led him through engagement with British abolitionists, alliance with Mexican Liberals, the Walker debacle in Nicaragua, and disillusionment with Southern filibusters in New Orleans.[160] In New York, other white Cuban exiles published pamphlets raising the possibility of abolition to acclaim or silent acceptance rather than outrage.[161] By the late 1850s, Goicuría and other exiles connected Cuban independence with emancipation in an effort to gain support from Northern audiences.[162] In 1859 lectures celebrating the "hot blowing wind of revolution," Santacilia praised the United States as the model for the "democratic idea" against monarchical Europe and celebrated filibusters like López while downplaying their ties to slave owners.[163] Cuban exiles were now ready to meet the Republican expansionists on the Republicans' own ground.

Domestic and international conflicts magnified the stakes of the 1860 election and helped prepare the way for the revolutionizing of the Republican Party. As the 1860 presidential election approached, Republicans developed their own expansionist arguments that foreclosed compromise and promised an apocalyptic battle for the world. Senator Hale derided Democrats for preventing the annexation of Canada. "If there is a geographical necessity for our expansion, let us go north," Hale said. "We have gone south long enough."[164] The abolitionist *National Era* called acquisition of eastern Canada "ten-fold more necessary" than annexation of Cuba, though it emphasized the importance of expansion northward by "legitimate and honest means."[165] Republicans even changed their tune toward Cuba. If Cuba ended slavery, Republicans like William Seward and Senator James Doolittle pledged to welcome its acquisition as part of what Doolittle called "the great national policy which is to control this continent."[166] Sagely, the *National Era* wrote that abolition on the island would "only serve to multiply the friends of annexation. It is true that the present friends of the measure would change front, and become its bitter foes, but the North would be unanimous for it."[167] In 1859 congressional debates, Republicans tried to substitute a homestead bill—parceling up land in the West for settlers—for the Democratic bill to acquire Cuba, substituting wage-labor settler colonialism for slave-labor settler colonialism. This contrast combined Kansas and Cuba into a common struggle between these two forms of empire. Anticipating contemporary scholarship that connects settler colonialism in the West to "overseas" empire, Republicans celebrated the antislavery civilization they meant to transport to the Great Plains and then to the world. The issue was "lands for the landless freemen," not "slaves for the slaveholders," as Seward said. Or, as Benjamin Wade crudely put it, in a form that reminds us that antislavery rhetoric could be both sincere and racist: "Shall we give niggers to the niggerless, or lands to the landless?"[168]

Cuba and the question of slavery's global survival helped unify Republicans around an ambitious international agenda. Influential antislavery editor Horace Greeley wrote that he would back any candidate who was "openly and unequivocally Anti-Slavery-Extending, anti-Cuba-Stealing, Anti-Filibuster."[169] One antislavery newspaper examined the parties' stances on "Foreign Diplomacy" to explain the centrality of the "One Paramount Question, Shall Slavery or Freedom determine the character, policy, and destiny of the American Union?"[170]

After Lincoln's election in November 1860, Southern states took the revolutionary step of seceding in order to salvage slavery's place in a world they could no longer control. But it was a defensive revolution. Secession marked recognition of the failure of the Slave Power to control the country; secession was a reactive move to sustain what they could before the Republicans turned the force of the United States against slavery; secession was an acknowledgment of, even a tribute to, the transformation of the Republican Party. Southern planters believed that the future of world slavery depended on them. As Southern politicians debated whether to leap into nationhood or to hold their cards until the elections of 1862 and 1864, they reached two crucial conclusions: Northern Democrats would never be able to deliver on any promises of expansion. More significantly, Republicans could implement a radical agenda for thwarting slavery and its power, at home and especially abroad. Lincoln and other politicians made much of Republican domestic moderation, noting that under the Constitution Republicans could only block the spread of slavery to territories, permit the flow of antislavery literature to the South, and build a patronage network in slave states. But internationally, Republicans could act quickly to isolate Southern states and to weaken slavery in Cuba and Brazil.[171] These defeats would deprive planters of the feel of inevitability, an eschatology of victory that they relied on and that Hammond famously emphasized in his "Cotton Is King" speech. Planters thus launched their own revolutionary project to save slavery not just in the United States but in the Americas. Planters ended up losing slavery when they turned to war, but they had already calculated the costs of peace.

During the secession winter, Lincoln demonstrated his commitment to thwarting Southern plans for Cuba, even if it meant war. Lincoln consistently explained that Republican opposition to the expansion of slavery was not defined solely, or even primarily, by the western territories. Nonexpansion was a policy for Cuba and the rest of the hemisphere, a brake against acquisition, a barrier against slavery's long-term survival. To powerbroker Thurlow Weed, Lincoln wrote in December 1860 that Republicans could not afford to compromise on slavery in the territories because "filibustering for all South of us, and making slave states of it, would follow in spite of us."[172] Even more than the Fugitive Slave Act or the extension of slavery to New Mexico, the acquisition of slave Cuba became the line Lincoln would not cross. Like many Republicans, Lincoln expressed moderation on many internal issues and deference to the powers of existing states. But Lincoln showed no moderation on the question of the expansion of slavery to new acquisitions. If Republicans compromised on that issue, he warned, "a year will not pass, till we shall have to take Cuba as a condition upon which they will stay in the Union.... There is, in my judgment, but one compromise which would really settle the slavery question, and that would be a prohibition against acquiring any more territory."[173] In last-minute negotiations to avert war in 1861, Lincoln wrote to William Seward that on the fugitive slave issue he wished to add due process protections but "I care but little, so that what is done be comely, and not altogether outrageous." In that same letter, Lincoln isolated the irreconcilable cause of the conflict: the effort to "put us again on the high-road to a slave empire."[174] In his inaugural address, Lincoln likewise dismissed other causes of the conflict. The "only substantial dispute" that could not be compromised was that "one section of our country believes slavery is *right*, and ought to be extended, while the other believes it is *wrong*, and ought not to be extended."[175] This stance against global slavery helped inspire the *New York Herald* to call Lincoln's election—in dismay—"the Second American Revolution."[176]

The radical new entry into global politics was not the Confederacy but the newly United States. The Confederacy offered to guarantee Spanish sovereignty over Cuba in return for recognition, evidence of the deep realism embedded in Southern politics before and (even more so) during the Civil War. Bemusedly noting that Louisianan John Slidell had once blocked U.S. guarantee of Spanish rule but now offered Confederate guarantees, a British diplomat described the "strange conversions of political principle brought ab[ou]t by the existing conflict in America."[177] So, too, were changes evident in the United States. The Lincoln administration indeed acted to restrain Atlantic slavery. For secretary of state, Lincoln selected prominent antislavery politician William Seward. Seward immediately, and notoriously, aimed to use expansionism to prevent civil war, urging Lincoln to resist the Spanish annexation of Santo Domingo, hint at the acquisition of Cuba, and "rouse a vigorous *spirit of independence* on this continent against European intervention" to convince Southerners to fight with the North against Europe. Lincoln, however, opposed both a foreign war and any suggestion of adding Cuba while slavery endured.[178] In Great Britain, antislavery diplomat Charles Francis Adams negotiated agreements on the slave trade. In Spain, German revolutionary refugee Carl Schurz lobbied to turn the Civil War toward abolition and encouraged Spanish abolitionists including the republican Emilio Castelar.[179] These were the kinds of transformations that the secessionists feared. This was the creation of an antislavery force in the Atlantic World, an alliance between the United States and the liberal party throughout the globe. Although the conflict in Mexico did not relate directly to slavery, the Lincoln administration showed its ideological (if rarely concrete) support for Juárez's Liberal government by appointing Thomas Corwin—a staunch opponent of the U.S.-Mexican War—as minister.[180]

Republicans' increasingly revolutionary expansionist project helped build bridges with many Northern Young Americans. Although John O'Sullivan (like Cuban creole ally Quintero) supported the Confederacy, many Northern Young Americans hitched their hopes for an expansive, powerful nation to the United States. August Belmont helped lead New York Democrats into support for the war, in part by moving loan sales through New York City. Daniel Sickles provides perhaps the clearest view of the transformations of the 1850s. A schemer, diplomat, and financier of slavery-backed expansion, Sickles now remade himself into a revolutionary against the Confederacy. Although Sickles in December 1860 called it an "illusion" to believe that the United States could be preserved by force, by January 1861, he turned militantly against the Confederacy in a speech titled "New Phases of the Revolution—How to Meet Them."[181] As the *Liberator* heard the "echoing, earthquake tread of the impending second American Revolution," Sickles and other Young Americans embraced the U.S. cause and infused it with revolutionary fervor. Over time Sickles followed the war to increasingly radical ends; by the first years of Reconstruction, Sickles would lead what he called a revolution on the ground to end slavery and create defensible rights for freedpeople. Antislavery expansionism had turned some Young Americans into Republican revolutionaries.[182]

From the Civil War's first days, the conflict seemed likely to reshape not just the United States but the Gulf, the Caribbean, and possibly even the broader

Atlantic World. Many people saw signs of a new set of power relations and ideologies displacing the Second American System, although no one could say confidently what shape this new system might take. Would the United States emerge a triumphant, imperialist antislavery power, ready to absorb and abolitionize Cuba and perhaps then fold Santo Domingo, Haiti, and even Mexico and Central America into a vast antislavery, republican empire? Or would the Confederacy prevail and establish either informal or formal relations with fellow slave powers in Cuba and Brazil, a triple alliance of bondage meant to defend the system against international pressure? If so, would the remaining United States become a sibling of Great Britain, a fellow antislavery force in the world? Or a competitor? Or a cacophony of continually seceding republics, akin to the city-states of Italy? So, too, could one imagine different futures unfolding for the Spanish Empire, for Jamaica, for Mexico, for Texas, for all the regions that were tied commercially but separated politically around the Gulf. Behind these political questions lay the economic issue that had driven the Gulf to crisis and then to revolution: What kind of labor system would predominate? For a quarter century, the tense balance between slavery and antislavery, monarchy and republic, held, but now it might all be washed away.

As political leaders tried to grasp these futures, the map of the greater Gulf began to shift. While the U.S. secession crisis bubbled, Spain reabsorbed its former colony of Santo Domingo.[183] "Spain would not have made this move if the United States had not become the dis-United States and the government in Washington been made almost contemptible by the revolt of the slaveholders," an antislavery newspaper complained.[184] Afro-Dominicans suspected that the Spaniards planned to reimpose slavery on the island, part of its consolidation of empire and slavery. Spain, Britain, and France intervened in Mexico against Juárez's government. France eventually invaded the country's heartland, captured Mexico City, and installed an Austrian prince as emperor of the new Mexican Empire. As Guatemala and other Central American states considered annexation to the Mexican Empire, Americans feared that France would next retake Haiti and launch a new triumphant wave of European colonialism. Partly in response, the United States recognized Haiti for the first time in July 1862, prompting speculation that the United States would then move on Cuba and Puerto Rico.[185]

On Cuba, everyone knew that the situation would change, but no one was sure how. Spanish officials believed that the "spirit of annexation" "has died entirely," Capt. Gen. Francisco Serrano wrote in November 1861. "To whom would Cuba annex today? To the South to dare the enmity of the North? To the North to conquest against the hatreds of the South? . . . The Cubans are not so destitute of good sense to think today, in the middle of such events" that annexation was possible.[186] Perhaps world conditions would make the "ever faithful" island of Cuba actually faithful and usher in a new period of stable Spanish rule. Serrano had his reasons for confidence. Serrano used the war to expand Cuba's economy and influence. Traders from both the United States and the Confederacy moved vessels in and out of Havana, and merchants made fortunes smuggling goods from Cuba to Confederate ports, turning Havana from an exporter of sugar and coffee to a way station for European goods heading to the Confederacy. Havana was a military and political center of Spanish operations in the New World, managing the Dominican annexation, a Spanish war with Peru and Chile, and, in part, the Mexican intervention. In these heady days, Serrano and others could see—some with hope, some with fear—a resurgent Spanish Empire reestablishing its dominion over much of the Americas, turning the early nineteenth-century revolutions into just a blip in the long history of empire.

Other Cubans saw different futures tantalizingly close at hand. Slaves sang songs to Lincoln and talked openly of the impact of U.S. emancipation on the island.[187] And many white Cuban creoles saw the Civil War as a way to tilt the balance of power permanently toward independence and republicanism. Santacilia and Goicuría pined for (and doubted the likelihood of) an alliance of Mexican and U.S. republics, and they moved weapons to the Mexican Liberals and lobbied the United States to support Juárez against the French invaders. Perhaps U.S. victory in the Civil War and Liberal victory in Mexico might even create a Third American System, a truly liberal order that would sweep away both colonialism and slavery, carrying Cuba along in the new tide of history.

Inside the United States, grand dreams of a new world endured even amid the crushing grind of battle. As the United States shifted toward abolition in 1862, talk circulated once again of revolutions abroad to match the one at home. The Civil War that began, in part, because of Cubans might end in an effort to conquer the island for freedom and, not incidentally, for the United States. "The system in Cuba and Brazil is only maintained by the example and influence of the United States," one newspaper editorialized. "With the civilization of the Christian world opposed to this monster evil and wrong, its universal extinction will only be a question of time."[188] As Charles Sumner said in October 1862, "The war which we wage is not merely for ourselves; it is for all mankind. . . . We conquer for Liberty everywhere. In ending slavery here, we open its gates all over the world."[189] For Sumner and for other U.S.

revolutionaries, the Civil War could not conclude with domestic transformations because it had not been animated solely by domestic causes.

The decades ahead would answer the questions of how the Civil War the world made would in fact remake that world. Or whether in fact it would remake the world at all. For the moment, it seemed possible to imagine a new Gulf or American System being born, one that would reshape governance, trade, diplomacy, and the political and economic life of the hemisphere. But so, too, was it possible to see the resilience of the old system even in the face of the transformations at hand. And Cubans, of various "races" and ideologies, prepared to meet that new world and to turn it to their own ends. The reality of the world the Civil War helped make did not of course live up to the fantasies unleashed during the conflict. But those same fantasies remind us that the hopes the Civil War sparked were as international as the causes that fueled the war. The transformation of the world, like the transformation of the United States, would be fraught, incomplete, and in many ways disappointing, but only such monumental dreams could produce such monumental disappointments.

THE WORLD THE CIVIL WAR
MIGHT HAVE MADE

I n 1873, eight years after the Confederate surrender at Appomattox, the Second American Revolution seemed to surge across the Atlantic Ocean to Spain, as democrats there cast away the monarchy, declared a republic, and prepared to end slavery in their colonies of Cuba and Puerto Rico. For a few months, the First Spanish Republic realized dreams of a triumphant, transatlantic antislavery republicanism. It seemed a turning point in Atlantic history. With extravagant but perhaps forgivable optimism, some Spaniards and Americans envisioned a new Atlantic system. Diplomatic and commercial power would shift from the British Empire to a U.S.-Spanish alliance. Political theory would turn less on the radical barricades and reactionary retrenchments in Paris than on the flow of ideas among Washington, Mexico City, and Madrid. Chattel slavery would disappear; so, too, would monarchs. The Republican Party, triumphant in the United States, would help to remake not just the nation but the world, with the help of like-minded allies.

To mark this triumph of republicanism, the new Spanish government and the U.S. minister in Madrid orchestrated a much-publicized recognition ceremony. The U.S. minister climbed the steps of the Cortes as congressmen applauded and bands played. Meeting the first Spanish president, the U.S. minister offered legitimacy, support, and encouragement; in return, the Spanish president acknowledged the postbellum United States as a role model and guide. In the celebratory cheers of U.S. editors and in the worried complaints of Spanish conservatives, the U.S. minister's tramp into the Cortes heralded the forward march of United States influence in Atlantic World affairs. From those steps, it seemed that the U.S. revolution had proven that a nation conceived in liberty could not only long endure but also reproduce. The war that ended slavery inside the United States might destroy it everywhere. Those could-have-beens help us assess one impact of the Second American Revolution: the World the Civil War Might Have Made.

It had taken eight years of internal consolidation and external transformation, but antislavery, republicanism, and U.S. power seemed ascendant by 1873. The path to transformation was quite a bit longer than many had expected at war's end. Back in 1865, there had been numerous signs of imminent change: fearful Spanish officials launched a study of the future of colonial government and colonial slavery; Cuban slaves talked openly of emancipation; white creoles and free people of color once again prepared to revolt; Spanish democrats and free traders formed the Sociedad Abolicionista Española in Madrid; U.S. politicians and soldiers bragged of driving slavery and monarchy from Cuba. Yet internal struggles confounded those quick hopes. Slowly—sometimes unbearably slowly—those dreams of power and virtue unfolded over the next eight years. In 1868, Cubans and Spaniards launched separate rebellions that looked to the United States for support. And by 1873, eight years of disappointed expectations seemed to evaporate in the figure of a new Spanish republic, a wedge against slavery and monarchy, a dream that the United States might still revolutionize the world.

Or perhaps those dreams—and even the Spanish republic itself—were simply a mirage. From those same Cortes steps, more jaundiced and, in the long run, more astute viewers saw that the U.S. minister and the Spanish republicans celebrated far too soon. What seemed a revolutionary wave to both celebrants and critics might be nothing more than a wish, a tale that lulled people into believing that they understood an irreducibly complex world. Conservative Spaniards glimpsed the resilient drag of the past in the very figure who walked up those Cortes steps. The same Daniel Sickles who in the 1850s had schemed to buy Cuba from Spain in order to save slavery now welcomed Spain as a sister republic, a shared model for the world. But Spanish conservatives and British diplomats ridiculed the notion that the United States was the inspiration for the First Spanish Republic; instead, they suggested, the United States was its puppet master, forcing the republicans into power in order to advance the United States' selfish interests. The Civil War had not produced a new United States; it had only laid a new veneer over the country's long-standing efforts to undermine other nations' stability. Although the United States' ideology had changed, its foreign relations remained the same, oriented around not the spread of a U.S. system of government but the expansion of U.S. might.

Looking beyond the figures on the steps, skeptics could see other reasons to doubt the arrival of a new moment in history. In the Spanish countryside, cantonalists, socialists, Carlists, and other royalists paid the new republic neither respect nor mind. They saw it not as a government but as a fraud. Their long-standing struggles for power could not be subsumed in the ideological clash between liberal republics and monarchism. Over time these Spanish civil wars revealed that the republic barely extended beyond the Cortes. The ceremonial meeting did not mark the birth of the republic; it marked its high tide.

Only perhaps a mile from the Cortes, skeptics would have seen a symbol of the many other waves that buffeted the country's shores. From his window in Madrid, a young Cuban rebel named José Martí responded to the Spanish Republic by waving the flag of the so-called Cuban Republic. Although Martí expressed some hopes for the Spanish Republic, he adamantly defended Cubans' revolt against Spain. "The rebelling insurgents do not yield," he wrote. "My country writes with blood its irrevocable resolution. Above the cadavers of its sons, it stands to say that it firmly wants its independence. . . . Cuba wants to be free." This nascent Cuban Republic represented yet another way of imagining a new world, one defined by anticolonialism, one that could not be enfolded under Spanish republicanism. Some of Martí's allies claimed that Cubans, not Spaniards, were the rightful heirs of the U.S. Civil War's battle against slavery and the proper recipients of U.S. support. If the Civil War remade the world for democracy and freedom, perhaps its fruits should be found in Cuba, not Madrid. Or, perhaps, as many Cubans would eventually argue, the struggle in Cuba was independent of the Civil War altogether, a product of the island's own history.[1]

The confusions and contradictions in the streets of Madrid remind us that the U.S. Civil War both raised and dashed hopes for a new Atlantic World. It was both more transformational, for a moment, and less transformational, in the end, than we might think. While the Civil War created expectations for the end of global slavery and the triumph of democracy, it did not in fact lead directly to either outcome. At the end of the 1870s, slavery limped along in reduced form in Cuba and Brazil, monarchies flourished, and U.S. politicians flailed against political and financial limitations on U.S. power. Although legal slavery died in the 1880s, the United States expanded its global reach in the 1890s, and monarchies toppled in the 1910s, those outcomes were only generically products of the U.S. Civil War, and those outcomes are more fruitfully understood in light of their immediate contexts: 1880s Spanish political crises, 1890s U.S. economic transformations, and 1910s warfare.

The hemispheric abolition of chattel slavery over the long nineteenth century may be divided into four key moments: the Haitian Revolution and the subsequent growth of Anglo-American abolitionism in the 1790s and 1800s; British abolition in the 1830s; the U.S. Civil War; and Cuban and Brazilian emancipation in the 1880s. The U.S. Civil War might best be understood as one among a handful of inflection points, rather than *the* turning point in the world war against slavery. The emancipations of roughly 1.5 million slaves in Brazil, Cuba, and Puerto Rico in the post–Civil War years was significantly smaller than the freeing of 4 million in the United States, yet larger than any other emancipation in American history and worthy of being treated as their own processes. The gap in years between the end of slavery in the United States and in Cuba and Brazil was nearly as long as the gap between abolition in the British Empire and in the United States. As Haiti had perhaps been necessary but not sufficient to explain later British abolition, and British abolition necessary but not sufficient to explain U.S. abolition, so, too, U.S. abolition might be necessary but not sufficient to end chattel slavery across the hemisphere. History was harder to turn than abolitionists and antislavery politicians imagined.

So, too, did the triumph of republics look illusory. The founding of the United States had helped legitimize the republican form of government, a form practiced in Switzerland and at times in England, Rome, and other regions, but one that had fallen into disrepute by the 1700s. Between 1776 and 1861, republics spread across the Americas, from Haiti to the continent, breeding, at times, optimism that monarchies were, like slavery, a relic of the past, doomed to extinction. Now that monarchies have been defanged and liberalized, the nineteenth-century association between republics and freedom can be puzzling; Britain today seems hardly less free than the United States despite having a monarch. But for many nineteenth-century liberals, republics were the only safe way to protect individual liberty against an otherwise oppressive crown. Still in 1861, democratic republics remained, as Abraham Lincoln told Congress, an "experiment."[2] More parochially, in 1862, Lincoln called the United States' defense of republican stability "the last best hope of earth."[3] And in the Gettysburg Address, Lincoln made the Civil War a test of whether "government of the people by the people for the people" would "perish from the earth."[4] Of course, Lincoln overstated; many Latin American nations remained republics. Nevertheless, Lincoln captured the pessimism of 1860s republicans, the optimism of monarchists as they watched the U.S. Civil War and the French invasion of Mexico. In turn, the victories of U.S. Republicans and Mexican Liberals sparked new hope for republicans in the Americas and Europe.[5]

More than most moments, revolutionary waves lead us to contemplate the transformation of human societies, the seeming velocity of history when the world seems turned upside down and sudden change is the order of the day everywhere, all at once, immediately. Many hopes bloom and spread. And then, just as suddenly, revolutionary waves crash; their mysterious energy disperses; the past endures with all its furniture still in place. Thus, revolutionary waves also help us grapple with the torpor of history.

Though much was taken by the U.S. Civil War, much abided. The Second American System inaugurated in the early nineteenth century had been challenged by the U.S. Civil War but not overthrown. The balance of power had shifted, but the Americas, and particularly the Gulf, remained a contradictory world, where monarchism and republicanism, slavery and free labor, endured side by side. It was a site of competition among both American and European powers, multipolar and multisided.

The late 1870s seemed a time of stasis or retreat inside the United States, Cuba, and Spain. In the United States, the retreat from Reconstruction over the 1870s and 1880s signaled the end of the Second American Revolution, the partial triumph of restorationism. Such restorationism was also visible in the successful reimposition of Spanish colonial rule over Cuba and in the crowning of a new monarch in peninsular Spain. To make sense of the relationship between these common stories, we need an extranational political history that combines foreign policy, international circulations, and formal and informal politics to analyze how people used their sense of the world to remake domestic politics and how they used domestic politics to remake the world.[6]

In exploring the Second American Revolution as a revolutionary wave, the previous chapter aimed to capture the domestic and international sources of that wave's energy. This chapter asks where that dynamism went and what became of it, what difference the Civil War actually made.

||||||||||||||||||||||||||||||||||||

From the war's first days, many people—inside and outside the United States—were certain that the Civil War would change the Gulf world by creating a new American system, replacing slavery and European power with U.S.-style free-labor republicanism. The preliminary Emancipation Proclamation turned the war into an antislavery crusade, at least rhetorically, and raised hopes that the U.S. war would lead to emancipation for the roughly 1.5 million people enslaved in Brazil, Cuba, and Puerto Rico. The proclamation would be the "the death-blow to slavery in the rest of the world."[7] At a Faneuil Hall celebration, Charles Sumner claimed that the proclamation "will revolutionize the world."[8] Freed from the shackles of proslavery politics, the United States would displace Britain as the most powerful antislavery force on the planet, the "daystar of the world."[9] The consolidation of the U.S. free-labor republic would propel free-labor republics across the remainder of the hemisphere and eject European monarchies and slaveholders from power. Often there was no mistaking the potential imperialism behind this antislavery triumphalism, the elements of expansion inside the language of crusade. One black orator in Louisiana predicted that the antislavery United States would next plant its flag in Cuba, Mexico, and Canada and even eventually over the Tower of London.[10] Inverting the Confederate pledge that Atlantic slavery depended on its survival in the South, U.S. orators increasingly argued that slavery's extinction in the United States would inevitably lead to its destruction everywhere.

Exiles and diplomats tied the U.S. Civil War to the broader Atlantic World through the European intervention in Mexico.[11] With the United States overwhelmed by its internal war, France, Britain, and Spain seized the Mexican port of Veracruz in 1861 to collect debts. As Benito Juárez's Liberal government struggled to survive, Mexican minister Matías Romero labored valiantly to convince U.S. politicians to treat the European intervention and the U.S. Civil War as a single struggle between bourgeois republicans and reactionary, landowning European sympathizers. This was a conjoined (if tendentious) reading of diplomacy and grand ideology, recasting French, British, and Spanish financial maneuvering into a coherent antirepublican, anti-American crusade and, even more tendentiously, the Confederacy into a pro-monarchist revolt. But the threats were real. In 1863, France invaded central Mexico, displaced the Liberal government, and helped reactionaries install an Austrian prince atop a new Mexican empire. Cuban exile Pedro Santacilia, now married to Juárez's daughter, acted as a kind of shadow Mexican minister inside the United States. In banquets and public speeches, U.S. and Latin American diplomats and politicians made the battle over Mexico a war over the future of republics. With his longtime mentor Domingo de Goicuría, Santacilia engineered arms deals for Juárez's government.

As long as the Civil War endured, these extranational connections remained tentative and abstract. After Confederate surrenders in April and May 1865, however, people inside the United States began to speak more clearly about what would follow battlefield fighting. Some soldiers dreamed of returning home in time for harvest. Generals and politicians increasingly saw that the war could not end with surrender but would continue through an occupation of the defeated South. And others like Ulysses S. Grant began to imagine a war that would extend beyond the national borders, that could not end until the United States helped drive the French from Mexico. Grant moved roughly fifty thousand U.S. troops to Texas in the months after Confederate surrender. U.S. officers dropped weapons on the border, secretly encouraged black soldiers to muster out and then join the Mexican Liberal army, and at times skirmished directly with Imperial forces in border towns, especially in the now-lost trading post of Bagdad. Although Secretary of State William Seward thwarted Grant's hopes for direct intervention, U.S. actions helped undermine French confidence and create space for Juárez's Liberal forces to regroup.[12]

But no place captured the twin ambitions of national power and expansionist antislavery more clearly than Cuba. With the Civil War's end, many Americans saw the island as the next front in the battle against slavery. To gain antislavery support, Goicuría in 1865 translated a Cuban speech against slavery. In New York, Santacilia helped organize a Cuban republican society to turn the filibustering "revolutionary efforts of the past" toward antislavery.[13] The Spanish minister warned of this alliance between "filibusteros and abolitionistas"[14] as white Cuban creoles and antislavery Americans knitted together two strains of Civil War nationalism: one emphasizing the new nation's power, the other its purpose. For U.S. Republicans this antislavery internationalism elicited the crusading language in both expansionism and antislavery.[15] At a mass gathering in Boston, an orator described the task remaining before them as to "impress, furthermore, upon the American people, that its holy mission is not purely national. And that mission is to carry on throughout the earth the noble principles of American democracy and to help all the nations in the attainment of the blessings of liberty and equality" by freeing slaves and creating republics.[16] When abolitionist leader William Lloyd Garrison suggested that the American Anti-Slavery Society disband, the *Christian Recorder* angrily responded that its work would not be done "as long as slaves breathe the air any where in the world."[17] On the ground, some black soldiers hoped to carry out Martin Delany's dream of a Gulfwide slave rebellion. In April 1865, a chaplain with the Twenty-Eighth U.S. Colored Infantry regiment wrote from newly captured Richmond, Virginia, that the men intended to fight until freedom was "proclaimed throughout the world. Yes, we will follow this race of men in search of Liberty through the whole island of Cuba."[18] For U.S. scholars it is tempting to treat these as narcissistic projects of U.S. fantasy, evidence of the nation's limitless ability to assume its own importance.

To Spanish officials, however, the interdependence of slavery in the United States and slavery on the island did not seem fantastic at all. In worried reports back to Madrid, they described how ripples from the United States might overthrow slavery on the island. They feared that U.S. abolitionists and Cuban exiles were working together to "organize a conspiracy of the blacks."[19] A Spanish officer reported that "the spirit of old filibusterism has revived in this country so different of that of four years ago. . . . The abolitionist party has no other idea than that of finishing absolutely and immediately with the slavery of the world."[20] And Spanish officials' confidence was undermined by the empire's struggles in Santo Domingo. As Afro-Dominicans rebelled against Spanish authority, officials turned pessimistic.[21] In November 1865, Spanish officers launched a sweeping investigation of slavery's future. As one wrote, the Civil War had decided the future of slavery on the island. "The opinion of America" was "so definitively formed on this point, that all discussion on it has come to be useless."[22] Puerto Ricans pressed the information-gathering committee for immediate abolition, and in response, panicked Cuban planters proposed gradual emancipation "under coercion of fear produced by late events in N. America," a British diplomat reported.[23]

Spanish officials had reason to be concerned about the state of slavery and Spanish authority on the island. In 1864, slaves around El Cobre plotted to rise up against their masters. Cuban slaves sang songs to Lincoln, songs that bespoke enslaved people's political awareness.[24] Officials worried that rumored Christmas insurrections in the United States would leap across the sea and inspire similar uprisings in Cuba. No one could quite tease out the relationship between rebellions against slavery in the United States and on the island, yet everyone searched for connections, from hope or from fear. When a U.S. squadron landed in Havana in August 1865, Cubans chanted "Liberty" and "Death to Spaniards."[25] After Dominicans rebelled against Spain, a heartened Santiago poet wrote that "Hispaniola was the cradle of [Spain's] empire, and today it is the tomb." Cuban exiles in New York smuggled supplies to the Dominicans and hoped that Spain's January 1865 retreat from the island would trigger rebellions on Cuba.[26]

Across the Spanish Empire, abolitionism grew. On April 10, 1865, in the days between the surrender at Appomattox and Lincoln's assassination, Spanish history professor Emilio Castelar helped lead students into the streets to protest monarchical rule. Spanish cavalry attacked, killing one hundred students. But Madrid was changing faster than the crown could manage. The population grew by 50 percent, or a hundred thousand people, between 1842 and 1860, and the number of newspapers sextupled between 1837 and 1868. Young intellectuals began to organize societies on political economy, tariff reform, and women's education. In 1865, Castelar and other democrats allied with free traders and supporters of a freethinking philosophy called

Krausism to create the Sociedad Abolicionista Española, arguing that slavery constrained the economic growth and political development of the colonies and of the home country. Puerto Rican abolitionists particularly argued that eliminating slavery would open the gates for self-rule and personal liberty on the island.[27] But a Spanish coup in 1866 sent Castelar and other democrats into exile. In 1867, wealthy planters and Cuban-tied merchants blocked a plan for abolition in the colonies. On the island, Spanish officials encouraged the importation of Chinese "coolies" as a bridge from slavery to other forms of coerced labor.[28] Meanwhile, Cuban sugar exports continued to rise, surpassing 40 percent of world sugar production by 1870.[29]

Still, the international situation was not yet ripe for a rebellion. Even though there were some small uprisings in 1866 and 1867, many Cuban rebels recognized that they needed to wait for stability in Mexico and the United States before they could call for help from those countries. In Mexico, many Cubans aided Juárez's forces as they slowly drove the Imperialists from northern Mexico, then Monterrey, then the capital.[30] Inside the United States, politicians could not yet focus on Cuba because they remained absorbed by the ongoing battle between President Andrew Johnson and congressional Republicans over Reconstruction.[31] During 1866, Republicans fought Johnson for control of the government, overriding his vetoes of the Civil Rights and Freedmen's Bureau bills and passing the Fourteenth Amendment. After fall 1866 midterm victories, congressional Republicans seized the reins in early 1867, sweeping away Johnson's temporary governments in all the rebel states but Tennessee, ordering generals to register freedmen as voters, and empowering this new electorate to draw up new constitutions. These domestic struggles convinced a Spanish diplomat that the United States was not interested in "filibusterism." "The interests of internal politics absorb the public activity and attentions," he wrote.[32] And the Jamaican uprising at Morant Bay in October 1865 sparked fears that emancipation would prove impossible to tame.[33] In the interim, it was Confederates who focused on Cuba and Brazil, as slave owners fled there, some with enslaved people, in hopes that they could sustain the institution.[34]

By 1868, however, Cuban insurgents believed that the time was ripe for revolution. Mexican Liberals and U.S. Republicans had prevailed and might support a republican advance across the waters in Cuba. Juárez captured and executed Emperor Maximilian and began to reestablish control over the country and promote a broad liberal agenda of individual rights and property reform. These triumphs over monarchism signaled the new political age, what Goicuría called a victory for "American Republicans." [35] The new

U.S. minister to Mexico likewise praised the "sister Republics" of the United States and Mexico and their "triumphant vindication of the American system of governments."[36] In his 1869 tour of Mexico, former secretary of state William Seward claimed that republicanism was "discussed" in Europe but won "on the field of battle in America."[37] Juárez's government supported a successful revolution in Guatemala and revolutionaries in other neighboring states.[38] Soon, the Benemérito of the Americas became an icon of continental Spanish-speaking republicans, eventually enshrined (with Lincoln and Simón Bolívar and Martí) in Havana's presidential palace, now the Museo de la Revolución. In Paris in 1871, communards, on entering a wealthy Mexican man's house, stopped at the portrait of Juárez, demonstrated their "respect," and departed without breaking or taking anything.[39] Inside the United States, congressional Republicans and freedpeople reaped the fruits of revolution in these years, as refashioned states approved the Fourteenth Amendment and installed Republican governments with biracial electorates and newfound commitments to education and social welfare. In November 1868, Ulysses S. Grant's election as president seemed to crown what the *New York Herald* called "this second American revolution."[40]

For many U.S. observers, including the *Herald*, the Cuban revolution of 1868 represented the next step in the Civil War's remaking of the world. But on the ground, the "revolution the world forgot" was as much a response to local conditions as it was to world affairs.[41] Like many revolutionaries, the Cuban insurgents used fractures in global power politics to try to achieve long-standing domestic goals. The struggle that would be called La Guerra de los Diez Años began in the eastern farming region of Yara, not far from hotbeds of 1850s revolutionary fervor. And the initial leader, planter Carlos Manuel de Céspedes, personally embodied continuities between 1850s and 1860s insurgencies. Like many other white Cuban creole rebels, Céspedes had been radicalized in the Narciso López uprisings of the 1840s and the echo rebellions of the 1850s. His initial list of grievances against Spain closely paralleled those decades-old complaints about martial law, lack of home governance, and Spanish misrule, as well as late 1850s protests against direct taxes and increased tariffs. As his uprising spread to familiar sites of insurrection like Puerto Príncipe and Santacilia's hometown of Santiago de Cuba, it seemed a continuation of earlier anticolonial struggles by marginalized elites. Like those 1850s rebels, Céspedes had close connections to U.S. trading interests, especially New York banker Moses Taylor, who housed, funded, and—some claimed—directed the rebellion.[42]

Yet in other ways Céspedes inhabited a new world. These rebels tried to gain support in what appeared to be a new balance of Atlantic power, as a vitalized and antislavery United States angled to displace Britain, Spain, and other European countries. Cuban insurgents calculated that the United States was fashioning a Third American System based on anti-European alliances that would drive the Europeans from the hemisphere.[43] To attach the insurgency to this new world, Cubans on the island combined their anticolonialism with antislavery. Céspedes's freeing of his own slaves in October 1868 signaled the new relationship between white creole rebellion and slavery. At first, however, Céspedes's forces treated slavery warily, pledging to accept into their ranks only voluntarily freed slaves. But enslaved people, drawing on their own politics of rebellion, wrenched the movement toward freedom. Formerly enslaved people like José Manuel disregarded Céspedes's caution and promised liberation as they marched onto plantations. By December 27, 1868, Céspedes declared that people enslaved by Spanish loyalists would be freed by the insurgents and welcomed into the army, although often in subordinate positions. Thousands of formerly enslaved people joined over the next month. In April 1869, the insurgents' constitution declared all inhabitants entirely free, although compulsory labor persisted until December 1870. On Christmas Day, 1870, Céspedes formally recognized the end of this forced labor. Slavery and plantations broke down amid the frictions and abrasions of war, as ex-slave soldiers proclaimed emancipation, even as moderate insurgent leaders tried to protect slavery on loyal plantations.[44]

Both formerly enslaved people and the international situation drew the insurgent leaders toward antislavery. Cuban rebels needed a firm antislavery stance to appeal to Republican-leaning Northern businessmen; no longer could they depend on the now-displaced Mississippi Valley planters. From offices on Broadway, Rosalía Hernández and Cuban women's committees raised money, penned articles, and purchased arms for the rebels. Taylor and railroad magnate Edward Plumb introduced Cuban insurgents to leading Northern congressmen, including Charles Sumner, John Sherman, Roscoe Conkling, and Lyman Trumbull.[45] The bonds between Cuban insurgents and Republicans—fledgling in Goicuría's late 1850s New York and expanding in Santacilia's mid-1860s sojourn—were now mature. "New York is today the laboratory of the intrigues of all the ambitious Cubans," one Cuban exile wrote.[46] Cubans rose in part because they had a "sympathetic echo in the Capitol of Washington," wrote one Cuban insurgent. "Every government sustains its own institutions, not only at home but abroad, especially in neighboring countries." Grant's November 1868 election not only "saved and redeemed the U.S." but inspired "visions of free and independent Cuba."[47]

Naively, U.S. politicians and editors celebrated the Cuban insurrection as proof that the Civil War had changed the Atlantic World. When Congress returned in December 1868, it rang with speeches celebrating the Cubans, especially by longtime expansionist Representative Nathaniel Banks. The American Anti-Slavery Society urged the United States to back the rebellion.[48] In these triumphant proclamations, antislavery internationalism blended easily with expansionism, even with imperialism. In Pittsburgh, a colored men's convention called for the annexation of Cuba and Haiti.[49] Soon many black voices inside the United States took up the cry. "Cuba is at this juncture a direct challenge to American Republicanism," the *New Orleans Tribune* wrote. "Let us not fail of our duty."[50] The *Christian Recorder* carried its mission to Cuba, a land that "needs America—our force of character, our modern ideas, our Democratic institutions, and last but not least our Protestant faith to do the work; and sooner or later it must have it."[51] The antislavery movement contained multitudes and was not limited to expansionists. Samuel Scottron and his Cuban Anti-Slavery Society sought extension of the United States' influence but not its borders, becoming forerunners of the civil rights and anticolonial coalition that flourished later in the century.[52] And other Americans feared that expanding to Cuba would bring in mixed-race or—to some, worse—Catholic citizens who could not be assimilated into U.S. republican citizenship.

Although U.S. politicians myopically emphasized their nation's impact, Cubans also looked to Mexican Liberals for inspiration and support. First in New York City and then in Mexico City, Pedro Santacilia was a vital broker between Cuban exiles and Mexican Liberals. As his father-in-law, Benito Juárez, reestablished his government in the capital, Santacilia shepherded the Juárez family back into Mexico, served as his father-in-law's secretary, and then was elected to congress. With fellow exiles Porfirio Valiente and Juan Clemente Zenea, Santacilia propagandized the Cuban insurrection as a natural outgrowth of Juárez's struggle for American republicanism in the many newspapers his friends edited, including *El Siglo Diez y Nueve* and *Diario Oficial*. As the revolutionary agent for one Cuban junta, Santacilia helped stitch together exile groups in Veracruz, New York, New Orleans, Key West, Charleston, Savannah, Kingston, Caracas, and Santiago, and steered demobilizing Mexican Liberal soldiers into the Cuban forces. To raise funds, Santacilia helped stage a Spanish production of *Uncle Tom's Cabin* in Teatro Hidalgo in Mexico City. Then on December 20 exiles sponsored another grand event celebrating that "democracy is the universal cause. The Republic is the world."[53] More tangibly, Santacilia and Goicuría brokered weapons deals through José

Spanish officials prepare to execute Domingo de Goicuría for his support of the
Cuban insurgency in 1870. Goicuría had conspired with proslavery Southerners in
the 1850s, allied with antislavery Northerners during the Civil War, traded weapons
for Benito Juárez's Mexican Liberals, and worked steadily with Pedro Santacilia
to propagandize Cuban independence during this period. Courtesy of the
New York Public Library, The Miriam and Ira D. Wallach Division of Art,
Prints and Photographs: Picture Collection, Image 814275.

Francisco Basora, a Puerto Rican abolitionist in New York. In Matamoros,
petitioners pressed Juárez's government to "listen to the voice of its brothers, the children of Cuba."[54] In a grim tribute to their effectiveness, Spanish
military commissions condemned Goicuría, Valiente, Santacilia, and others
to death, and in 1870, Spanish forces captured and killed Goicuría.[55]

The new North American order gave Cuban rebels confidence that they
could now prevail. New 1860s governments in the United States and Mexico
would surely recognize and aid the insurgents, giving them both legitimacy
and money. And in fact, there were signs of a popular pro-Cuban swell in
U.S. public opinion. An African American meeting in Washington resolved to
back independence, for "wherever our race suffers in bondage we shall not be
particular about the rights of nations, being content to consult first of all the
rights of man."[56] At a May 1869 American Anti-Slavery Society meeting, both
Frederick Douglass and Henry McNeal Turner called for recognition of the

Cuban insurgents.[57] Banks campaigned in the House and in public meetings for recognition, and Cuban diplomats lobbied administration officials and the public. The same *New York Herald* editorial that praised Grant's role in the second American revolution also predicted—inaccurately—that Grant would use his inaugural to endorse recognition of the Cubans as belligerents. Although recognition of belligerency seemed inadequate to some Cuban supporters, belligerency would have helped Cuban rebels operate in public in the United States, eased the path for U.S. volunteers to fight, and set the stage for later recognition of the Cuban republic as an independent nation.

But foreign relations and self-interest overwhelmed ideological affinities. The United States could not act freely on belligerency in 1869; British and French recognition of the Confederates as belligerents during the Civil War loomed heavily over discussions of the Cuban case, as did unusually fraught postwar negotiations with Britain over Britain's toleration of vessel sales to the Confederacy. Grant's administration thus could not recognize other belligerents while complaining about European recognition of Confederate belligerency. And Secretary of State Hamilton Fish and other administration officials were distracted by a different expansionist project, one that tied directly back to Cora Montgomery and her husband, William Cazneau, as well as to Spain's imperial struggles. The Cazneaus had schemed to buy Samaná Bay from the again-independent nation of Santo Domingo, and in 1869, those negotiations suddenly expanded into a draft treaty to annex the entire country. Although this treaty went down to defeat in the Senate, debates about incorporating Dominicans into U.S. citizenship sharpened opposition to Cuban annexation.[58] The Civil War also weighed heavily in the minds of U.S. officials. The "epoch of filibusterism in the United States has passed—our people now know too well what war is, and what preparations, money, trains, and supplies are necessary for any expedition," the U.S. consul to Havana assured the captain general.[59] More cynically, the British minister in Washington believed that the Grant administration dithered because it preferred to expand northward into Canada, "where the inhabitants are of a kindred race."[60] U.S. racism might well have blocked Cuban annexation in the end, but the practical barriers to recognition of belligerency prevented politicians from testing their will to make a new state in the Gulf of Mexico.

In Mexico, Cubans garnered more sympathy but no more luck. Although José Martí and other Latin American intellectuals contrasted Mexican support for the Cubans with U.S. reluctance, the Mexican government was similarly slow to move. At first there was reason for optimism. The Mexican government permitted Cuban ships to enter Mexican ports flying the new Cuban

A SIGHT TOO BAD!

Struggling Cuba: "You must be awfully near-sighted, Mr. President, not to recog-nize me."

U. S. G(rant): "No: I am far-sighted; for I can recognize France."

President Grant ignores the pleas of Cuba for aid as he instead surveys France and Europe in this critique of U.S. failure to support the Cuban insurgency. Courtesy of the New York Public Library, The Miriam and Ira D. Wallach Division of Art, Prints and Photographs: Picture Collection, Image 1246619.

flag, and the Mexican congress voted to support recognition. Many Mexican and U.S. newspapers optimistically but inaccurately reported that the Mexican government had recognized the rebels.[61] But in fact, Juárez declined to recognize them as belligerents. Instead, Juárez used the fraught Cuban situation to persuade Spain to forgive older Mexican debts, taking advantage of Spanish prime minister Juan Prim's connections to a Mexican property-holding family. Thus Juárez failed officially to back the Cuban revolution, even as he at times supported revolutionaries in Colombia, Paraguay, Guatemala, and the state of Panama. When Cuban insurgents pressed Mexico's government for support, minister of foreign relations José María Lafragua wrote that "no one can doubt the sentiments of the Mexican people respecting slavery" but that Mexico could not treat "the theoretical question of the abolition of slavery" because Mexico was bound by its pledge of neutrality.[62] Santacilia was disappointed but not surprised by his father-in-law. "The Mexican liberals sympathize at heart with the cause of Cuba but the political condition of the country does not make it possible to do anything for the island," he wrote in 1872.[63]

Revolutionary waves crash against the entrenched self-interest of nations. The countries that recognized the insurgents were those recently in conflict with Spain—Peru, Chile, and Bolivia.[64] Mexico and the United States remained eager to preserve good relations with Spain and to pay down their own debts. For editors and orators, this gap between belief and action was untenable, a betrayal of allies and of each nation's own self-image. For the politicians who maneuvered through these shoals, caution reflected a commitment to a belief even more central than that of republican ideology in the nineteenth century, a belief in the nation.

And then there was a terrible irony: the United States and Mexico withheld recognition not because of too little revolutionary fervor but because of too much. The Cuban revolution was not the only transformation of the late 1860s. A nearly simultaneous revolution in Spain confounded U.S. and Mexican policy and transformed the international situation precisely as the Cubans revolted. The 1868 Spanish revolution was led by moderate monarchist Juan Prim[65] and backed by republican abolitionists like Emilio Castelar. This revolution elicited the same kinds of sympathy as the Cuban rising, the same hopes that the U.S. example had been exported to the Atlantic World. The evidence lay in the overthrow of a monarchy and the promise that the new Spanish government would attack colonial slavery.[66] Over time, these twin Cuban and Spanish revolutions—each partly a product of the North American revolutions of the 1860s—would raise the broadest hopes that the Civil War might remake the Atlantic World and prove most clearly why in fact that world would not be so easily remade. American republicans could not easily balance their support for Cuban and Spanish revolutionaries, no matter how similar their ideologies. While Cuban and Spanish revolutionaries shared ideological commitments, they differed on the fundamental question of who should control the island of Cuba.

Spain's revolution burst from the country's own internal fissures. A few weeks before the Cuban rebellion at Yara, Spanish general Juan Prim rose against Queen Isabella II and her increasingly autocratic rule. Backed by disgruntled generals, progressive monarchists, republicans, and socialists, Prim drove Isabella from the throne and established an interim government to write a new constitution and then, he hoped, select a new, constitutionally constrained monarch.[67] At once Prim represented both midcentury Spanish expansionism and restraint; the general led the victorious war in Morocco and its occupation of Veracruz and—more controversially—thwarted conservative plans to join France's invasion of central Mexico. Later he expressed grave respect for Juárez and helped reestablish relations between Spain and Mexico. Prim had also witnessed republics' power firsthand when he observed U.S. forces in Virginia in 1862.[68] Yet Prim was certain that Spain and other European countries would always be monarchies, though he hoped that they would be constitutionally restrained. In 1866, he led a failed coup. Had Prim failed again in 1868, it is easy to imagine the United States and Mexico intervening to aid the Cuban insurgents against a reactionary Spain.[69] But Prim's successful coup in 1868 changed the calculus for the United States.

So, too, did Prim's coup open up new revolutionary possibilities for Spaniards. Labor unions, socialists, and anarchists claimed power, and republicans won victories in new local elections. Spanish abolitionists in turn used the revolution to promote their cause in mass meetings, such as a five-hour gathering in October 1868 where liberal ministers and abolitionist Carolina Coronado lobbied the government to end slavery in the colonies.[70] For exiled history professor Emilio Castelar, the moment represented the culmination of the dreams he had developed during his travels, when he wrote paeans to the Swiss republics and to Lincoln, and celebrated Juárez's Mexican Liberals as the "government which has saved democracy." In biweekly columns for Mexico City's *Monitor Republicano*, Castelar narrated the emergence of the Spanish republic for Mexican Liberals. On the founding of the republic, the Mexico City newspaper published a poem dedicated to Castelar. Mexico and Spain, "by liberty blessed, we form a single people."[71]

Hurrying back to Spain in 1868, Castelar sought to fashion common ground on the left by proclaiming, "I want the republic of the Girondins, the republic of the Helvéticos, the republic that engendered the two premier magistrates of the modern world, Washington and Lincoln."[72] At a large unity meeting in November 1868, Castelar called for "popular revolutions," abolition, and a republic patterned on Mexican and, particularly, U.S. models. Over the 1860s, the often-fractured Spanish left unified around shared projects of building a republic and ending slavery. Past (and future) rivals like the socialist Francisco Pi y Margall and the republican Castelar helped stitch together fragile but meaningful alliances between socialists and republicans, federalists and centralizers, all focused on undermining the monarchy.[73]

As the Spanish government debated a new constitution in 1869, Castelar, Pi y Margall, Nicolás Salmerón y Alonso, and other republicans unsuccessfully lobbied to eliminate the monarchy altogether and to drive out slavery.[74] Castelar explained that both the U.S. Revolution and the U.S. Civil War evolved into broad revolutions, and he expected the same in Spain. Castelar also argued for seating Cuban and Puerto Rican representatives so that the islands would "not be a monstrous exception in the grand American democracy." Spain had to permit the islands some self-rule because they "had a grand example near [their] eyes: the glaring example of the United States."[75] A glowing U.S. biographer wrote, "There is something marvelous" in Castelar's knowledge about U.S. institutions and "the accuracy of his interpretation of them."[76] Like Cuban and Mexican republicans, Spaniards used Harriet Beecher Stowe's *Uncle Tom's Cabin* to connect their cause to global abolition. Of course, the United States was not the only potential model for Spanish politicians; radicals looked to France, republicans to Mexico, constitutional monarchists to Britain. But still the United States' example, and the particular lessons of the Civil War, loomed large.[77]

The uprisings in Spain and Cuba shook the Atlantic World. For international socialists and French republicans, the rebellions raised expectations of broader revolutions to come. In London, these rebellions provoked fears that the United States was displacing Britain in the Americas. In the courts of Berlin and Paris, politicians dreamed of naming the next monarch of Spain, a rivalry for control that helped spark the Franco-Prussian War. Prussia's victory in turn destroyed Louis Napoleon's government and led to the rise of the Paris Commune and the eventual Third French Republic. And across the Americas and Europe, abolitionists waited in hopes that the new Spanish government would attack slavery.

Instead of a single revolutionary wave, the U.S. and Mexican wars helped swell several different revolutionary ripples as Cubans and Spaniards each tried to harness the movement's energy. The Spanish and Cuban revolts posed a terrible quandary to U.S. republicans. Oblivious to local causes, they asked, which was the rightful fruit of the U.S. Civil War? A fledgling Spanish government, potentially a republic, with leaders who looked to the United States as a model? Or a Cuban insurgency backed by familiar exiles? Many American politicians backed the Cuban rebels, out of a mix of longing for the island and sympathy for independence movements. But others saw greater hopes in Spain. To antislavery activist Lydia Maria Child, the moment called for "expediency," not blind faith. The United States should give Spain a chance before committing to Cuban insurgents. Although the United States had deep ties to the Cuban revolt, "the friends of freedom deserve our sympathy, whether they are in Spain or Cuba," Child wrote.[78] The *National Anti-Slavery Standard* also looked to the "Spanish Revolution" to remake not only "the people of Spain, and of Cuba" but the entire "cause of Republicanism in Europe."[79]

The irrepressible Daniel Sickles intended to steer the wave from Washington to Madrid, not Havana. To Sickles, a new government in Spain would prove the impact of the United States on the Atlantic World. For the first four years of the Grant administration, Sickles played an outsized role in shaping U.S. policy as the minister to Spain. To Sickles, the new Spanish government represented the chance to complete three seemingly contradictory strands of his revolutionary career: expansionism, antislavery, and personal enrichment. In the 1850s, Sickles rose through Young America circles in New York politics and finance. As James Buchanan's aide in London, he helped craft the Ostend Manifesto and angled to best New York financier August Belmont in the scramble for bond contracts for the purchase of Cuba. Like many other Young Americans, Sickles mingled self-interested expansionism and sincere revolutionary beliefs. And, like many, he seemed unconcerned with slavery, never an enemy to Southern planters but also not quite a pawn. During the secession crisis, Sickles at first responded with confusion but soon joined other Northern Young Americans in supporting the war of national unification. After losing his leg at the Peach Orchard in Gettysburg, Sickles tried desperately to regain his reputation by carrying out a secret mission in Colombia, perhaps to broker an "alliance of all the American Republics" (as the British suspected), perhaps to negotiate a trans-isthmus passage.[80] Back in the United States during what he called the revolution of Reconstruction, he acted boldly as commander of the Carolinas to protect the rights of freedpeople. Pressured out of office by Andrew Johnson, Sickles championed Ulysses S. Grant and the completion of Reconstruction in the 1868 campaign, then lobbied for the posting to Madrid.[81]

Self-interested and self-dealing, Sickles in the 1870s used the same financial techniques to end slavery that he had used in the 1850s to save the institution. For these reasons it is common (and often correct) to portray him as a scoundrel, an opportunist, or a crook.[82] These efforts to establish coherence in Sickles's life represent an understandable, perhaps even admirable, effort to impose unity on an unruly world. But revolutionary history, like most history, suggests that human behavior is not nearly so consistent, human agency not nearly so meaningful. Revolutionary situations compel people to judge their self-interest anew, to act boldly where once they were cautious, to back positions they previously opposed. Revolutions transform crooks into radicals, just as the absence of revolutionary situations may turn bold radicals into blowhards. Sickles's transformation, therefore, tells us less about his personal character than about the transformations the Civil War's revolution fostered. Sickles had always been an opportunist. The Civil War taught him that the only way to sustain his opportunism was by also being an abolitionist. Of such metamorphoses are revolutions made.

In Madrid, Sickles offered many plans for Spain to end slavery and to relinquish some of its authority in Cuba and Puerto Rico. All his proposals centered on Spanish abolition, Cuban home rule, an end to trade barriers between the United States and the island, and a hundred-million-dollar payment from the United States to Spain. At times, Sickles imagined that figure as compensation for the direct purchase of the island, but Sickles also offered to pay for Cuban independence, knowing that the island might "fall into our hands in a few years."[83] At other moments, Sickles offered the money to change Spanish policy even if not to end Spanish rule; the hundred million dollars might compensate the planters for abolition, or the Spanish government for loss of customs revenue in a free-trade Cuba. In these different plans, we see several models of imperialism: explicit expansionism, the creation of client states, and the extension of trade privileges. Sickles's proposals were, he admitted "the revival of an old plan of my own—with significant modifications—which I proposed to Mr. Buchanan at London + afterwards to Pres[ident] Pierce" but now transformed from a plan to save slavery to one to end bondage.[84] For Sickles, and for the United States, self-interest and high-minded idealism worked hand in hand; freeing slaves would make him rich.[85] Even as politicians, editors, and exiles called for the U.S. government to recognize the Cubans as belligerents, Sickles insisted that the best hope for remaking Cuba and ending slavery was in Madrid.

But Sickles found it hard to make a deal. Prim and his advisers were trapped by Spanish popular opinion, which strongly opposed any sale. "The question of Cuba is not the question of parties, it is the question of national

honor," argued *La Época*.[86] While some Spanish officials considered it inevitable that Cuba would be independent, none could risk the massive public
outcry that would follow its sale. Ministers therefore repeatedly suggested
that they were close to a deal but then insisted on impossible conditions.[87]
John Hay, Sickles's aide, wrote in October 1869 that "the Government here is
crazy to accept our offered mediation but does not dare."[88]

   To defend slavery, Spanish merchants, colonial officials, trade protectionists, and Cuban planters constructed a Liga Nacional, a "league against
liberty," through branches of the Havana Casino and the Spanish colonial
clubs. Those clubs empowered Manuel Calvo y Aguirre, Ignacio González
Olivares, and others to bribe government officials to prevent any change on
the island.[89] "Slave holders are the friend + supporter of the interests + govt
of Spain," British minister Austen Henry Layard wrote.[90] This Slave Lobby
convinced Spanish politicians (and perhaps Layard himself) that American
abolitionists were solely self-interested, aiming only to "detach" Cuba from
Spain for the United States.[91] Sickles wrote that Cuban slaveholders "have
sent a large sum of money to Spain" "to be used in in manipulating the venal
Press + venal politicians" by paying editors to publish articles against abolition. "They also know that slavery is the bulwark" of the Spanish colonies
"and that with Emancipation the dreadful evils of Spanish colonial administration will cease to feed the Spanish vampires."[92] As the debate over slavery
dragged on, the Slave Lobby sent "mountains of gold to the court to hinder
the path of these reforms."[93] Spanish political support for colonialism was
tied to agricultural protectionism; Cuba absorbed 20 percent of Spanish exports, behind only Great Britain and France, and was a crucial market for
Spanish grain farmers.[94]

   In the face of Spanish resilience, Sickles turned to international opinion to
break the logjam over Cuba's future. In a sign of the transformations the decade had wrought, Sickles emerged as a leading figure in Atlantic antislavery.
Working with the Spanish abolitionist society, he hosted republican abolitionist meetings in his house and became close friends and allies with dense
intellectual and political networks of abolitionists.[95] At a mass gathering, and
to thunderous applause, he lifted his pants to show the mangled stump of his
leg, his sacrifice for "the sainted cause of abolition of slavery."[96] Sickles wrote
long analyses of immediate emancipation in the United States to prove the
"prosperity" that followed "free labor."[97] Sickles lobbied international abolitionists to pressure their own governments to act against slavery.[98] "So far England has done little or nothing on the subject of Emancipation in Sp[anish]
America," Sickles complained. "I have had all the work on my shoulder."[99]

It was a head-spinning moment. Within a decade, the world's greatest pro-slavery power had remade itself into the most aggressively antislavery nation, and a Southern-aligned politician into a global crusader against the Slave Power. Such are the fruits of revolution. The acceleration of history ate away at Spanish conservatives' confidence. Seeing the swell of antislavery propaganda and diplomacy, even Spanish opponents recognized "the double change that the triumph of North America and the Constitution of 1869 in Spain had produced in the Antilles. Slavery was virtually impossible."[100]

In 1870, abolitionist lobbying, the ongoing insurgency, and Sickles's constant pressure nudged the Spanish government to take a first, partial step toward emancipation. The Cortes passed the Moret Law, which gave liberty to children born after its execution, to the elderly, and to those confiscated from slave ships or those who fought for Spain against the Cuban insurrection. This was a partial fruit—and a limited one—of the U.S. Civil War. But even freeborn children of slaves were to be held in an unpaid state of *patronato* until age eighteen and paid half rates until twenty-two. When conservatives denounced the bill, colonial minister Segismundo Moret explained that U.S. abolition had made slavery unsustainable. Cuban rebels "familiar with North American customs" "have been able to give the insurrection a special character, presenting it as the flag of liberty against the flag of tyranny."[101] In floor debates, abolitionists like Castelar argued that a free Spain could be "in Europe what the U.S. is in America: it will be the ideal and the hope of all the people."[102] Castelar's comparisons to the United States were not superficial; he cited Lincoln's path from gradual emancipation to immediate abolition as an example of "wisdom and political prudence" in the face of changing events.[103] An exuberant John Hay mailed one speech to Charles Sumner, calling Castelar's delivery "glorious" and "miraculous."[104] After Castelar delivered a tribute to Lincoln, Hay wrote that Castelar had "a fire and fury of utterance equaled by no living being . . . you can easily imagine what an intense intellectual pleasure I had for two splendid hours."[105]

Prim hoped to use the Moret gradual emancipation law to ease international tension, so that he could crown a new constitutional monarch, Amadeo I. But outraged republicans argued that Prim moved against the tides of history. In speeches about the "the force of the grand superior organisms" of "republican government," Castelar drew on George Bancroft's histories of the United States to denounce monarchism as a weak vestige of the past.[106] But Prim prevailed, then was mysteriously assassinated shortly after Amadeo's coronation. From the start, Amadeo faced challenges from supporters of the Carlist monarchical line, anarchists and labor unions around

Barcelona, backers of the deposed queen Isabella, and Cuban planters. Sickles lobbied the king frantically for a British commonwealth model, making Cuba into Canada, an essentially self-governing province, in hopes that the king would "hit upon a bait" in a one-hundred-million-dollar loan.[107]

In Cuba, the revolutionary situation expanded as Cuban planters around Havana and Matanzas launched an un-proclaimed revolution against both Spain and the island's rebels. As rumors circulated that Spain might shift toward emancipation, slave owners on the island all but declared independence, professing loyalty to Spain but deciding to "ignore whatever comes by the Cable" and to govern the island by their own lights.[108] Planters raised Voluntarios, soldiers in a privately funded army that obeyed their orders and could be used against both insurgents and potentially reform-minded Spanish appointees. When Prim named abolition-friendly reformer Domingo Dulce as captain general, Voluntarios and leading planter Julián Zulueta forced him from power. It was a "revolution," a Cuban wrote.[109] A British diplomat noted that "in fact a second 'insurrection' against Spanish rule has, as it were, taken place in Cuba. . . . The armed volunteers of Havana . . . are at present in reality the rulers of the island."[110] Cuban planters then intimidated the Spanish government into suspending the Moret gradual abolition law, and they executed poet Juan Clemente Zenea when he arrived to conduct negotiations. The government is "more afraid of the Spanish Volunteers in the Island, than of the Cubans themselves," Hay wrote. Soon the next governor resigned, too.[111]

Planter restorationism prodded insurgents toward a bolder revolution of their own. Over 1869 and 1870, the Spanish army and volunteer forces successfully drove insurgents from parts of Oriente and Puerto Príncipe, scattering rebels into the countryside and prompting many elites to abandon the insurgency. In Guantánamo, the absence of local elite support and the relatively weak history of white creole annexationism there opened space for free men of color and former slaves to emerge as leaders, most famously the "Bronze Titan," Afro-Cuban José Antonio de la Caridad Maceo y Grajales, and Policarpo Pineda. Pineda (known as Rustán) had allegedly fought with an Ohio infantry regiment in the Civil War. When Rustán was injured, Quintín Bandera, a free man of color, assumed command. The Cuban insurgency was becoming a multiracial struggle against slavery.[112]

Frustrated in Cuba, abolitionists turned their eyes to the smaller colony of Puerto Rico, where slavery was less central to economic life and local deputies supported its overthrow. There, the Moret Law did slowly undermine slavery, but abolitionists pressed for an immediate emancipation law. Sickles warned Amadeo's cabinet that immediate emancipation was a "concession due to the public opinion of America and Europe—that it was a fulfillment of the Spanish Revolution of 1868 and the pledges made in the Democratic Constitution of 1869."[113] When Spain failed to act, President Grant temporarily recalled Sickles. Spanish editors cheered his departure, denouncing Sickles's "arrogant propositions" and "inadmissible pretensions," and government officials hoped he would not return. "It is less damaging to have enemies than pretended tutors," one Madrid newspaper opined.[114] By the fall, however, the desperate Spanish government began to take up Puerto Rican emancipation, and Sickles sailed back. The Spanish "abolition movement gains strength," Sickles wrote approvingly. "And I say Amen."[115] The British minister reported that the Havana Slave Lobby once again gave "very costly" bribes to block the legislation before it created a precedent for Cuban abolition.[116]

Grant's reelection and the peaceful conclusion of negotiations with Britain over the *Alabama* controversy shifted the situation again in 1872 by clearing the way for the United States to turn its attention to Spain and Cuba. "Now that we have adjusted our own domestic questions and (the English business)," Sickles warned the Spanish cabinet, "our hands are free for a move towards Mexico and Cuba."[117] The Spanish minister in Washington wrote, "The question of slavery is the touchstone of our relations with the United States."[118] After the Grant administration threatened to boycott Cuban sugar and Congressman Banks called on Europe and the United States to settle the Cuban crisis, the Spanish government promised on December 2, 1872, to back a bill for immediate abolition in Puerto Rico. That day Grant delivered a blistering indictment of Spanish rule in his written State of the Union. "We have succeeded in making the colonial questions foremost in the Cabinet and in the Press," Sickles wrote.[119]

Spanish historian Emilio Castelar used this newfound political space to fuse abolition and republicanism once again. Castelar had spent much of 1872 writing about revolution and "American" forms of republicanism for *Harper's* and Argentine and Mexican publications, as he tried to sustain a politics of hope. That hope emerged from his confident reading of the lessons of Mexico and the United States, although at times Castelar, like all Spanish republicans, looked to France and to medieval Spain for models. In a December 1872 Cortes speech against slavery, Castelar described the Spanish as "the mediators between the old and the new world." Once Spain carried European practices of Catholicism to the Americas; now it would bring American republicanism to Europe. To accomplish this, Spain had to follow Lincoln—whom Castelar quoted at length—by killing slavery in one blow.

Despite differences in culture and religion, Spanish abolitionists shared a race with Lincoln "because we have pronounced without fear the word liberty."[120] An exultant Sickles compared Castelar and his allies to Edwin Stanton and Wendell Phillips and distributed the speech to abolitionists in the United States and Europe.[121] Meanwhile, Spanish newspapers asked cynically, "Who has played the ministers on this occasion, the government of the U.S. or of Spain?"[122] Critics charged, "There are strong reasons to believe that the government has begun under instructions and at the suggestions of the representative of the United States in this court."[123] Abolition was nothing more, they complained, than the continuation of U.S. expansionism. "Time and circumstances have changed their arguments . . . but the procedure comes always to be the same."[124] Privately Sickles speculated that a "strong Republican 'blue pill'" might remake Spain entirely if the king did not bend to U.S. pressure.[125] As the Cortes debated Puerto Rican slavery in late 1872, petitions on slavery flooded into Madrid, including more than one hundred anti-abolition petitions. But abolitionists pressed forward. In January 1873, more than ten thousand people gathered in a mass meeting in Madrid. An abolitionist denounced slave plantations in Cuba and Puerto Rico as "special schools, breeding grounds for reactionary elements. . . . It is not in vain that they breathe the poisoned atmosphere of slavery."[126]

Trapped between proslavery protectionists and republican abolitionists, Amadeo abdicated, opening the way for a new revolution in Spain. As constitutional monarchists divided among their different candidates, Emilio Castelar and other republicans declared the First Spanish Republic. Conservative Spanish newspapers denounced the government as a product of Yankee manipulation and sarcastically argued that the republic should change the law to state "that the sovereignty resides solely in the United States."[127] Privately, British diplomats drew on decades of experience with Sickles to interpret his behavior as an extension of filibusterism. The British minister believed that Sickles had "contributed in no small degree to the fall of the dynasty" and the establishment of the republic. "He was in league with the republican party here" who "were in the habit of meeting at his home" and "consulted him in what they did," and "many of the documents which they published were written under his inspiration."[128] These "extraordinary steps" went beyond both Washington's instructions and diplomats' standards of behavior, they argued.[129] The British minister grumbled about the United States' "filibustering policy" and repeated gossip that Sickles should "be President."[130] Sickles himself wrote, "All I have done—no more and no less—have been to persuade the Republicans to be patient and wait until they could command a majority of the chamber." The key work, Sickles wrote, was Castelar's speech, which "fused the Republican and Radical Elements."[131]

Unlike Cuban insurgents, Spanish republicans gained support from the United States. While European diplomats denounced the republic, on February 15, 1873, Sickles became the first minister to pay his respects. As he approached, members of the Cortes gathered on the portico to welcome him, and a "battalion of volunteers" played music and waved flags to line his path. Sickles cheered the "immense efficacy" of "free institutions." The new Spanish president celebrated the United States' "perfect equilibrium" as a "dignified example that I will not forget" as he worked to resolve the "difficult problem of uniting democracy with liberty." [132] In response a Spanish newspaper proclaimed, "Filibusterism has ended in America."[133] More concretely, Sickles called on the U.S. Navy to reinforce "my Spanish Republic" with ships in case of an uprising.[134] "It seems like a dream," Sickles wrote to John Hay. Sickles in these heady moments placed republicanism over expansionism, warning the United States not to destroy the republic by selfishly grabbing Cuba. Although Sickles acknowledged that the United States might one day claim Cuba and Puerto Rico if the republic fell, he lobbied the United States to prop up the government. "If the Republic be just to the Antilles it will leave us nothing to desire," he wrote.[135]

Spanish republicans used abolition to prove their legitimacy on a world stage reconfigured by an antislavery United States. The short-lived republic's four presidents—Estanislao Figueras, Pi y Margall, Nicolás Salmeron, and Castelar—all shared sincere abolitionist beliefs and a confidence that emancipation would prove the republic's power to the United States. A bill to abolish slavery in Puerto Rico became the test. Conservatives never ceased characterizing abolition as evidence of U.S. meddling, as "reforms made by suggestion of the North American politicians. . . . All the world knows that the policy of the U.S. is and always has been the acquisition of the Antilles." Conservatives argued that abolition destroyed economies in Haiti, the British and French Empires, and the Southern United States. And conservatives, with impressive specificity, quoted Lincoln's 1862 letter to Horace Greeley— in which Lincoln pledged to emancipate only as many slaves as he needed to win the war—to illustrate the thinness of U.S. commitment to antislavery.[136] Conservatives also attacked the relation between freedom and coercion in their critique of Reconstruction. Comparing military governors like Sickles to captains general, they argued that immediate emancipation required a "tyrannical and despotic domination" that denied slave owners "even the rights of citizens" while under the "imperial sable."[137] Another skeptic complained that abolition led to the "Freedmen's Bureau and the military governments of the South."[138] Charging that the United States extended wartime powers for years after "peace," one critic said that the story of Reconstruction "begins with the occupation of New Orleans by General Butler, and concludes with the ruin of the same New Orleans."[139] In ways that anticipate current analyses of the interaction between U.S. westward expansion and international imperialism, Spanish papers mockingly asked if the country should offer to intervene in the United States' Modoc War in California. Although meant in jest, the invocation of internal imperialism captured the logic of the Republican Party, a party sincerely committed at once to ending slavery and to extending free-labor settler colonialism.

Castelar and his allies used the example of the United States to justify their actions. Although Castelar at times mangled his facts—once doubling the number of slaves in the United States—he drew an impressively nuanced portrait of the wartime United States as he assessed Lincoln's suspension of habeas corpus, Reconstruction's reliance on force, and Republicans' impeachment of Andrew Johnson. Yes, the United States had to rely on brute power to end slavery, but the U.S. example proved that republics could govern successfully. For its part, Reconstruction demonstrated that republics could generate "a force, a prestige that today, we do not deceive ourselves, it [Spain] does not have."[140] Castelar wrote to Lew Wallace, former general and soon to be author of *Ben-Hur*, that "our nations will be brothers" as the "modern Republics."[141]

But antislavery republicanism did not necessarily mean anticolonialism, either for Spanish republicans or for U.S. Republicans. The revolutionary wave buffeting Spain would not cost them Cuba, Spanish republicans promised. To rebut charges that they lacked patriotism, Castelar and other republicans pledged that abolition would cement Cuba's ties to Spain, ties they would never relinquish even as they granted more home rule. When anti-abolition deputies warned that "liberty is beautiful" but "above all is the homeland,"[142] Castelar swore to "die 1000 times before we are content to diminish an atom of territory of the homeland."[143]

When the Cortes passed Puerto Rican abolition in 1873 and freed the island's twenty-nine thousand remaining slaves, many U.S. abolitionists celebrated the legislation as a culmination of the Civil War. Sickles formally recognized the Spanish republic in a much-covered ceremony in May. Riding in a carriage with leading Spanish congressmen, Sickles marched through a company of flag-waving and music-playing soldiers to a reception with the republic's ministers.[144] The Spanish president emphasized the common "form of government which has arisen between us." The United States was a "grand and glorious" guide to the "three grand elements of progress: liberty, democracy, and the republic."[145] In the United States, editors cheered. "WELL DONE," the *Christian Recorder* wrote. "These Spanish Republicans know the worth of a precedent. . . . Naught remains for the new Republic, but to continue the good work" in Cuba.[146] Already, in his March 1873 second inaugural, Grant had celebrated "that the civilized world is tending toward republicanism, or government by the people through their chosen representatives, and that our own Great Republic is destined to be the guiding star to all others."[147] Castelar, familiar to U.S. editors from his many published essays in English and Spanish, was foreign minister, and a powerful example of the virtue of the republic and the apparent influence of the United States. "The soul of Democracy is marching on," the *Christian Recorder* wrote. "Don Emilio Castelar . . . worships at the shrine of Republicanism and Liberty, with the devotion of our own Sumner. . . . Slavery in Cuba may be set down as a thing of the past."[148] But some U.S. abolitionists, especially Henry Highland Garnet and Samuel Scottron and Congressman Banks, continued to doubt Spain's intentions and favored Cuban insurgents. "Cuba must be free," Henry Highland Garnet said, "God has decreed it."[149] The *Christian Recorder* stated that it was "high time that liberty be brought in, even if Spain has to be kicked out.[150]

The Spanish republican revolution of 1873 birthed dreams of a never-ending series of revolutionary waves that would remake the world. In these heady moments, both Castelar and Sickles described new epochs to match the new form of government. Some Spanish republicans turned to thoughts of expansion, perhaps by attacking Portugal, deposing its monarch, and installing a republic there or even annexing Portugal as a state.[151] In his airier moments, Emilio Castelar sketched out plans for a United States of Europe, a federation of republics that was one nineteenth-century precursor to twentieth-century discussions of a European Union.[152] Castelar's dreams later seemed foolish, but in these heady years at the end of the 1860s and the start of the 1870s, many people saw new signs of hope. On Cuba, formerly enslaved people pressed a politics of abolition and racial equality, helping create the foundation for an antiracist ideology. In the United States, supporters of Reconstruction also imagined a revolution against racism, a transformation not only of freedpeople's legal rights but of their place in society. Others like Lucy and Albert Parsons dreamed that the Reconstruction of Southern labor might spur a new place for working people across the United States.

Daniel Sickles, too, seemed caught in flights of imagination inconceivable even a year earlier. After a lifetime spent combining revolutionary republicanism with expansionism, Sickles seemed to pause, stunned by the force of what he could not resist seeing as his own creation, and to contemplate a new world being born. Instead of trying to steal Cuba, he proposed something much bolder: a United States of Spain, in which the United States would finance the cost of emancipation in Cuba, and Spain would eliminate trade barriers with the United States and declare Cuba a self-governing state within the Spanish nation.[153] This would inaugurate a new moment in Atlantic history. An allied United States of America and United States of Spain would form a vanguard of free-trading republics that would stretch across the Atlantic, displace Great Britain commercially and diplomatically, and inspire the creation of free-trading republics throughout Europe. "The Spanish Republic will surely exert more influence on the politics of the continent during the next decade," Sickles wrote.[154] As Spanish Republicans debated a new constitution, Sickles wrote, "I believe we shall feel the scythe and the sickle at work very soon and then you will see Slavery, caste privilege, monopoly, church establishment and all the old weeds cut away and mowed down."[155] Still, Sickles would get his money. Who else, after all, should gain the commissions for the bonds to pay for abolition? But Sickles's dreams of a new Atlantic World baffled some U.S. diplomats and outraged some more moderate politicians. In private, Grant doubted the republic's future, and Secretary of State Fish asked, "Is Sickles being bamboozled? Or does he believe in these people?"[156]

The Spanish Republic struggled against the very utopian dreams it unleashed. Worker revolts in Barcelona and elsewhere paralyzed legislators. Cantonal uprisings in Cartagena undermined the government, Carlists gained ground in the north, Catalans declared autonomy, members of the First International proclaimed new social republics, anarchists took to the streets, and army officers threatened coups. One republican president after another departed. The tenuous alliance forged among left-liberals in 1864 dissolved as decentralized federalists and socialists under Pi y Margall assumed control and then resigned. After yet another president quit, the republic seemed to be collapsing.

In this chaos, Emilio Castelar assumed the presidency and inaugurated a quest for order, an effort to prove that republics possessed sufficient force to survive. In September 1873, the Spanish congress turned over dictatorial power to him and adjourned. Until it returned in January 1874, Castelar could try to build a republic through martial law.[157] Drawing explicitly on the examples of Lincoln and Juárez, Castelar embraced military power and reached an understanding with local general Manuel Pavía. As Castelar contemplated the United States, Mexico, and other republics, he wrestled with the relation between democracy and stability. "Democracy is liberty, but it also is authority; movement, but also stability; action but also brake on this action; individual rights but also discipline and social authority," he said during the Puerto Rico debate.[158] For this Friedrich Engels called Castelar an "undisguised bourgeois."[159] But Britain's minister saw signs by October that "the streets are no longer infested by an armed mob" and "public confidence to a certain extent [has] been restored," even though he still doubted that the republic could survive.[160] An exultant Sickles called Castelar "one of the greatest men of the Epoch. . . . This is what Spain + the Republic now need."[161] In October, Sickles sent him a picture of George Washington and compared him to the "Father of his country."[162] Castelar praised Washington's "grand examples" of the "liberty of men and for the integrity of the country," to be "free and grand," protect its "rights" and "conserve its territories."[163] Sarcastically a conservative newspaper reported that it was "false" that Sickles attended cabinet meetings. Instead, "What happens is that the ministers accepted his advice."[164]

But revolutions test the relation between abstract beliefs and concrete self-interest. No matter how much the Spanish talked of republican self-rule, they could not resolve the basic problem of Cuba. Cuban insurgents rebelled in the name not only of liberalism or republicanism or abolition but of Cuban national self-determination, a cause that placed them in direct conflict with the Spanish Republic. As Martí demonstrated when he flew the Cuban, not Spanish, flag in the streets of Madrid, most Cuban insurgents wanted, not a "Spanish Republic," but a "Republic of their own. What they aspire to is independence, and for this, as they know, they must fight."[165] Many Cubans denounced the Spanish Republic as a "vain delusion" that tyrannically "crucified in Cuba the same ideas it was defending" in Spain.[166] Santacilia cheered the Spanish Republic only because he assumed that it would die quickly, and its collapse would "facilitate" the "triumph of our glorious revolution."[167] Meanwhile, Spanish republicans moved slowly on colonial reform and abolition, fearful of provoking a counterrevolution. "They all say yes—and do nothing," Sickles complained.[168]

On Cuba, planters and Voluntarios took advantage of the revolution in Spain to assert their own authority. With the creation of the republic, planters' loyalty oozed "out at their fingers' ends," a reporter wrote.[169] A British diplomat believed that the volunteers "do what they please and have practically taken power out of the hands of the Viceroy. It is not clear that if abandoned by Spain they would not carry on the pro-slavery war on their own account."[170] A British consul in Puerto Rico reported that if the government put the islands under a republican government, Cuban planters "had resolved to resist it by force of arms, + if necessary to join in proclaiming the independence of the island."[171] Pro-Spanish Cuban planters acted boldly because they saw a chance to shatter an insurgency already divided over strategy and the role of men of color. Maceo and commander Maximo Gómez pressed for a cross-island invasion to bring the war to Havana and the west, but other insurgents feared the growing presence of men of color in the military. "Do we liberate ourselves only to share the fate of Haiti and Santo Domingo?" one asked.[172]

And the international situation that aligned the United States with the Spanish Republic was more fragile than it seemed. In late 1873, the alliance collapsed with the capture of the *Virginius*, a small event that forced the United States to choose between the Spanish Republic and Cuban insurgents, an event with significance far out of proportion to its details. In October 1873, Cuban planters saw their chance to drive a wedge between the United States and Spain when Spanish authorities seized the ship *Virginius* owned by the Cuban Junta of New York. The *Virginius* itself was a product of the Civil War, constructed in Scotland for the Confederate States in 1864. By 1873, the ship had spent three years carrying men and supplies from the United States and Caribbean to Cuba while illegally flying the U.S. flag. In October 1873, the *Virginius* docked at Kingston, Jamaica, and gathered U.S., British, and Cuban soldiers to join the insurgency. As the ship turned toward Haiti to pick up weapons, Spanish vessels captured it and carried it into Santiago de Cuba. The passengers revealed the international nature of the Cuban revolution. Among those on board were General Bernabé de Varona, a young Cuban who had studied in the United States; William Ryan, a Civil War veteran and British citizen; Henri Céspedes, brother of the president of the Cuban insurgents and nominally a U.S. citizen; and ship captain Joseph Fry, a former U.S. and Confederate naval officer.[173]

Cuban officials and planters sagely used the ship to separate the United States from the Spanish Republic. Under the influence of the Voluntarios, Cuban officers executed fifty-three men in eight days. At first, Sickles responded cautiously, working with Castelar to draft orders to stop the firing squads. But the republic lacked the authority to enforce its will; Voluntarios had just circulated pamphlets urging Cubans to ignore any directives from Spain.[174] In the face of this rebellion, the captain general "discontinued the convenience of obeying the orders of the government!" Castelar's minister wrote. "You cannot figure the obstinacy, the blind resistance of these men; they believe they can eat the United States. . . . Here exist two rebellions: one a yell of independence and the other of Viva España."[175] The British minister in Washington likewise believed that Spain encountered "two insurrections" in Cuba: the insurgents and the Volunteers, "who completely controlled the authorities sent from Madrid and would not allow the orders of the Govt to be obeyed."[176] In Spain, conservatives defended the executions by once again comparing settler colonialism to imperial colonial rule. "If the United States has the right to exterminate the Modoc Indians . . . it cannot deny the right to Spain against those who attack its national integrity."[177]

The executions outraged U.S. editors and politicians, swamping sympathy for the Spanish Republic under a tide of popular nationalism. Newspaper columns and public speeches called for war. As black filibusters met in Savannah, New Orleans, and South Carolina, it seemed that Martin Delany's dream of a joint rebellion might again be in the offing. In Savannah, Henry McNeal Turner promised "5000 colored citizens are ready to enlist for Cuba to teach the Spanish authorities respect for the American flag."[178] In New Orleans, Cuban insurgents, Mexican Liberals, former Confederate lieutenant general James Longstreet, and black Republican politician P. B. S. Pinchback gathered in a mass meeting to raise support for a Cuban invasion.[179] Influential *Chicago Tribune* publisher Joseph Medill mocked the "maudlin sympathy" on behalf of the "slavery and barbarism which [Charles] Sumner calls by the sweet name of 'Sister Republicanism' in our 'Struggling Sister Republic' of Spain."[180]

Hearing calls for war, Daniel Sickles reinvented himself once again, this time from the Spanish Republic's champion to its bitterest foe. Humiliated by his inability to control the Spanish government, Sickles suddenly struck out against his friends and allies. Sickles began making impossible demands, hoping to provoke a war between Spain and the United States. In Madrid, crowds stormed Sickles's home and rallied outside the U.S. legation.[181] Baffled, fellow diplomat Elihu Washburne wondered if Sickles "has become mad with the whole world and is striking out wild."[182] More astutely, Secretary of State Hamilton Fish believed that Sickles had mistaken newspaper editorials for popular support for a war, and so Sickles "was preparing his sword & epaulettes to be at the head of the Movement."[183] Lustful for glory, Sickles had ridden proslavery filibusterism in the 1850s, antislavery revolution in the 1860s, and now, he believed, U.S.-Spanish war in 1873.

But there was no war. Self-interest had limited the connection between the Spanish Republic and the United States, and now self-interest limited the break. After the previous year's economic crash, the United States could not afford an extended conflict. Fish cut off Sickles and personally negotiated terms with the Spanish minister in Washington: release of the remaining U.S. citizens, a formal salute to the U.S. flag, and the return of the *Virginius*.

Fittingly, on its way back to the United States, the ship sank. So, too, did Sickles's reputation, as he marched at the head of a war column that did not form, leading it to a battle that did not take place. Sickles lashed out at Fish and Grant: "Out of a sentimental + foolish deference to this phantom," the United States "lost the best occasion possible" to acquire Cuba.[184] In these wild moments, Sickles revealed himself not as the savvy plotter he saw in the mirror but as an incorrigible romantic, a man who could accept any degradation other than boredom, who preferred revolutionary glory to mundane policy.

A month after Sickles abandoned his dream for international revolution, Castelar's hopes came to their own end. In January 1874, the Cortes judged his efforts to create public order through martial law. Allegedly, General Pavía offered to block the Cortes from convening and thus to sustain Castelar as dictator. Castelar, still a republican, declined. On the Cortes's first day, discontented federalists argued that Castelar had gone too far toward centralization. In response, Castelar presented a simple, fearful choice. With a positive vote affirming his use of extraordinary powers, Castelar argued, he could solidify the alliance between republicans and military leaders and save the republic. "Do not forget, however, that we are in war; that we must sustain this war . . . that there is no politics possible outside of the politics of war." What turned on the outcome, he believed, was the future of republics in Europe. "Saving the republic, I put this above liberty, above democracy, above all. . . . Before the liberal, before the democratic, I am a republican, and I prefer the worst of the republics to the best of monarchies; and I prefer a military dictatorship inside of the Republic to the most kind of all kings." Once again, Castelar invoked the U.S. Civil War as a guide. The United States "could not save itself without ten years of dictatorship" in the war and Reconstruction, he argued, with only mild and justifiable exaggeration.[185]

Castelar's struggle to reconcile force and the republican form of government was emblematic of the age. As Castelar noted, Lincoln and congressional Republicans repeatedly turned to martial law to sustain a republic that could not otherwise defend itself. So, too, did the recent history of Mexico suggest the role of steel in sustaining the Liberal project. There Juárez turned to military power to save his state both during the French intervention and in struggles against internal chieftains. When Juárez's family found the president dead in his chair, the president was holding in his hands Eugène Lerminier's *Cours d'histoire des législations comparées*, annotated with Juárez's final written notes: "When a society is threatened by war, the dictatorship or the centralization of power is a necessity as a practical remedy to save institutions, liberty, and peace."[186]

The future of the Spanish Republic, and perhaps of the nineteenth-century republican idea, hung on a question that had plagued both the U.S. and Mexican revolutions: how to sustain both democracy and order.

For Spanish federalists, Castelar had gone too far, prioritizing power and order over liberty. By 100–120, they voted him from office and swept away his government. In response, General Pavía swept away the republic. As soldiers poured into the chamber, congressmen fled for their lives. Soon the army established a government under former Cuban captain general and Liga Nacional leader Francisco Serrano. "The volunteers in Cuba are rejoicing over it," the British minister to the United States wrote.[187] In 1874, the military government reappointed Slave Lobby favorite José Gutiérrez de la Concha to a third term as captain general in Havana. The following year, the army named a new king. Abolition faded. Restorationism prevailed.

Embittered, Castelar saw the death of republics. "Our Republic, not our Republic, our Nation is lost. The socialist utopia which some have cherished; the federal utopia, which I had also supported; destroyed a country, the work of so many centuries. . . . I had no army, and I recruited it; it had no discipline and I re-established it. It had no order and I founded it."[188] Although Castelar could forgive Daniel Sickles, he could not forgive his fellow Spanish republicans. After a time in self-imposed exile, Castelar reemerged as a self-styled *posibilista*, a man who fought only for what he believed was possible to achieve. From running a newspaper called *La Democracia*, he now ran one called *El Orden.* Increasingly, to Castelar, the lesson of the U.S. and Mexican republics was a bleak one. Republics survived by surviving. Not by elevating liberty but by massing force against their enemies.

But the United States' break with Spain did not lead the United States toward support for Cuba. Cuban insurgents struggled to hold their ground in the face of Spanish counterattacks. Although island revolutionaries made gains in 1874, they fought in small bands rather than as an organized army.[189] As Cuban insurgents struggled, the United States turned away from them, too. In his December 1875 annual address, Grant called recognition of Cuban independence "impracticable and indefensible" and saw no "marked or real advance on the part of the insurgents" to merit recognizing the state of belligerency.[190] Ten years after Appomattox, the United States' dreams of expansion had mostly vanished, buried by political dissent, the economic Panic of 1873, and a gradual diminishment of national ambition. Cora Montgomery's plan to annex Santo Domingo had died in the U.S. Senate; the hopes for Cuba sank with the *Virginius.* The Civil War had not made a new Atlantic system. In despair, many Cuban exiles, especially those with ties to New York Young Americans and Cuban planter Miguel Aldama, switched to the Democrats in 1876.[191]

In Cuba, the last years of the revolt turned into a dramatic, doomed slave rebellion. Leading insurgents agreed to a peace in 1878 that guaranteed emancipation for roughly sixteen thousand ex-slave soldiers. But Maceo and others refused to surrender without complete abolition.[192] Against official U.S. indifference, Henry Highland Garnet desperately sustained the American Foreign Anti-Slavery Society. "If the veteran abolitionists of the United States had not mustered themselves out of service, I believe that there would not now have been a single slave in the Island of Cuba," Garnet told a biracial and bilingual crowd in late 1877.[193] But some insurgents ceased fighting in 1878, others in 1880. When the next Cuban revolution sprang up in the 1890s, it would be led by some of the same warriors, but they would never again have faith in the United States as an ally.

The retreat of the United States abroad was matched by and perhaps intertwined with a parallel retraction at home. As the Ku Klux Klan attacked in 1870–71, Sickles urged Grant to strike back hard at this "second rebellion" and mused that he almost wished he could leave the Cuba negotiations to "go back to the Carolinas and take hold of those unruly devils."[194] But the 1873 economic crisis doomed Reconstruction and sapped away Northern support for the Republican Party. In 1874, restorationist White Leagues in Louisiana seized several parishes by force and briefly toppled the state government. That fall Democrats won vast majorities in the U.S. House midterm elections. Republicans made one last, desperate, and unsuccessful effort to extend military power over the South in early 1875 but then retreated. The Republicans were too "much depressed by the victories of their opponents in the recent elections," the British minister to Washington wrote, to pursue either an aggressive foreign or domestic policy.[195] In 1875, Democrats drove Republicans from power in Mississippi, and in 1876, they captured Louisiana, Florida, and South Carolina.

‖‖‖‖‖‖‖‖‖‖‖‖‖‖‖‖‖‖‖‖‖‖‖‖‖‖‖‖‖‖‖

The nearly simultaneous collapse of republican ambitions in the South, in Cuba, and in Spain may inspire historians to reconsider the impetus and ultimate limits of Reconstruction. Had imperialism abroad inspired revolutionary ambitions at home? Were civil rights for domestic minorities tied in some direct or indirect way to the potential exploitation of other people outside the nation's borders? Wendell Phillips made the connection between Reconstruction and internationalism a practical one: "The moment the black man puts his hand on the helm at Washington, we will have a politics that shall dictate to Cuba." Black senators and secretaries of state would send black admirals to protect the Americas from European monarchs and defend "the natural rights of every race."[196] Frederick Douglass likewise tied together "the interest of the negro," the "interest of patriotism," and the "interest of liberty" in the United States and Cuba.[197]

More abstractly, advances at home and abroad seemed to inspire mutually reinforcing confidence in the force of government and in the direction of history. Hope is admittedly a difficult concept to quantify, or even estimate, but it remains a crucial engine of human history. Reconstruction leaders drew sustenance from many sources—religious, ethical, moral, but also teleological, a faith that history was on their side. Both domestic Reconstruction and U.S. intervention against global slavery benefitted from, and perhaps depended on, a crusading mentality, a broad vision that inspired and energized its followers yet also, like other crusades, may become militant to the point of militaristic.[198] When defeat fractured that faith in the future, the international and the domestic revolutions died in tandem. Untangling the relation between antislavery and expansionism may help historians reassess the generative force and ultimate disappointments of Reconstruction.[199]

By the late 1870s, slavery limped along in Cuba and Brazil, and republics either teetered into chaos or solidified into antidemocratic oligarchy. In Cuba, the colonial government finally proclaimed the eventual end of slavery in 1880, with a system of apprenticeship to last for eight years. Over time this *patronato* system wore down the institution of slavery, as enslaved people pressed for freedom. During the first three years almost fifty thousand *patrocinados* gained their freedom, leaving roughly fifty thousand enslaved people in 1886, when the colonial government ordered the end of slavery on the island two years early.[200] Meanwhile, the grand dreams of U.S. Reconstruction ebbed to Jim Crow disfranchisement, U.S. Republicans into a defense of corporations, Mexican Liberalism into a one-party, and soon one-candidate, state.[201] With a sense of that end, we might be prepared to assess a question posed by global historians: What difference did the Civil War actually make in the Atlantic World?[202]

In the extravagant expectations that circulated around the Gulf, we see an Atlantic World the Civil War Might Have Made, glimmering perhaps with a touch of blinded romance, of naive hope. To engage in what might-have-beens is to risk ahistoricism but also to see clearly the possibilities embedded in the post–Civil War moment. In the upheaval of the nearly simultaneous struggles in the United States, Mexico, Cuba, and Spain, participants saw the chance to remake the Gulf World and the Atlantic World. To reimagine their economies, their politics, their relations to one another, even the way they saw themselves and formed their own identities. A history that does not address the plausibility of those hopes cannot capture the realm of dreams and expectations, mysterious engines of history.

Yet history must also assess the disappointment of those dreams, the poverty of some of those hopes, the illusive nature of those expectations. To address those limits, while still taking their potential seriously, we might ask whether the Civil War would have influenced the Atlantic World more if it influenced it less, if its limits were embedded not in its failings but in its seeming success. Had Spaniards not deposed their queen, perhaps the United States and Mexico would have backed Cuban revolutionaries and helped guide a process to independence and abolition on the island. Or, had Cuban insurgents not judged it their time to strike, perhaps the United States might have been able to negotiate some form of home rule and abolition with revolutionized Spain. But these conjoined, oppositional revolutions paralyzed U.S. policymakers and laid bare the thinness of the idea of a historical time that transcended local and national contexts. Trapped between the competing claims of Cuba and Spain, U.S. officials lost their sense of revolutionary momentum, and with it their sense of timing, until the moment of confidence passed. The World the Civil War Might Have Made helps us see that hope and also help us weigh more carefully the deeply buried forces, dull and unremarkable as they seem, that sink like a stone those dreams of a different, perhaps better, world.

A FINISHED REVOLUTION

The Sorrow of Stubborn Hours

By 1880, the Second American Revolution had come to its end, Frederick Douglass told a crowd in Elmira, New York, and the end was all too perilously close to its beginning. "The old master class is to-day triumphant, and the newly-enfranchised class in a condition but little above that in which they were found before the rebellion," Douglass said. During the 1870s, the planters' counterrevolution overthrew Southern state and local governments, drove freedpeople and their allies from office, won control of the U.S. House of Representatives, and reasserted social, cultural, and political power over much of the South. "Do you ask me how, after all that has been done, this state of things has been made possible?" Douglass continued. "I will tell you. Our reconstruction measures were radically defective. . . . In the hurry and confusion of the hour, and the eager drive to have the Union restored, there was more care for the sublime superstructure of the republic than for the solid foundation upon which it could alone be upheld."[1] Douglass's interpretation was already becoming commonplace in 1880, and that argument has endured ever since: the Second American Revolution ended because it had been poorly designed from the beginning, undone by haste and indifference.

But in the same speech Douglass raised an even bleaker possibility: perhaps the Second American Revolution's limits revealed a flaw not just in the American character but in the American constitutional system or in liberal democracy. "Great and valuable concessions have in different ages been made to the liberties of mankind," Douglass told the crowd. "They have, however, come not at the command of reason and persuasion, but by the sharp and terrible edge of the sword."[2] From a different political angle, former president Ulysses S. Grant reached a somewhat similar conclusion in the late 1870s. "Looking back over the whole policy of reconstruction, it seems to me that the wisest thing would have been to have continued for some time the military rule," Grant told a reporter. "The trouble about military rule in the South was that our people did not like it. It was not in accordance with our institutions."[3]

Douglass and Grant explored a tension that haunts—or should haunt—the United States: Could the same constitutional order that had denied rights to black people now protect people's newfound rights? In the 1860s, many Republicans practiced what I call bloody constitutionalism, a plan to build a sustainable, more just political order by forcing alterations of the Constitution through martial law, then returning to normal political time. Force changed the political order; a resumption of peace embedded that new order in the stability of the old. Or so they hoped. In the face of the 1870s counterrevolution, Douglass and Grant—and many other Republicans—wondered whether they had erred, whether bloody constitutionalism had been a miscalculation, not because of the force but because of the constitutionalism. Republicans could bully through changes, but they could not hold the fruits of victory.

The ends and endpoints of the Second American Revolution should trouble our understanding of U.S. political history and of the United States' political project. The Second American Revolution's gains are an affront to narrow constitutionalism, and the counterrevolution against Reconstruction the most damning evidence of constitutionalism's limits. In a nation that tries desperately, and nobly, to combine constitutionalism and personal freedom—to make the two synonymous—the Second American Revolution and the restorationist counterrevolution raise the question of whether black people's personal freedom depended, perilously, on the suspension of constitutional limits. The great flaw in Reconstruction, as both Douglass and Grant acknowledged, may have been that the revolution closed. Wartime and its special powers ended. Freedpeople and their allies lost their ability to deploy force to protect individuals or create further change. With the revolution's close, freedpeople—and the broader notion of individual rights—had to depend on courts and bureaucracies, instead of martial law. Although that trade seems worthwhile from the vantage point of a twenty-first-century government, in the nineteenth century, courts and bureaucracies turned out to be thin reeds. Legalism and restraint were other names for abandonment.

The Second American Revolution was thus a finished revolution. It arose from 1850s international and domestic crises, turned revolutionary in 1861, then ended in stages between 1871—when the legal powers of wartime expired—and 1878—when congressional Democrats barred the military from intervening in most domestic affairs. Over 1879 and 1880, congressional Democrats continued to strike at the army's authority. By 1880, Douglass looked back on a period defined by powers that no longer existed, a revolutionary era that had come to an end. Preserving the Second American Revolution had depended on normal constitutional and bureaucratic tools, tools not sufficient for the task.

To assess the Second American Revolution, we may need to set aside, at least for a time, Eric Foner's much-loved description of Reconstruction as an "unfinished revolution," the single-most influential historical argument ever made about this period. This is a risky endeavor, far riskier than simply shifting vocabulary. The phrase "unfinished revolution" has helped a generation of scholars think through what Reconstruction did and did not accomplish. To say that Reconstruction (and thus the entire Second American Revolution) was unfinished was to acknowledge what Douglass confronted: Reconstruction had not accomplished Republican goals of establishing legal and political rights, much less the longed-for but fiercely resisted dream of racial equality. And, more optimistically, to call Reconstruction unfinished was also to connect that period to the post–World War II civil rights movement and the American rights revolution. Seen together, Reconstruction and the civil rights movement shared some aspirations, technologies of governance, and tactics.

The unfinished revolution framework is a great deal to give up. So why should we? We should let go of the unfinished revolution so that we might see the Second American Revolution as a finished revolution on its own terms, not as a prelude for the civil rights movement. It many respects it was a successful revolution, one that culminated in four million people's freedom, perhaps the greatest emancipation in world history, and perhaps the greatest confiscation of property in world history. That freedom had consequences we should never overlook: formerly enslaved people now created legal families, bought property, bargained over their terms of work, moved, filed lawsuits, testified in court, founded thousands of schools, educated their children, chartered thousands of churches, and forged the institutional structures for African American cultural, economic, and family life. None of these powers were inevitable in 1861 or even 1865, and in their aggregate they made an enormous difference for freedpeople. So, too, did emancipation disrupt the power of a planter class that had attempted to rule not merely the South but the nation and the world. The Second American Revolution's forcible methods remind us that none of these gains was inevitable or simple to achieve or even constitutional, and those methods warn us against the idea that fundamental change might be easy to enact.

But it has been challenging to remember the boldness of the Second American Revolution. Republicans made it harder for us by their decision to whitewash their revolution. In the decades after the Civil War, many Republicans domesticated the conflict, softened its revolutionary rhetoric, turned away from its revolutionary methods. Some did so to appease former Confederates. Others whitewashed the revolution in hopes of saving it. By making their gains seem constitutional and normal, Republicans aimed to depoliticize emancipation and its legacies. Without enough proper propagandists, the Second American Revolution disappeared behind the mystifying fog of unionism, part of a continuous story of American freedom.

And the revolution was finished because it was partly overthrown. Southern planters launched a restorationist counterrevolution that aimed to displace both freedpeople and the Republican whitewashed narrative. Planter counterrevolutionaries overthrew Republican governments, intimidated freedpeople and white Republicans from voting, punished freedpeople for negotiating labor contracts, policed freedpeople's movements, raped freedwomen, and murdered tens of thousands of African Americans. In the 1890s, counterrevolutionaries led massive efforts to disfranchise freedmen and create a Jim Crow segregationist caste society. The Supreme Court acquiesced in many of those actions in the *Slaughterhouse* decision, the *Civil Rights Cases*, *Williams v. Mississippi*, and other lawsuits that emptied the new constitutional amendments of much of their meaning. By the late century, white Northern Republicans acquiesced as well, and hopes for racial equality died amid a resurgence of brutal, bitter racism. Decades later W. E. B. Du Bois wrote gloomily that "the slave went free; stood a brief moment in the sun; then moved back again toward slavery. . . . Democracy died save in the hearts of black folk."[4] Despite Du Bois's blurring of distinctions between Jim Crow and slavery, some parts of the revolution endured even in the face of counterrevolution. Restorationists could weaken the Second American Republic, but they could not restore the First. Defeated planters lost some of their economic hold over the region and a great deal of their national power; not for a century would Southern politicians dominate national political life, and never again would they set the nation's economic course. So, too, did the words of the Constitution endure, even if they seemed illusory or nearly useless in the early twentieth century; birthright citizenship, equal protection, and due process remained mostly latent within American life, even if a quite different era would be required to revive them. And freedpeople and their descendants did continue to acquire property, educate children, move northward in search of opportunity, and develop thick cultural institutions that could not be forged so directly in slavery. Restorationists stunted the Second American Republic and its Second Constitution, but they could not displace it completely.

Just as Du Bois wrote, however, a Third American Republic was slowly coming into being. As much an evolution as a revolution, this Third American Republic emerged so differently than the first two that the name "revolution" may not fit. The Third Republic was established not by armed force and suspension of civil law but by reform, legalism, and executive action. Between the 1930s and 1960s, a new civil rights movement shook the nation and the world and at times found common cause with a constitutional transformation launched by the New Deal. Third Founders—activists, lawyers, and Supreme Court justices—took bold new constitutional steps, some far beyond the aspirations of most Second Founders, but also took care to whitewash their own bold actions, clothing their decisions on school desegregation and racial discrimination in the amendments that created the Second Constitution, especially the Fourteenth. In a kind of liberal originalism, justices and lawyers defended twentieth-century decisions as the true fruit of the Second American Revolution, helping make the civil rights movement seem more American, less radical, less creative than it actually was. At their most optimistic, celebrants of the civil rights movement tied their work to Reconstruction to make the American rights revolution the central story of U.S. history, Jim Crow restorationism an aberration, the three republics into one.[5] Yet the rhetorical connections between the Second Republic and the Third may be stronger than the analytic ones; Reconstruction may have been more a useful fiction than a precedent for the civil rights movement.

Separating the Second Republic from the Third may help scholars see the Second American Revolution, and particularly its revolutionary methods, more distinctly. In fact historians of the Second American Revolution once emphasized its bloody constitutionalism—its forcible means—but primarily to disparage and delegitimize Reconstruction. Early twentieth-century books portrayed martial law, bayonet rule, and the tenuously legal machinations of a peculiarly constituted Congress. Since the civil rights movement, however, Third Republic scholars have turned away from force and methods and have mirrored the civil rights movement's grassroots activism and legal struggle back onto Reconstruction, defanging Reconstruction's revolutionary moment and perhaps even the entire notion of revolution, which now too often becomes simply a synonym for change. By distinguishing between the two periods of fundamental transformation, we might see the civil rights movement more clearly, as well.

In turn we may find new things to say about the United States, about its instability and vulnerability, about the limits of law in shaping the nation, and about the space for politics beyond the law. Abraham Lincoln called for such rethinking in his second annual message to Congress. "As our case is new, so we must think anew and act anew," Lincoln wrote in 1862. "We must disenthrall ourselves, and then we shall save our country."[6] Perhaps we, too, must disenthrall ourselves from the concepts and lingo that we have inherited, and perhaps we too may find this disenthralled vision of the United States—of a republic without guardrails—a means to preserve or even save the country. Shed of our fantasies that the Constitution or the Supreme Court will ride in to rescue us, perhaps we will learn from postbellum Republicans' constitutional boldness. Instead of explaining why the political situation is stacked against us, it is time to save ourselves by reimagining the U.S. republic, perhaps even by inventing a Fourth Republic and a Fourth Constitution. Or at least by re-examining the tools that 1860s-1890s Republicans used to try to save the country: the creation of new states, the transformation of Supreme Court membership, federal oversight of elections, forceful protection of voting rights, constitutional amendments. The disenchantment of Reconstruction lies in the recognition that no one is riding in to save us from the collapse of republican dreams and liberal rights. But in that realization we may also discover a new boldness, a new determination.

And that disenchantment with the U.S. story may also help us read the Second American Revolution back into its international revolutionary situation. The United States' restorationist counterrevolution was part of a reactionary wave that overthrew revolutionary hopes in the United States, Spain, Cuba, and Mexico. By looking outward to other intertwined nineteenth-century revolutions, we may disenthrall ourselves from the belief that the Civil War era tells us something particular about the United States and learn what it tells us about the period more broadly.

To these ends, it is worth asking whether the despair of the Second American Revolution is quite as exceptional—and therefore as American—as we think it is. The crises of the Civil War era should be read within the sequences of counterrevolution and despair that shaped Cuba, Spain, and Mexico. Just as the U.S. Civil War emerged from a swirl of transatlantic hopes, so, too, did it sink in a current of transatlantic sorrows, when midcentury dreams died and when previously bold and even revolutionary actors descended into gloom. In this way we might be able to assess which parts of that sorrow are particular to the U.S. Civil War, which parts belong to the broader revolutionary currents of the midcentury, and which parts to what historian Yuri Slezkine calls the "Great Disappointment" that follows the common, human realization that "Moses had died, the promised land had been reached, but there was no milk and honey. . . . The real day had come, but there was still death and mourning and crying and pain."[7]

The parallels are powerful and painful to contemplate. By 1876, the revolutions in the United States, Cuba, Mexico, and Spain all teetered. In the United States, disputed returns from four states prompted a grave constitutional crisis, and white Southern Democrats claimed control over the remaining ex-Confederate states and began to roll back the political gains of Reconstruction. Over the next years, congressional Democrats stripped away the military's power to intervene to protect civil and political rights. But these were not just U.S. sorrows. At almost exactly this moment, Mexican general Porfirio Díaz overthrew Juárez's successor, Sebastián Lerdo de Tejada, defeating government forces in November 1876 and claiming the presidency. In Cuba, the insurgents teetered on collapse, eventually acceding to Spanish power between 1878 and 1880. And in Spain, the republican dream died for a half century. For Pedro Santacilia and his fellow Cubans and Mexicans, the 1870s were both a political and a personal catastrophe. As Porfirio Díaz accumulated power, Santacilia was exiled for a brief time.[8] When reunited with his family, Santacilia abandoned politics, devoting his attention to poetry and constructing a new Mexican national literature.

Across the sea in Spain, Emilio Castelar drifted through his own disillusionment. After writing a long series of essays in the early 1870s for *Harper's*, he was dropped in December 1875 because, the editor wrote, U.S. readers had turned with the coming centennial to "domestic topics."[9] A careful observer of Latin America, Castelar wrote sensitively of the political upheavals of the rest of the century. At times, he could be an apologist for monarchical Spain, defining himself still as a republican but celebrating the incremental gains of democratic monarchism. At times, Castelar took solace in what he hoped was a progressive liberalization of society underneath the constitutional monarchy. Castelar wrote that he "withdrew into myself and resolved to restore all we had lost by that reaction. To do this, I realized that it was necessary to change our methods. During the revolution we had acquired a revolutionary temperament; it behooved us to throw off that temperament and to accommodate ourselves to a slower but surer method—that of evolution." He wrote that "a creative generation like ours must be an unhappy generation. Among the various forms of government that might be deduced from national sovereignty, we looked for anchors in our liberties, and lo! We could not find them. . . . Revolutions are like wars after all; and in wars we can forge heroic warriors, but we cannot educate good citizens endowed with that juridic conscience and that respect for law that the moderate and legal exercise of liberty demands."[10]

Perhaps these gloomy narratives may help us understand the despair inside the United States. Few of the characters mentioned in this book came to happy ends. Cora Montgomery and her expansionist dreams sank to the bottom of the sea. Martin Delany made brief alliances with White Supremacy Democrats and then turned to thoughts of exile, chairing the finance committee of a joint stock company for a ship to carry black South Carolinians to Liberia. Soon, he left the South altogether, not for Liberia but for Ohio, where he died. Henry McNeal Turner lost faith in the American experiment and urged his fellow African Americans to contemplate a future in Africa. Dan Sickles lived in squalor in New York City, pompously telling absurd stories of his time as "Yankee King of Spain" and allegedly stealing money from the Gettysburg memorial. Frederick Douglass and Ulysses S. Grant doubted democracy itself.

One of the costs of the closing of the Second American Revolution was the collapse of the dreams the revolutionary situation and the revolutionary wave had inspired of an alliance between the United States and Spanish-speaking republics. In the mid-nineteenth century, many U.S. Republicans hoped—naively but not foolishly—that the destinies of the United States, Cuba, Spain, and Mexico might converge. Undoubtedly this convergence was intended to benefit the United States, especially its merchants. And yet it would be too cynical to suggest that it was only cynicism. The midcentury United States birthed revolutionary impulses that might have created a Third American System of free-trading antislavery republics, an unequal but still mutually interlinked network that connected the United States, Cuba, Spain, Mexico, and others. Or, perhaps, that too was simply an unrealistic dream.

But the crushing of the Second American Revolution meant that the 1890s Cuban Revolution occurred in an entirely different revolutionary situation. Cubans in the 1890s launched a bold revolution to remake the country, a movement that generally expected no aid from the United States. Like José Martí, many Cubans had learned that the United States of the late century was no friend to republicanism or anticolonialism but was an imperial power of its own. After Cuban rebels defeated the Spanish forces, the United States intervened and overwhelmed the island, turning it into a quasi-colony. At first, Santacilia cheered even as it became clear that the United States would steer Cuba's future to its own imperialist ends. "Only one thing consoles me when I think on the possible abuse of the Yankees; I prefer *todo, todo, todo* to the government of Spain and to the dominion of the Spanish."[11] But by

1910, a decade after the achievement of his life's goal of Cuban independence, Santacilia wrote that he was so "disenchanted" that he no longer worried over politics at all.[12] So, too, when Mexican revolutionaries launched their own movement in the 1910s, the United States would be the opponent, not even a putative ally. The Third American System that developed in the early twentieth century was largely a unipolar, oppositional system, one often dominated by the United States.

Perhaps it is even more depressing to see United States despair in context than to see it alone. If the disappointment is the nation's, then it is somehow specific, perhaps even salvageable. But what if it is the world's story? Perhaps American exceptionalism, even at its most critical, endured because it carried within itself a seed of hope, a notion that if only the United States had overcome its racism or its middle-class aspirations or its narrow attachment to prosperity, things might have been better. Perhaps international history, by reminding us that things are rough all over, by pointing toward a tragic view of human history, steals some of our anger and some of our hope. It is not hard, for people who take history seriously, to come to doubt hope. And yet, it may also be true that lasting hope, the kind that can endure the crushing disappointment and years in the wilderness that greet most efforts to improve the human condition, can only be forged in the face of hopelessness.[13]

In a discussion with Irving Howe, the scholar Gershom Scholem described what he called "plastic hours." "There are in history what you could call 'plastic hours,'" he told Howe. "Namely, crucial moments when it is possible to act. If you move then, something happens." Scholem raised these moments to contrast them to the stubbornly disappointing times in which they now lived.[14]

A history of change must reckon with those plastic moments like the Second American Revolution, of course, but also, more troublingly, with their opposite, what we might call stubborn hours, the times when the times are not a-changing. Such moments can drag us toward the abyss of despair, an awareness of the disappointment not only in one's life but in life, not only in one's moment in history but in history, not only in the times but in time itself. Of course, it is difficult to judge stubborn hours when we live among them. Just as people often mistake the plasticity of moments and act futilely, so, too, do they overrate the stubborn hours and acquiesce when they shouldn't. But a sense of history, and of how to act within it, and even more of how to sustain action in the face of history, depends, I suspect, on a sincere reckoning with those stubborn hours, with that sense that the world may not be turned, or at least not for the better, no matter how hard we strive. Without that sense, we risk fostering a naive optimism that cannot survive contact with reality.

The particular despair the characters in this book faced may be one we are well primed to contemplate now and one that may even be useful to us. Like them, we are well situated to understand that liberal republics do not float down on clouds from heaven but are products of human creation and therefore liable to die at human hands, perhaps even our own. And rights can turn quickly into mere parchment barriers no matter how venerable the parchment. Knowing this is true, from History, does not solve our problems but helps us see them more clearly. How exactly should republics defend themselves from existential threats? How might we navigate Castelar's dilemma that a republic without force was a farce but a republic with only force was a tyranny? How should we respond to Juárez's judgment that perhaps only dictatorship saved the republic? How should we guard against and also make use of revolutionary situations? The United States still has not addressed the basic role of brute force in shaping its own republic, with a new constitution made through martial law, and we therefore have failed to take seriously some of the basic dilemmas of American life or of life inside a democracy.

Many of us have quoted an epigraph from William Butler Yeats, published as World War I approached: "In dreams begin responsibility." Twenty years later, in the heart of the Great Depression, the great writer Delmore Schwartz slightly broadened the phrase in titling his classic short story "In Dreams Begin Responsibilities." Perhaps now, in our own crises, we might ponder reordering those lovely words. If—as some read it—the phrase suggests the duties that should, and that must, weigh on dreamers, perhaps we might consider the converse. For all their limitations, the revolutionaries who shaped the midcentury possessed the courage and clarity to contemplate the idea that in responsibilities begin dreams.[15]

NOTES

ABBREVIATIONS

AHN   Archivo Histórico Nacional, Madrid
ANC   Archivo Nacional de la República de Cuba, Havana
BNA   British National Archives, London
BNC   Biblioteca Nacional de Cuba José Martí, Havana
BNE   Biblioteca Nacional de España, Madrid
NA   National Archives, College Park, Maryland
NYHS   New-York Historical Society, New York
NYPL   New York Public Library, New York
SRE   Archivo Histórico Genaro Estrada de la Secretaría
       de Relaciones Exteriores, Mexico City

INTRODUCTION

1. David Armitage and Gaines M. Foster analyzed the various names for the conflict and the emergence of the "Civil War" as the dominant sobriquet in the early
twentieth century. Although only some of Foster's queries included "Revolution,"
the naming appears in his appendix with varying levels of support. Word searches
for "Revolution" in congressional debates and newspapers inevitably run into the
challenge of distinguishing between references to the (first) American Revolution
and the use of the word to refer to what we now call the Civil War. My argument is
not that "Revolution" was more common than "Rebellion" or "Civil War" but that
it is more analytically useful today. Foster, "What's Not in a Name"; Armitage, *Civil
Wars*, 161–95.

2. "The Inauguration and the Inaugural of President Grant—the New Epoch,"
New York Herald, March 4, 1869.

3. Ibid.

4. In fact, the *Herald* had long been more antimonarchical than antislavery. Its
(temporary) embrace of the antislavery internal revolution served its larger goal of
republican (and U.S.) expansion.

5. Based on Abraham Lincoln's restorative rhetoric, James M. McPherson called
Lincoln a "conservative revolutionary" who "wanted to conserve the Union as the
revolutionary heritage of the founding fathers." This is accurate as a portrayal of
the language, though not, as I suggest later, of the actions, and is hard to square
with McPherson's comparisons of the U.S. Civil War with the French Revolution.
McPherson's later description of Lincoln as a "pragmatic revolutionary" is more
convincing. McPherson, *Abraham Lincoln and the Second American Revolution*, 41.

6. Thomas, *Civic Myths.*

7. Halstead, *War Claims of the South,* 36.

8. On the displacement of violence in U.S. history, see, e.g., Kelman, *Misplaced Massacre*; Blackhawk, *Violence over the Land*; Emberton, *Beyond Redemption*; Williams, *They Left Great Marks*; Williams, "The Wounds that Cried Out"; Feimster, "'What If I Am a Woman'"; and Hahn, *Nation under Our Feet.*

A general amnesia about the foundational role of violence in U.S. political history has fed into and in turn been heightened by the myths of the civil rights movement that make nonviolent political change not only theoretically possible in the proper context but universally possible, even inevitable. This may not describe the 1960s, and of course it may tell us even less about the methods for transformative social change today. See, e.g., Cobb, *This Nonviolent Stuff'll Get You Killed*, and Tyson, *Radio Free Dixie.*

9. Slezkine, *House of Government*, 121–22.

10. For decades sociologists of revolution focused on great revolutions in ways that divided historical epochs. While recognizing the different uses of the word "revolution" in early modern and classical periods, many historical comparative sociologists diagnosed a small number of moments when great powers experienced cataclysmic popular uprisings that seemed to introduce new ideological and state-building frameworks to the world. "First wave" revolutionary theorists—drawing from Atlantic historian Crane Brinton, among others—assessed great revolutions in naturalistic terms, studying their common causes and progressions. A "second wave" of modernization theorists—including Samuel Huntington and Talcott Parsons—emphasized the impact of mass material discontent in undermining existing institutions. After Barrington Moore and Charles Tilly critiqued modernization theorists for failing to acknowledge the range of revolutionary causes, a "third wave" emerged in the wake of Theda Skocpol's social structure theory about state collapse. In the process "revolution" became what one critical scholar called "an almost metaphysical category, an invented social concept that bore little resemblance to actual experience" that "stemmed from a romanticism that equated revolutions with heroic fights to the finish. . . . This disguised a much more complex relationship between revolutions and violence." Lawson, "Negotiated Revolutions," 475–76. See also Crane, *Anatomy of Revolution*; Malia, *History's Locomotives*; Walzer, *Revolution of the Saints*; Arendt, *On Revolution*; Eisenstadt, *Great Revolutions*; Skocpol, *States and Social Revolutions*; Moore, *Social Origins of Dictatorship and Democracy*; Hobsbawm, *Age of Revolution*; Hobsbawm, *Age of Capital*; Hobsbawm, *Age of Empire*; McAdam, Tarrow, and Tilly, *Dynamics of Contention*; Foran, *Taking Power*, 7–15; Goldstone, "Rethinking Revolutions," 18–21.

11. Goldstone, "Toward a Fourth Generation of Revolutionary Theory"; Goldstone, *Revolution and Rebellion in the Early Modern World*; Kurzman, *Unthinkable Revolution in Iran*; Kurzman, "Can Understanding Undermine Explanation?"; Goodwin, "Why We Were Surprised (Again) by the Arab Spring."

12. This is not unlike the process by which the Glorious Revolution was drained of both its drama and its revolutionary nature by later British scholars seeking to domesticate their country's uproarious past. See esp. Pincus, *1688.* In a different

way, David Blackbourn and Geoff Eley argued that the failure to understand what Blackbourn called Germany's "silent bourgeois revolution" had, in Eley's words, "structured our general understanding of the German past. It affects both the questions we ask and where we look for the answers." Blackbourn and Eley, *Peculiarities of German History*, 51, 176.

Although the distinctions between the historical treatment of the U.S. Civil War era and the Haitian Revolution are so profound as to discourage any facile analogizing, historians of the United States could nevertheless benefit from contemplating Michel-Rolph Trouillot's words about "formulas of erasure" that "empty a number of singular events of their revolutionary content so that the entire string of facts, gnawed from all sides, becomes trivialized" in what he termed "formulas of banalization." Trouillot, *Silencing the Past*, 69.

13. On revolutionary waves, see Katz, *Revolutions and Revolutionary Waves*; Sohrabi, "Historicizing Revolutions"; Sohrabi, "Global Waves, Local Actors"; Patel and Bunce, "Turning Points"; Hale, "Regime Change Cascades"; Weyland, "Diffusion of Revolution"; and Beissinger, "Structure and Example in Modular Political Phenomena." For a critique of wave theory, see Way, "Real Causes of the Color Revolutions."

Among historians, Jeremy Adelman most thoroughly captured this sense of revolutions that "transpired when international pressures of competing sovereignties broke down state systems; it is not so easy to find a sharp boundary between internal and external dynamics of large-scale social change—in large measure because instability, not immutability was central to sovereignty." Adelman, *Sovereignty and Revolution in the Iberian Atlantic*, 5. In *The French Revolution in Global Perspective*, Suzanne Desan, Lynn Hunt, and William Max Nelson described the interdependence of international and domestic politics and asked how the world made the French Revolution, not just how the French Revolution made the world. Parker, *Revolutions and History*, 2–4; Armstrong, *Revolution and World Order*, 3; Walt, *Revolution and War*; Kimmel, *Revolution*, 220; Paquette, *Imperial Portugal in the Age of Atlantic Revolutions*; Desan, Hunt, and Nelson, *French Revolution in Global Perspective*, 1–4.

14. Ada Ferrer wrote, "Americanist historians [have] generally neglected the complex history of insurgency and counterinsurgency that unfolded in the three decades preceding the United States' declaration of war on Spain. As a result, they have overlooked the extent to which conditions in Cuba—and the internal story of the revolution itself—shaped the possibilities for U.S. intervention." Ferrer, *Insurgent Cuba*, 5.

15. Bender, *Nation among Nations*; Tyrrell, *Transnational Nation*; Pérez, "We Are the World," 558–66; Hahn, *Nation without Borders*.

16. Rugemer, *Problem of Emancipation*; McDaniel, *Problem of Democracy in the Age of Slavery*; Blackett, *Divided Hearts*; Blackett, *Building an Antislavery Wall*; Dal Lago, *American Slavery, Atlantic Slavery, and Beyond*; Schoen, *Fragile Fabric of Union*; Horne, *Race to Revolution*; Clavin, *Toussaint Louverture and the American Civil War*; Field, "'No Such Thing as Stand Still'"; Kenny, *Contentious Liberties*; Roberts, "Chickasaw Freedpeople at the Crossroads of Reconstruction"; Rothera,

"Civil Wars and Reconstruction in America." Classic works on the global history of abolition include Davis, *Problem of Slavery in the Age of Revolution*; Davis, *Inhuman Bondage*; Davis, *Problem of Slavery in the Age of Emancipation*; Drescher, *Abolition*; and Blackburn, *American Crucible*.

17. Langley, *Struggle for the American Mediterranean*; May, *Manifest Destiny's Underworld*; May, *Slavery, Race, and Conquest in the Tropics*; Opatrný, *U.S. Expansionism and Cuban Annexationism*; Guterl, *American Mediterranean*; Baptist, *Half Has Never Been Told*; Johnson, *River of Dark Dreams*; Karp, *This Vast Southern Empire*; Diaz, "To Conquer the Coast"; Lightfoot, "Manifesting Destiny on Cuban Shores." A classic work on U.S. diplomacy in this period is Jones, *Blue and Gray Diplomacy*. New work on diplomatic history includes Schoen, "Civil War and Europe," and Eichhorn, "North-Atlantic Trade in the Mid-Nineteenth Century."

18. Doyle, *Cause of All Nations*. For a rich telling of cross-national interactions, see the essays in Doyle, *American Civil Wars*, esp. Schmidt-Nowara, "From Aggression to Crisis"; Eller, "Dominican Civil War, Slavery, and Spanish Annexation"; Sabato, "Arms and Republican Politics in Spanish America"; Childs, "Cuba, the Atlantic Crisis of the 1860s, and the Road to Abolition"; and Marquese, "Civil War in the United States and the Crisis of Slavery in Brazil."

19. Eller, *We Dream Together*; Schmidt-Nowara, *Slavery, Freedom, and Abolition*; Schmidt-Nowara, *Empire and Antislavery*; Fradera, *Colonias para después de un Imperio*; Lazo, *Writing to Cuba*; Naranjo, *Nación soñado*; González-Ripoll et al., *Rumor de Haití en Cuba*; Ferrer, *Freedom's Mirror*; Ferrer, *Insurgent Cuba*; Scott and Hébrard, *Freedom Papers*; Scott, *Degrees of Freedom*; Schneider, *Occupation of Havana*; Pérez, *Cuba*; Tomich and Zeuske, "Second Slavery"; Tomich, *New Frontiers of Slavery*; González-Ripoll and García, *Caribe en el period independiente*; de la Guardia and Pan-Montojo, "Reflexiones sobre una historia transnacional"; González, *Cuestión de honor*; Sánchez, "Quitter la Très Fidele."

20. See esp. Pani, *Series de admirables acontecimientos*, and Pani, *Segundo Imperio*.

21. Ackerman differs from my analysis in emphasizing the popular, rather than military, roots of this constitutional revolution. See esp. the essays in "Symposium: Moments of Change: Transformation in American Constitutionalism," a response to Ackerman, *We the People*.

22. More recently Andrew Zimmerman challenged the liberal nationalist republican framework in Zimmerman, "From the Second American Revolution to the First International and Back Again"; Zimmerman, *Civil War in the United States*; and Zimmerman, "From the Rhine to the Mississippi." Beard and Beard, *Rise of American Civilization*, 2:52–53; Moore, *Social Origins of Dictatorship and Democracy*, 111–15; Foner, *Reconstruction*; Hahn, *Nation under our Feet*; Bender, *Nation among Nations*, 116–80; Doyle, *Cause of All Nations*; Parrish, *Civil War*; McPherson, *Abraham Lincoln and the Second American Revolution*, 3–42; Fleche, *Revolution of 1861*; Blight, *Frederick Douglass' Civil War*; Levine, "Second American Revolution"; Levine, *Fall of the House of Dixie*; Gannon, "Civil War as a Settler-Colonial Revolution"; Downs, "Why the Second American Revolution Deserves as Much Attention as the First"; Guelzo, "History of Reconstruction's Third Phase"; Guelzo, *Reconstruction*.

Guelzo's argument seems to represent a development from his prior claim in the *Encyclopedia of Political Revolutions* that the Civil War was "only superficially revolutionary in nature." Guelzo, "United States Civil War." This shift likely reflects the increasing salience of both revolution and of Reconstruction in U.S. history.

The Beards' arguments about an economic revolution tied to the Civil War produced an impressive literature on the war's economic impact, one well summarized by Ransom, "Fact and Counterfact"; Ransom, "Economics of Civil War"; and Ransom and Sutch, "Conflicting Visions." Although these economic arguments remain important, my argument centers on the forcible remaking of the political order, not the question of whether revolutionary economic changes were the cause or consequence of the Civil War.

23. This is especially puzzling since in many respects the North American revolutionary wave had much broader and more long-lasting effects on world history than the 1848 revolutions that Eric Hobsbawm called the end of "political revolution." World historians of the nineteenth-century struggle to place even the U.S. Civil War within the global story. Where the Civil War appears, it is generally a generic example of the nineteenth-century crisis of sovereignty—as nations faced expansive claims to regulate their peripheries even as their populaces were well armed to resist them—or as a late-arriving end of slavery. Jürgen Osterhammel diagnoses "upheavals of revolutionary dimension" in the postwar United States but has virtually nothing to say about midcentury Mexico, Cuba, or Spain; instead, he toys with and then discards the idea of a "revolutionary cluster" connecting 1848 in Europe, the Taiping Rebellion in China, the 1857 Sepoy Mutiny, and the U.S. Civil War. There remains a tendency to treat U.S. and, particularly, Cuban abolitions as completions of an already established process, just as there is a tendency to treat liberal republican forms as reproductions of existing structures. Maier, *Leviathan 2.0*, 67–68, 160–61; Osterhammel, *Transformation of the World*, 514–15; Bayly, *Birth of the Modern World*, 161–65; Hobsbawm, *Age of Capital*, 2, 10; Hawgood, "Liberalism and Constitutional Development," 211; Dal Lago, *Age of Lincoln and Cavour*; Dal Lago, *William Lloyd Garrison and Giuseppe Mazzini*; Dal Lago, "Lincoln, Cavour, and National Unification."

24. McPherson's well-developed notion of a Second American Revolution found less support than his other influential ideas in part because ambiguity in the social science study of revolution left him with a vague "common-sense working definition of revolution" as "the overthrow of the existing social and political order by internal violence," and the Reconstruction scholarship underplayed the military's intervention in political life. McPherson, *Abraham Lincoln and the Second American Revolution*, 15–16.

25. Eliot, *Four Quartets*, 46–47.

CHAPTER ONE

1. Cong. Globe, 41st Cong., 2nd Sess. 658–59 (1869).

2. Cong. Globe, 40th Cong., 1st Sess. 519–22 (1867).

3. Ibid., 22–23.

4. "Letters from New York," *Liberator*, December 8, 1865.

5. John Sherman to William T. Sherman, May 7, 1863, and William T. Sherman to John Sherman, February 28, 1866, *Sherman Letters*, 203, 265.

6. Quoted in Nicoletti, *Secession on Trial*, 2.

7. McPherson, *Abraham Lincoln and the Second American Revolution*, 4-7.

8. The desire to turn away from Republicans' actions and words is powerful. Although probably never a majority, many more Republicans spoke openly of revolution than most histories suggest. It is striking that Michael Les Benedict, perhaps the greatest constitutional historian of the era, bypasses these easily available quotations to declare, "Never did [Republicans] admit that their actions made the ratification of the Civil War amendments 'unconventional.'. . . Never did they concede that they were revolutionizing the federal system." Benedict, "Constitutional History and Constitutional Theory," 2030.

9. The Second Founding phrase gained some public prominence in the anniversaries of the Civil War and Reconstruction and was used by both the U.S. Senate and President Barack Obama. On second foundings, see Quigley, *Second Founding*; Holland, *Body Politic*, 94,103; Rosen and Donnelly, "America's Unfinished Second Founding"; S. Res. 198, June 10, 2015; and "Presidential Proclamations— Establishment of the Reconstruction Era National Monument." Eric Foner's *The Second Founding* appeared too late to be incorporated into this book, but I have been influenced by his public talks and private discussions.

10. Here I follow Lawson, "Negotiated Revolutions," quotation at 479; Goldstone, "Analyzing Revolutions and Rebellions," 178-80; Tilly, *European Revolutions*, 9-14; Droz-Vincent, "Military amidst Uprisings and Transitions in the Arab World"; and Trimberger, *Revolution from Above*.

11. On tragic views of history, see Blight, *American Oracle*, 22-24. Tragedy may be redemptive in certain cases, perhaps in the Civil War, but I emphasize here Blight's invocation of a tragic view that does not seek redemption for suffering or transcendence of oppression. On redemption, see Emberton, *Beyond Redemption*.

12. Although historiographical debate about the Civil War's impact has assumed many shapes over the decades, currently the most vigorous engagement is between those scholars who find its radicalism in its antislavery origins, particularly James Oakes, and those who find its conservatism in its enduring Unionist, preservationist origins, particularly Gary Gallagher, Daniel Crofts, Mark Summers, Adam I. P. Smith, and Caroline Janney. Oakes, *Freedom National*; Oakes, *Scorpion's Sting*; Gallagher, *Union War*; Crofts, *Lincoln and the Politics of Slavery*; Summers, *Ordeal of the Reunion*; Smith, *Stormy Present*; Janney, *Remembering the Civil War*.

13. Scholars wrestled increasingly with this after 1989, as revolutions in the former Soviet Bloc and then the Arab Spring led social scientists to displace revolutionary origins for the idea of revolutionary situations. McAdam, Tarrow, and Tilly, *Dynamics of Contention*; Foran, *Taking Power*, 7-15.

14. Plummer, *Haiti and the United States*; Horne, *Confronting Black Jacobins*; Hunt, *Haiti's Influence on Antebellum America*; Clavin, *Toussaint Louverture and the American Civil War*; Gaffield, *Haitian Connections in the Atlantic World*.

15. Gemme, *Domesticating Foreign Struggles*; Roberts, *Distant Revolutions*.

16. Bassler, *Collected Works*, 3:29.

17. Davis and Wilson, *Lincoln-Douglas Debates*, 14.

18. "The New Era of the Anti-Slavery Agitation," *New York Herald*, November 25, 1859, 4.

19. *Official Proceedings of the Democratic National Convention, Held in 1860*, 57–58.

20. "The Second American Revolution," *New York Herald*, October 18, 1860, 2.

21. Antislavery constitutionalism included several strands. Some embraced a radical constitutionalism that saw the Constitution as a purely antislavery document not in need of amendment; others, especially William Lloyd Garrison, as a proslavery document in need of replacement; and Free-Soilers like Salmon P. Chase saw its denial of federal support for property in man as an opening for antislavery where states did not rule. This Republican vision of the Constitution has been well described by Fehrenbacher, *Slaveholding Republic*; Wiecek, *Sources of Anti-Slavery Constitutionalism*; Vorenberg, *Final Freedom*; and Oakes, *Freedom National*. Sean Wilentz extended this argument to claim that the Constitution was genuinely antislavery, not simply that Republicans argued for this interpretation, in *No Property in Man*. Wilentz provided excellent historical background for the Republicans' retrospective view but did not address other solutions to the mystery he posed of how a proslavery Constitution might have produced antislavery constitutional politics. In the process he underestimated the intelligence and creativity of 1850s Republicans and refused to consider the notion that the 1865 amendments overthrew, rather than fulfilled, the Constitution. For the view of the Constitution as a proslavery document, see Waldstreicher, *Slavery's Constitution*, and Finkelman, *Slavery and the Founders*.

22. Brooks, *Liberty Power*.

23. Bassler, *Collected Works*, 4:27.

24. "Territorial Slave Code," *National Era*, February 9, 1860.

25. "Princeton Centennial Celebration," *Liberator*, July 6, 1860.

26. "Free Speech Outraged," *Douglass' Monthly*, January 1861.

27. "Declaration of the Immediate Causes."

28. Quoted in Slotkin, *Long Road to Antietam*, 64.

29. "Declaration of the Causes which Impel."

30. Wakelyn, *Southern Pamphlets on Secession*, 337.

31. "Jefferson Davis' First Inaugural Address."

32. Stephens, "Corner Stone Speech."

33. Bassler, *Collected Works*, 4:265–71.

34. Ibid., 4:434, 441.

35. Because neo-Confederates invoke the alleged right to secession to turn attention away from slavery, historians have been tempted to overstate the argument for the unconstitutionality of secession. But constitutional histories have noted the complex debate over secession and a compact theory of government. See esp. Nicoletti, *Secession on Trial*, 318, 326, and White, "Recovering the Legal History of the Confederacy."

36. "Kentucky," *Observer* (Fayetteville, N.C.), March 7, 1861.

37. Bancroft, *Speeches, Correspondence and Political Papers*, 1:227–29.

38. Bassler, *Collected Works*, 1:438–39.

39. "John Stuart Mill on the Contest in America," *National Anti-Slavery Standard*, March 1, 1862.

40. Taylor, *Destruction and Reconstruction*, 233–34.

41. Basler, *Collected Works*, 7:281–82.

42. Lydia Maria Child to George W. Julian, April 8, 1865, container 5, Joshua R. Giddings and George W. Julian Papers, LoC.

43. McPherson, *Battle Cry of Freedom*, 73–76.

44. Hamilton grouped habeas corpus with the Constitution's bar to ex post facto laws as singularly important protections. Hamilton, "Federalist No. 84."

45. *Ex parte Merryman*.

46. McPherson, *Battle Cry of Freedom*, 289.

47. Steiner, *Life of Reverdy Johnson*, 107.

48. Volck, "Knight of the Rueful Countenance."

49. Greeley, *American Conflict*, 500.

50. Basler, *Collected Works*, 6:261–69.

51. States of exception and emergency have emerged again as fields of study in relation to the U.S. government's response to the 9/11 attacks. For theorist Carl Schmitt, states of exception were restorative moments that forestalled revolution. I argue that the Civil War and Reconstruction created a state of exception in order to embed a permanent, if demarcated, revolution before returning to normal legal time. On states of exception, see Witt, *Lincoln's Code*; Dudziak, *War Time*; Schmitt, *Political Theology*; and Agamben, *State of Exception*.

52. See the somewhat different estimates of Neely, *Fate of Liberty*, 168; Hart, "Military Commissions and the Lieber Code," 4; and Witt, *Lincoln's Code*, 267–68.

53. Lincoln was careful not to misuse these powers. Early twentieth-century historian James G. Randall argued that Lincoln's "humane sympathy, his humor, his lawyerlike caution, his common sense, his fairness toward opponents, his dislike of arbitrary rule . . . operated to modify and soften the acts of overzealous subordinates and to lessen the effects of harsh measures upon individuals." A leading political theorist likewise used Lincoln as an example of "constitutional dictatorship" in order to capture both the wartime expansion of presidential authority and its temporary status that distinguished it from unconstitutional dictatorship. Lincoln's reliance on martial law was, indeed, a "'perfect platform for a military despotism,' but more than a platform it never became." Randall, *Constitutional Problems under Lincoln*, 513–20; Rossiter, *Constitutional Dictatorship*, 223–24, 236.

54. Amy Murrell Taylor argues for the presence of women and children during this first flight in Taylor, *Embattled Freedom*, 3–4, 251; "General Orders No. 100: The Lieber Code"; Witt, *Lincoln's Code*; Oakes, *Freedom National*.

55. Cong. Globe, 38th Cong., 1st Sess. 2987–88 (1864).

56. Consider Richard Slotkin's admonition that "we cannot appreciate the character and significance of the strategic decisions taken by Lincoln and Davis unless we understand that they were not acting as the heads of stable national governments, defending well-established constitutional systems, but as leaders of embattled political movements whose regimes were vulnerable to the play of uncontrollable social and political forces." Slotkin, *Long Road to Antietam*, xvi.

57. Quoted in "Abolition of Slavery in the District of Columbia," *New York Times*, May 22, 1862.

58. Nevins, *War for the Union*; Slotkin, *Long Road to Antietam*; Blackburn, *Unfinished Revolution*.

59. Zimmerman, "From the Second American Revolution to the First International and Back Again."

60. Basler, *Collected Works*, 7:281–82.

61. Cassius W. Clay to Anson Burlingame, November 23, 1863, box 2, Burlingame Papers, LoC. Many thanks to Aaron Sheehan-Dean for sharing this document.

62. Randall, *Constitutional Problems under Lincoln*, 383–84.

63. McPherson, *Political History of the United States of America*, 231.

64. Oakes, *Freedom National*, 393–429.

65. Ibid., 293–300; Cong. Globe, 37th Cong., 2nd Sess. 3316–19 (1862).

66. Lincoln himself did not press for the new western states before the presidential election, and Republicans' electoral college majority made the votes of Nevada, West Virginia, and Kansas (added in 1861) not crucial. Cong. Globe, 39th Cong., 1st Sess. 2372–73 (1866); Pomeroy, "Lincoln, the Thirteenth Amendment, and the Admission of Nevada," 113–20.

67. Cong. Globe, 38th Cong., 1st Sess. 2987–88 (1864).

68. Ibid., 2992; Oakes, *Freedom National*, 430–88; Vorenberg, *Final Freedom*.

69. Cong. Globe, 38th Cong., 1st Sess. 1367 (1864).

70. Ibid., 2989.

71. "The News," *Chicago Tribune*, February 3, 1865, 1.

72. *Army and Navy Journal*, April 29, 1865, 568.

73. Cong. Globe, 38th Cong., 1st Sess. 1490 (1864).

74. Cong. Globe, 38th Cong., 2nd Sess., app. 54–55 (1865).

75. Ibid., 527–31.

76. Grant, *Personal Memoirs*, 2:483–85; Porter, *Campaigning with Grant*, 463–64; Simpson, *Let Us Have Peace*, 82.

77. *War of the Rebellion*, ser. 1, vol. 47, part 3, 335–36, 410–11.

78. "Hereditary Patriotism," *New York Times*, June 25, 1865.

79. *War of the Rebellion*, ser. 1, vol. 47, part 3, 538.

80. Although Johnson's opposition to black civil rights can prompt cynicism about his 1865 determination to end slavery, Johnson in 1864 had said, "now is the time to secure these fundamental principles, while the land is rent with anarchy and upheaves with the throes of a mighty revolution." McPherson, *Handbook of Politics for 1868*, 46; Harris, *Presidential Reconstruction in Mississippi*, 52–54; Bergeron, *Papers of Andrew Johnson*, 9:325, 329.

81. Quoted in *Columbia (S.C.) Daily Phoenix*, December 14, 1865, 1.

82. Thomas, *Constitution of the United States of America*. S. Doc. 112-9, 112th Cong., 2nd Sess., 30; Vorenberg, *Final Freedom*; Kyvig, *Explicit and Authentic Acts*, 164–65.

83. Quoted in Litwack, *Been in the Storm so Long*, 389.

84. "Letters from New York," *The Liberator*, December 8, 1865.

85. Cong. Globe, 39th Cong., 1st Sess. 3–4 (1865).

86. Welles, *Diary of Gideon Welles*, 2:387, 412.

87. Wilson, "Reconstruction of the Southern States."

88. Basler, *Collected Works*, 4:434; *Report of the Joint Committee on Reconstruction*, xi; Belz, *Reconstructing the Union*.

89. Bruce Ackerman wrote that "so long as the Convention/Congress continued to exclude the Southern states, nothing the Republicans might say would fool anybody into thinking their 'Congress' was a perfectly legal assembly. Of course, like all revolutionaries, the Republicans thought that their break with the constitutional system was entirely legitimate." Ackerman, "Revolution on a Human Scale," 2307. McPherson, *Political History of the United States of America during the Period of Reconstruction*, 369.

90. Cong. Globe, 39th Cong., 1st Sess. 585–86 (1866).

91. Ibid., 1151–53.

92. Michael Vorenberg for this reason calls the Civil Rights Act the "most revolutionary" Reconstruction statute. Vorenberg, "1866 Civil Rights Act," 68.

93. Cong. Globe, 39th Cong. 1st Sess. 1829 (1866).

94. Ibid., 570.

95. Ibid., 2459–60.

96. Ibid., 1829.

97. *Journal of the Senate of the United States of America*, June 22, 1866, 563. Congress, however, had established the two-thirds of the quorum standard in passing the Twelfth Amendment in 1803. Kyvig, *Explicit and Authentic Acts*, 170.

98. Niven, *Chase Papers*, 5:89.

99. *Army and Navy Journal*, March 10, 1866, 460.

100. Cong. Globe, 39th Cong., 1st Sess. 4304–5 (1866).

101. Niven, *Chase Papers*, 5:142–43; Bergeron, *Papers of Andrew Johnson*, 11:xii–xiii, 448–49, 611; Brock, *American Crisis*, 183.

102. McPherson, *Handbook of Politics for 1868*, 118–19.

103. Blair, *With Malice toward Some*, 160–233.

104. William P. Fessenden to James S. Pike, April 6, 1866, James Shepherd Pike Papers, LoC.

105. Simon, *Papers of Ulysses S. Grant*, 16:330–31.

106. Thomas F. Bayard to My Dear Father, December 2, 4, 1866, container 11, Thomas F. Bayard Papers, LoC.

107. Cong. Globe, 39th Cong., 2nd Sess. 168 (1866).

108. "Veto Message on Admitting Nebraska."

109. Cong. Globe, 39th Cong., 2nd Sess. 1440–41 (1867).

110. Fessenden, Sherman, and other moderates' frequent backing of Reconstruction measures convinced Benedict that the measures themselves were moderate, but Ackerman rightly responded that the fact that "such an achievement was the work of 'moderates' only emphasizes how revolutionary that would have appeared ten years earlier." Ackerman, "Revolution on a Human Scale," 2305.

111. *Army and Navy Journal*, June 22, 1867, 700.

112. Cong. Globe, 39th Cong., 2nd Sess. 1972–76 (1867).

113. Ibid., 509; 40th Cong., 1st Sess. 519–22, 546, app. 1–3 (1867).

114. Cong. Globe, 39th Cong., 2nd Sess. 1729–33 (1867).

115. Welles, *Diary*, 2:18.

116. McPherson, *Political History of the United States of America during the Period of Reconstruction*, 142.

117. Bergeron, *Papers of Andrew Johnson*, 13:269–71.

118. Cong. Globe, 39th Cong., 2nd Sess. 250–53 (1867).

119. Ibid., 1290–92.

120. Cong. Globe, 40th Cong., 1st Sess. 22–23 (1867).

121. Hamilton, *Correspondence of Jonathan Worth*, 2:1050–51, 1106, 1192.

122. Hamilton, *Reconstruction in North Carolina*, 291.

123. Quoted in Nicoletti, *Secession on Trial*, 98.

124. Simon, *Papers of Ulysses S. Grant*, 17:294–300.

125. Hogue, *Uncivil War*, 56–59; Simpson, *But There Was No Peace*, 181.

126. Bergeron, *Papers of Andrew Johnson*, 12:297–98.

127. Cong. Globe, 39th Cong., 2nd Sess. 501–2 (1867); Friedman, "History of the Countermajoritarian Difficulty, Part II," 2; Ackerman, *We the People: Transformations*, 196.

128. Huebner, *Liberty and Union*, 227–28.

129. *Nation*, January 17, 1867, 50, quoted in Friedman, "History of the Countermajoritarian Difficulty, Part II," 25. On cultural responses to *Milligan*, see Thomas, *Civic Myths*, 102–23.

130. Cong. Globe, 40th Cong., 2nd Sess. 2119–22 (1868); Bergeron, *Papers of Andrew Johnson*, 13:471–72; Hyman, *More Perfect Union*, 503–5.

131. Cong. Globe, 40th Cong., 2nd Sess. 2170 (1868).

132. "Veto Message on Legislation Amending the Judiciary."

133. Benedict, *Trial*, 102–3.

134. Cong. Globe, 40th Cong., 2nd Sess. 2396 (1868).

135. Because Kansas was seated during the secession winter, I do not count it among the states created by the fractional Congress.

136. Cong. Globe, 41st Cong., 2nd Sess. 2810 (1870); Kyvig, *Explicit and Authentic Acts*, 172–76.

137. Fletcher, *Our Secret Constitution*, 2, 10.

138. Epps, *Democracy Reborn*, 262; Bond, "Original Understanding of the Fourteenth Amendment"; Aynes, "Unintended Consequences of the Fourteenth Amendment."

Historians and constitutional theorists have argued for decades about change and continuity across the Civil War era, with much of the discussion turning on the radical or moderate nature of the Thirteenth, Fourteenth, and Fifteenth Amendments. Harold Hyman emphasized constitutional adequacy to meet the Civil War's challenges and Republican desires to sustain the nation's constitutional forms, ideas expanded by Michael Les Benedict, William Nelson, and others. Phillip S. Paludan used this constitutional continuity to explain Reconstruction's disappointing outcome. Earl Maltz and Herman Belz emphasized continuity to an even greater extent. Scholars arguing for bolder constitutional discontinuity include Robert Kaczorowski and Eric Foner. Recent work by Michael Vorenberg argued for a nuanced approach. To Vorenberg the Thirteenth Amendment "represented a turn against the nation's fathers" but "was no act of patricide. By altering the Constitution without eviscerating it, Americans could remain firm in the belief that they were building on the founders' structure rather than tearing it down." Of course, one may kill one's fathers without announcing it or even intending to, nor do actors' beliefs (or self-delusions) resolve questions of interpretation. Vorenberg, *Final Freedom*, 6; Hyman, *More Perfect Union*; Benedict, *Preserving the Constitution*; Nelson, *Fourteenth Amendment*; Paludin, *Covenant with Death*; Maltz, *Civil Rights, the Constitution, and Congress*; Maltz, "Reconstruction without Revolution"; Belz, *Reconstructing the Union*; Kaczorowski, "'To Begin the Nation Anew'"; Kaczorowski, "Revolutionary Constitutionalism in the Era of the Civil War and Reconstruction"; Foner, *Reconstruction*.

Constitutional theorist Bruce Ackerman placed discussions of a second constitution within different contexts by portraying U.S. constitutionalism as inherently subject to higher lawmaking. Ackerman, *We the People: Transformations*, 99–252. For responses to Ackerman, see "Symposium: Moments of Change."

139. Amar, *America's Unwritten Constitution*, 81–94. Amar's argument against the "eccentric" view that the Fourteenth Amendment is a nullity because improperly ratified is true as far as it goes. Amar, however, conflates the success of the Fourteenth Amendment in establishing a new constitutional regime with its constitutionality; finding it impossible to justify contemporary U.S. politics or constitutional life without the Fourteenth Amendment, he claims that the Fourteenth Amendment must have been validly passed. The Fourteenth Amendment's necessary validity does not prove that the process was constitutional; it proves that the amendment created a new order.

Elvin T. Lim described a different Second Founding, the constitutional convention itself, and a long interplay between First Founding antifederalism and Second Founding federalism that manifests itself in the Civil War era and at other moments. Lim, *Lovers' Quarrel*.

140. Bruce Ackerman has argued that Reconstruction transformed the Constitution based on "unconstitutionally keeping the reconstructed states out of the Union until they gave their consent to the new nationalizing amendments." Ackerman, however, underplays the military nature of Reconstruction and attributes its transformations to a "higher lawmaking" available at other moments in U.S. history. Ackerman, *We the People: Foundations*, 46; Ackerman, *We the People: Transformations*, 99–252; Ackerman, "Living Constitution," 1747–49; Ackerman, "Higher Lawmaking"; Levinson, "Accounting for Constitutional Change"; Levinson, "Ten Year War."

141. Fletcher, *Our Secret Constitution*, 2, 10.

142. Magliocca, *American Founding Son*, 2. For a challenging reading of the impact of the amendment's shift from volitional to a narrower birthright citizenship, see Mathisen, *Loyal Republic*, 8, 167–69.

143. Gerstle, *Liberty and Coercion*, 89–148.

144. Cong. Globe, 41st Cong., 2nd Sess. 3607–9 (1870); Varon, *Armies of Deliverance*.

145. Dana, "'Grasp of War' Speech," 259.

146. There remains a great deal of wisdom in Benedict's observation, "It is one of the paradoxes of Anglo-American constitutional history that proponents of radical change have regularly portrayed themselves as conservators rather than transformers." Benedict, "Constitutional History and Constitutional Theory," 2032; Nicoletti, *Secession on Trial*, 12; Cox, "Reflections on the Limits of the Possible."

147. Cong. Globe, 41st Cong., 1st Sess. 658 (1869).

148. Cong. Globe, 40th Cong., 3rd Sess. 652 (1869).

149. Turner, "Fifteenth Amendment"; Kyvig, *Explicit and Authentic Acts*, 181–83.

150. From the dataset at "Amending America." Amendments offered between 1850 and 1859 are on lines 831 to 854 of the spreadsheet; those between December 1860 to March 1861 run from line 855 to line 1089; those from August 1861 to March 1865 from line 1090 to line 1183; and those from December 1865 to March 1871 from line 1184 to line 1528. Similar, though differently numbered, data are available at Ames, *Proposed Amendments to the Constitution*, 353–93, and Bernstein and Agel, *Amending America*.

151. "Message Proposing Constitutional Amendments."

152. On the expansive possibilities Reconstruction unleashed, see Dudden, *Fighting Chance*; Jones, *Goddess of Anarchy*; Jones, *Intimate Reconstructions*; Smith, *Freedom's Frontier*; Stanley, *From Bondage to Contract*; and Downs and Masur, *World the Civil War Made*.

153. Cong. Globe, 41st Cong., 1st Sess. 599–601 (1869).

154. Cong. Globe, 41st Cong., 2nd Sess. 220 (1869).

155. Cong. Globe, 41st Cong., 3rd Sess. 571, 575, app. 125 (1871); *Army and Navy Journal*, September 2, 1871, 35; Coakley, *Role of Federal Military Forces*, 308–10; Gillette, *Retreat from Reconstruction*, 25–26, 53; Calhoun, *Conceiving a New Republic*, 20–22, 26–33; Sefton, *United States Army and Reconstruction*, 222–24; Simpson, *Reconstruction Presidents*, 155–57; Trelease, *White Terror*, 374–80; Valelly, *Two Reconstructions*, 106–7; Foner, *Reconstruction*, 454–57; Williams, *Great South Carolina Ku Klux Klan Trials*, 44–47; Wang, *Trial of Democracy*, 49–133; *Annual Report of the Secretary of War 1870*, 2–4, 16–17; Goldman, *Free Ballot and a Fair Count*.

156. Cong. Globe, 41st Cong., 2nd Sess. 1257 (1870).

157. Ibid., 3607–9.

158. Ames, *Chronicles from the Nineteenth Century*, 216–17.

159. Quoted in McPherson, *Abraham Lincoln and the Second American Revolution*, 21.

160. Painter, *Exodusters*; Hahn, *Nation under Our Feet*.

161. McPherson wisely noted that skeptics of the Civil War as revolution compare it to ideal types, not to other, necessarily limited, revolutions. Neither the English Civil War nor the French Revolution completely destroyed older societies, and both were followed by counterrevolutions that undid much of their work. McPherson, *Abraham Lincoln and the Second American Revolution*, 21.

162. "Transcript of Gettysburg."

163. "Inaugural Address," March 4, 1861.

164. "Transcript of President Abraham Lincoln's Second Inaugural."

165. Quoted in Nicoletti, *Secession on Trial*, 323.

166. On cultural efforts at reunification, see Blight, *Race and Reunion*; Thomas, *Literature of Reconstruction*; Janney, *Remembering the Civil War*; and Silber, *Romance of Reunion*.

CHAPTER TWO

1. "Political Aspects of the Times," *Frederick Douglass' Paper*, November 26, 1852. This appears to be Douglass's only letter signed by "H," and the writer's identity is not clear from contextual clues. My thanks to Leigh Fought, Diane Barnes, Richard Newman, and Justin Leroy for assistance in trying to track down the author.

2. "The New Test," *National Era*, October 30, 1851.

3. Quoted in "Cuba," *Frederick Douglass' Paper*, October 29, 1852.

4. Quoted in McDaniel, *Problem of Democracy*, 203.

5. Basler, *Collected Works*, 2:255, 276. Caleb McDaniel discovered the source of Lincoln's quotation and explained its relevance in "New Light on a Lincoln Quote." See also McDaniel, *Problem of Democracy*, 210–11.

6. Forty years ago David M. Potter captured the interplay of domestic and international politics in 1854 when he wrote that "at the height of the Kansas-Nebraska crisis, there was also a Cuba crisis" and chided historians for writing about "past events as if each one occurred in isolation, neatly encapsulated in a sealed container, or chapter, which keeps it from being mixed up with other events in their own containers." Potter, however, argued that after 1854, international issues receded and the national ones took center stage. Potter, *Impending Crisis*, 177, 189.

7. Cong. Globe, 35th Cong., 1st Sess. 961–62 (1858).

8. Ibid., 944.

9. Robert E. May and Lester Langley developed this international lens forty years ago, and proslavery expansionism has been taken up in recent work by Amy Greenberg, Brian Schoen, Howard Jones, Jay Sexton, Matthew Pratt Guterl, Gerald Horne, Matthew Karp, and Maria Angela Diaz and in syntheses by Walter Johnson and Edward Baptist. May, *Southern Dream of a Caribbean Empire*; May, *Slavery, Race, and Conquest in the Tropics*; Langley, *Struggle for the American Mediterranean*; Greenberg, *Manifest Manhood and the Antebellum American Empire*; Schoen, *Fragile Fabric of Union;* Jones, *Blue and Gray Diplomacy*; Sexton, *Monroe Doctrine*; Guterl, *American Mediterranean*; Horne, *Race to Revolution*; Karp, *This Vast Southern Empire*; Diaz, "Rising Tide of Empire"; Johnson, *River of Dark Dreams*, 303–422; Baptist, *Half Has Never Been Told*, 354–74; Guyatt, *Bind Us Apart*. See also Sexton, "Toward a Synthesis of Foreign Relations in the Civil War Era."

10. This international lens thus fortifies the revived history of the Northern, antislavery origins of the Civil War that focuses on domestic causes and counters origins stories that emphasize Southern planters as the causal agents of the Civil War. See Barnes, *Antislavery Impulse*; Dumond, *Antislavery Origins of the Civil War*; Sewell, *Ballots for Freedom*; Foner, *Free Labor, Free Soil, Free Men*; the recent work of James Oakes, esp. *Freedom National* and *Scorpion's Sting*; and Brooks, *Liberty Power*. For an overview of the vast historiography on secession and the Civil War, see Towers, "Partisans, New History, and Modernization." For new historiographies of

antislavery, see Brooks, "Reconsidering Politics in the Study of American Abolition-ists," and McDaniel, "Bonds and Boundaries of Antislavery."

11. On the rigidity of "the sequence," see Huston, "Meaning of the Events Leading to the Civil War," and the counterfactual sequence in Kornblith, "Rethinking the Coming of the Civil War."

Many fine scholars have delineated the role of international antislavery, inter-national legal precedents, and hemispheric slave rebellions in bringing about the Civil War and have placed the war within broader Atlantic World struggles to save republicanism from monarchical conquest. The story of these antislavery interna-tional visions helps answer Edward Rugemer's call to take an "Atlantic approach to the antebellum United States" to break the now routine march through domestic events that preceded the Civil War, a march that at times substitutes sequence for analysis. Rugemer, *Problem of Emancipation*, 6; Rugemer, "Slave Rebels and Abolitionists," 180. For international antislavery, see Davis, *Problem of Slavery in the Age of Revolution*; Davis, *Inhuman Bondage*; Davis, *Problem of Slavery in the Age of Emancipation*; Blackett, *Building an Antislavery Wall*; Scott, *Common Wind*; Drescher, *Abolition*; and Dal Lago, *American Slavery, Atlantic Slavery, and Beyond*. On antislavery and international law, see esp. Oakes, *Scorpion's Sting*.

Over the past decade, Caleb McDaniel, Bethany Johnson, Robert E. May, Doug-las Egerton, Matthew Clavin, Gerald Horne, Justin Leroy, Gale Kenny, and Joseph Murphy have examined the domestic implications of an internationalized anti-slavery, and Manisha Sinha and Patrick Rael have incorporated this international lens in their syntheses of antislavery. McDaniel, *Problem of Democracy*; McDaniel and Johnson, "New Approaches to Internationalizing the History of the Civil War Era"; May, *Slavery, Race, and Conquest in the Tropics*; Egerton, "Rethinking Atlan-tic Historiography in a Post-Colonial Era"; Clavin, *Toussaint Louverture and the American Civil War*; Horne, *Race to Revolution*; Leroy, "Empire and the Afterlife of Slavery"; Kenny, *Contentious Liberties*; Murphy, "British Example"; Sinha, *Slave's Cause*; Rael, *Eighty-Eight Years*.

For studies of the Civil War in an era of republican revolution, see esp. McDaniel, *Problem of Democracy*; Efford, *German Immigrants, Race, and Citizenship*; Fleche, *Revolution of 1861*; Dal Lago, *Age of Lincoln and Cavour*; Dal Lago, *William Lloyd Garrison and Guiseppe Mazzini*; Eichhorn, "'Up Ewig Ungedeelt'"; Kelly, "North American Crisis of the 1860s"; Butler, *Critical Americans*; Bonner, *Mastering Amer-ica*; Roberts, *Distant Revolutions*; Messer-Kruse, *Yankee International*; and Zimmer-man, "From the Rhine to the Mississippi." For a vivid synthesis, see Doyle, *Cause of All Nations*, and Doyle, *Secession as an International Phenomenon*. For broader views of the Civil War as part of an international moment, see Bender, *Nation among Nations*; Tyrrell, *Transnational Nation*; Maier, *Leviathan 2.0*; Osterhammel, *Transformation of the World*; and Bayly, *Birth of the Modern World*.

12. Louis A. Pérez, Rebecca Scott, and Ada Ferrer played particularly important roles in bringing Cuban history to the attention of historians of the United States and in encouraging an extraordinary group of younger scholars of Cuba and the Spanish Empire. Eller, *We Dream Together*; Ferrer, *Freedom's Mirror*; Ferrer, *Insur-gent Cuba*; Schmidt-Nowara, *Slavery, Freedom, and Abolition*; Schmidt-Nowara,

Empire and Antislavery; Sartorius, *Ever Faithful*; Scott and Hébrard, *Freedom Papers*; Scott, *Degrees of Freedom*; Schneider, *Occupation of Havana*; Pérez, *Cuba*.

13. Two important recent books explore why U.S. historians should pay more attention to U.S. perceptions of Latin America in the early nineteenth century: Naish, *Slavery and Silence*, and Fitz, *Our Sister Republics*.

14. Residents of Cuba included large groups of Spanish-born "whites," Cuban-born "whites," free people of color, slaves, indigenous people, "mixed-race" people, and others. Spanish officials and Cuban writers emphasized the political, social, and legal distinctions between "white Cubans" born in Spain (peninsulares) and "white Cubans" born in Cuba or in other colonies (criollos). I use the awkward phrases "white Cuban creoles" or "white creoles" to capture colony-born people considered to be white or of Spanish descent. Of course, race was constantly being reconstructed in Cuba. See Sartorius, *Ever Faithful*; Hébrard and Scott, *Freedom Papers*; Ferrer, *Insurgent Cuba*; and Lazo, *Writing to Cuba*, 141–68, among many others.

15. Folio for Pedro Santacilia, Luis Hernández, and Bienvenido Hernández, legajo 115, no. 6, 1853, esp. 43–46, 70–71, Comisión Militar, ANC; "Expediente relativo a la orden del Gobernador de la Provincia de Cuba sobre que sean depatriados de la Isla D. Luis y D. Bienvenido Hernández, D. Pedro Santacilia y D. Antonio Manuel Mariño a la Península por procesos en aquella ciudad, alterando el orden público," March 5, 1852, legajo 218, no. 19, Asuntos Políticos, ANC; "Carbonell, *Pedro Santacilia*, 5–9; Prida Santacilia, *Apuntes biográficos*, 12–13; Carrión, "Pedro Santacilia"; Martínez, "Pedro Santacilia y Palacios," 1:lxiv–vi; "Proceso militar contra Pedro Santacilia," 1:3–8; Lazo, *Writing to Cuba*, 28, 37, 54, 180–81. For the politics of royal balls in Cuba, see Schmidt-Nowara, *Empire and Antislavery*, 26.

16. "Documentos, segregado, del Expediente relativo a varios individuos de Santiago de Cuba," March 5, 1852, legajo 218, no. 2, fol. 88, Asuntos Políticos, ANC.

17. The ties themselves are at times referred to as striped or as black and white or as white moons on a blue sky. Folio for Pedro Santacilia, Luis Hernández, and Bienvenido Hernández, legajo 115, no. 6, 1853, esp. 43–46, 70–71, Comisión Militar, ANC.

18. On "integrated history," see Tutino, "Introduction."

19. On this "great revolutionary wave," see most recently Fradera, *Imperial Nation*.

I somewhat promiscuously slide from American (meaning hemispheric) to Gulf to Gulf plus Caribbean, recognizing that these systems of trade and governance did not end neatly at geographic boundaries. The United States, Mexico, and Cuba disproportionately influenced one another because of their geographical proximity and trade connections, but islands beyond the Gulf—especially Hispaniola and Jamaica—were also key parts of this reformulation, as to a lesser degree were the mainland South and Central American nations, particularly proslavery Brazil.

20. Schneider, *Occupation of Havana*.

21. On complex zones of sovereignty, see esp. Benton, *Search for Sovereignty*, and for postindependence layering of political sovereignties and commerce, see Gaffield, *Haitian Connections in the Atlantic World*.

22. For a Gulf view of the American Revolution, see DuVal, *Independence Lost*, and

Clavin, *Aiming for Pensacola*. For a Gulf view of the Age of Revolutions, see Landers, *Atlantic Creoles in the Age of Revolutions*.

23. Fick, "From Slave Colony to Black Nation."

24. Tutino, "Introduction," and Tutino, "Americas in the Rise of Industrial Capitalism."

25. Literature on the "second slavery" has placed Cuban slave expansion in concert with expansion of slaveries in the Mississippi Valley and Brazil. See Tomich and Zeuske, "Second Slavery"; Marquese, Parron, and Berbel, *Slavery and Politics*; Kaye, "Second Slavery"; and Mathisen, "Second Slavery, Capitalism, and Emancipation."

26. Lazo, *Writing to Cuba*, 8.

27. Data from Eichhorn, "Civil War Trade Statistics," tables 1–4, 15–17; Eichhorn, "North Atlantic Trade"; Sexton, "Steam Transport"; Schmidt-Nowara, *Empire and Antislavery*, 5–6; and Bonner, "Salt Water Civil War."

28. Many countries fashioned hybridized systems, as historian Josep Fradera argued, with republics fashioning "imperial constitutions" and empires striving to emulate republican claims of homogeneity and rights-making, as both competed against the other. Fradera, *Imperial Nation*, 6–9; Marquese, Parron, and Berbel, *Slavery and Politics*; Eller, *We Dream Together*.

29. Venegas Delgado, *Gran Colombia*; Tarragó, *Experiencias políticas*, 50–55; Rojas, *Repúblicas de aire*; Horne, *Race to Revolution*, 28–44. For fascinating views of an earlier rebellion, see Childs, *1812 Aponte Rebellion*, and Ferrer, *Freedom's Mirror*, 271–328.

30. Hemispheric historians, especially those working from the Spanish and Portuguese Empires, have long noted the nineteenth century as the fulcrum when economic and political power in the hemisphere shifted from the South to the North. Still, it remains difficult to pin down a Second American System that is not simply a forerunner to the more explicitly imperialist aims of an empowered United States in the 1890s. Fernández-Armesto, *Americas*; Dunkerley, *Americana*; Cañizares-Esguerra, *Puritan Conquistadors*; Sanders, *Vanguard of the Atlantic World*. Marquese, Parron, and Berbel define a separate third American system of slavery stretching from the U.S. Civil War to Cuban and Brazilian abolition in *Slavery and Politics: Brazil and Cuba, 1790–1850*, 261–65.

31. "Sobre les renunicas de la Ciudad de Holguin," December 22, 1836, legajo 38, no. 5, p. 38, Asuntos Políticos, ANC; D. Zeferino Joaquín Pizarro to Excmo. Sr. Predte. Gubernador y Capitán General," December 22, 1836, legajo 38, no. 6, Asuntos Políticos, ANC.

32. A. P. Friss to John Forsyth, November 29, 1836, vol. 7, M899, RG 59, NA; Tarragó, *Experiencias políticas*, 44; data from *Trans-Atlantic Slave Trade Database* queries; Pérez, *Cuba*, 78–83; Knight, *Slave Society in Cuba during the Nineteenth Century*; Schmidt-Nowara, *Empire and Antislavery*, 22–25.

33. Capitán General to Excmo. Sr. Primer Secto del Despacho de Estado, September 9, 1849, legajo 5588, exp. 4, no. 51, Estado, AHN; Drescher, "From Empires of Slavery to Empires of Antislavery."

34. Barcia, *West African Warfare*; Finch, *Rethinking Slave Rebellion*; Reid-Vazquez,

Year of the Lash; Paquette, *Sugar Is Made with Blood*; Fradera, *Colonias para después de un imperio*, 283–89.

35. Eller, *We Dream Together*, 9.

36. Robert Campbell to Capitán-General Leopoldo O'Donnell, June 28, 1844, vol. 19, M899, RG 59, NA; Finch, *Rethinking Slave Rebellion in Cuba*; Reid Vázquez, *Year of the Lash*.

37. "The Mission of Democracy, No. 2," *National Era*, April 20, 1848; "Juan Placido," *North Star*, December 7, 1849.

38. Letter, February 19, 1848, *North Star*, March 3, 1848; "Annexation of Cuba," *North Star*, April 27, 1849; Mirabal, *Suspect Freedoms*, 42–43.

39. "Communications: The Redemption of Cuba," *North Star*, July 20, 1849; Brock, "Back to the Future," 15–16.

40. Greenberg, *Wicked War*; DeLay, *War of a Thousand Deserts*; Guardino, *Dead March*.

41. Campbell to James Buchanan, January 8, 1846, vol. 21, M899, RG 59, NA.

42. Campbell to Buchanan, April 17, 1847, vol. 21, M899, RG 59, NA.

43. J. Kennedy to Lord Palmerston, August 23, 1850, no. 39, FO 72/771, BNA; on the centrality of Great Britain to U.S. internal politics, see Karp, *Vast Southern Empire*.

44. John Gregory to B. Hawes, June 17, 1850, copy in T. Elliott to H. Addington, July 29, 1850, FO 72/776, BNA.

45. On the broader American phenomenon of annexationism, see Eller, *We Dream Together*, 11. For a clear analysis of different visions of annexation in Cuban letters and historiography, see Lazo, *Writing to Cuba*, 4–16.

46. Brock, "José Agustín Quintero," 17–19.

47. "Copia de parte de la comunicación de 20 de Junio ultimo a que se refiere la de esta fecha, dirigido al SM Ministro de Estado," legajo 4645, exp. 39, no. 5, Ultramar, Cuba Gobierno, AHN; Jos. T. Crawford to Palmerston, July 18, 1848, no. 22, FO 72/748, BNA; Crawford to Palmerston, August 18, 1848, no. 24, FO 72/748, BNA. For a profound rethinking of the López incidents, see Lightfoot, "Manifesting Destiny on Cuban Shores." See also Franco, *Revoluciones y conflictos internacionales*.

48. For the investigation of the López case, see the files in legajo 84, no. 1, Comisión Militar, ANC. For a count of people investigated for conspiracy, I tabulated names listed in the card records for files from legajo 84, no. 1, to legajo 128, no. 5. Of course, scholars must be careful not to take at face value all the rumors that circulated on the island or even the Spanish court records, since problems of communication and manipulative officials could produce "greatly exaggerated" claims of uprisings, military pronunciamientos, and general discontent. See, e.g., the changing view of the U.S. consul between August and September 1849 in Campbell to John Clayton, August 27, 28, September 7, 1849, roll 22, M899, RG 59, NA.

49. Capitán-General to Exmo. Sr. Primer Secto del Despacho de Estado, September 9, 1849, legajo 5588, exp. 4, no. 51, Estado, AHN.

50. "Pro-Slavery," *National Anti-Slavery Standard*, June 8, 1848; Sperber, *European Revolutions, 1848–1851*.

51. "Documentos sueltos relacionados con planes revolucionarios en Jamaica contra la Isla de Cuba," July 18, 1848, legajo 43, no. 28, Asuntos Políticos, ANC; "Summaria," legajo 85, no. 1, p. 5, Comisión Militar, ANC.

52. Santacilia, *Arpa del proscripto*, 109. On the 1848 revolutions and their impact in the United States, see Roberts, *Distant Revolutions.*

53. On the John Lytle case, see J. L. O'Sullivan to Buchanan, July 23, August 8, 13, 1848, Campbell to Buchanan, June 19, July 7, 1848, Campbell to Count of Alcoy, June 19, 1848, and Charles B. Ruy, William P. Powell, Chas. L. Reason, and James McCune Smith to Buchanan, July 22, 1848, roll 22, M899, RG 59, NA; "'The Peculiar Institution,'" *National Anti-Slavery Standard*, August 10, 1848; and Graden, *Disease, Resistance and Lies*, 176.

54. May, "Lobbyists for Commercial Empire"; Hudson, *Mistress of Manifest Destiny.*

55. "The Scheme Unfolding—The Future," *National Era*, August 12, 1847.

56. "Policy of Cuban Annexation," *National Era*, December 2, 1852; Rojas, *Repúblicas de aire*, 281–95; Hudson, *Mistress of Manifest Destiny*; Eyal, *Young America Movement*, 135; Sampson, *John L. O'Sullivan*, 213–15; Greenberg, *Manifest Manhood.*

57. "Speech of Mr. Wilmot," *National Era*, August 17, 1848; "Further Annexations," *National Era*, September 7, 1848.

58. De la Cova, "Taylor Administration versus Mississippi Sovereignty"; Chaffin, *Fatal Glory.*

59. O. L. Dabelsteen to Ministro de relaciones interiores y exteriores, May 10, 1850, L-E-133, SRE; de la Cova, "Taylor Administration versus Mississippi Sovereignty."

By contrast, Walter Johnson turned filibusters and Narciso López into comic foils, fools for Southern expansionists, based on his dependence on English-language sources and U.S. historians who have relied on them. Johnson, *River of Dark Dreams*, 330–64. Edward Baptist's synthesis is much more even-handed and also more attentive to Northern interest in López's expeditions. Baptist, *Half Has Never Been Told*, 355–57.

60. Richards, *California Gold Rush and the Coming of the Civil War.*

61. David Potter called the Compromise of 1850 an "armistice" and raised the disconcerting question of whether the North got the better of the deal. By contrast, most historians term the compromise a massive Southern victory, a "sell-out" or an "appeasement." See Potter, *Impending Crisis*, 113, 120; Freehling, *Road to Disunion*, 509–10; Finkelman, *Millard Fillmore*, 81, 88; Blackett, *Captive's Quest for Freedom*, 14; and Maizlish, *Strife of Tongues.*

62. Blackett, *Captive's Quest for Freedom*, esp. 69; Harrold, *Border War.*

63. "Red Rag of Cuba for the South," *Charleston Daily Mercury*, February 26, 1858.

64. "Speech of Hon. Charles Durkee," *National Era*, July 4, 1850. Recent work has captured the endurance of bonded labor in California, especially Indian slavery, and the endurance of African slavery in some parts of the state. See esp. Smith, *Freedom's Frontier*, and Reséndez, *Other Slavery*, 266–314.

65. For a study of the institutional explanations for the collapse of politics and the coming of the Civil War, see Holt, *Rise and Fall of the American Whig Party.*

66. For a nuanced study of the struggle over land in the western territories, see Morrison, *Slavery and the American West.*

67. Jélomer, *Pedro Santacilia,* 1:465; Lazo, *Writing to Cuba.*

68. Jélomer, *Pedro Santacilia,* 2:597–600.

69. Prida Santacilia, *Apuntes biográficos,* 23–25.

70. Sometimes rendered Goicouría or Goicuria.

71. Muller, *Cuban Émigrés and Independence in the Nineteenth-Century Gulf World,* 23–27; Gruesz, *Ambassadors of Culture,* esp. 111–48; Poyo, "Evolution of Cuban Separatist Thought"; Poyo, *"With All and for the Good of All"*; Martínez-Fernández, *Torn between Empires*; Mirabal, *Suspect Freedoms*; Opatrný, *U.S. Expansionism and Cuban Annexationism*; López Mesa, *Comunidad cubana de New York.*

72. Jélomer, *Pedro Santacilia,* 1:318, 340, 435.

73. *La Verdad,* February 10, 1853.

74. A. Calderon de la Barca to Exmo. Sr. Primer Secretario de Estado, November 12, 1849, legajo 5588, exp. 4, no. 95, Estado, AHN.

75. George Bancroft to Buchanan, March 10, 1848, no. 65, box 3, George Bancroft Papers, NYPL.

76. Jane Cazneau to Moses Beach, January 8, 1850, Cazneau (Jane McManus Storms) Papers 3H135, Center for American History, University of Texas, Austin.

77. Montgomery, *King of Rivers,* 9–12, 95–97, 116–17; Greenberg, *Manifest Manhood.*

78. Cazneau to My Dear Friend, June 25, 1855, Cazneau Papers.

79. Campbell to John Clayton, May 22, 1850, roll 23, M899, RG 59, NA.

80. May, *John A. Quitman.*

81. "Draft, Lord Howden," August 22, 1850, no. 28, FO 72/764, BNA.

82. Jélomer, *Pedro Santacilia, 1:*435; Lazo, *Writing to Cuba,* 22.

83. Campbell to Buchanan, July 17, 1848, roll 22, M899, RG 59, NA; Eller, *We Dream Together,* 77; Schmidt-Nowara, "'España Ultramarina.'"

84. Matthew Karp provides the subtlest argument for Southern power in his recent, well-crafted work *This Vast Southern Empire.* Although historians have emphasized the Slave Power for generations, the actual record of Southern accomplishment after 1845 remains thin, and Southern defeats were extensive. For studies of the extremely effective Slave Power rhetoric, see Richards, *Slave Power,* and, more skeptically, Davis, *Slave Power Conspiracy and the Paranoid Style.*

85. "A Don José de la Concha, nombrado Gobernador Capitán General de la Isla de Cuba, Madrid 30 de Setiembre de 1850," legajo 4645, exp. 1, no. 34, Ultramar, AHN.

86. Leopoldo O'Donnell to Sr. Ministro Plenipotenciario, October 8, 1846, legajo 4626, exp. 20, no. 4, Ultramar, AHN.

87. Pedro Pidal to D. W. Barringer, May 6, 1850, translation, copy in Barringer to John Clayton, May 10, 1850, no. 17, roll 36, M31, M31 Dispatches from United States Ministers to Spain, 1792–1906, RG 59, NA.

Increasingly the United States had good reason to fear Spain's navy. While small, it was being rebuilt in the late 1840s in response to U.S. aggression and was much more threatening than Mexico's navy. In 1849, Spanish *moderado* governments purchased one steamer for Cuba defense, and then added several more in 1850, and still more over the 1850s; Zaforteza, *"Moderado* Party and the Introduction of Steam Power."

88. "1852 Democratic Party Platform."

89. "Whig Party Platform of 1852."

90. William Sharkey to C. M. Conrad, November 8, 1852, roll 25, M899, RG 59, NA.

91. "Inaugural Address of Franklin Pierce."

92. "Manifestations," *Frederick Douglass' Newspaper,* January 14, 1853.

93. "Cuban Annexation," *National Era,* January 6, 1853.

94. "Our Foreign Policy," *National Era,* February 3, 1853.

95. "Cuba," *Frederick Douglass' Paper,* December 31, 1852.

96. "Mr. Soulé," *National Anti-Slavery Standard,* April 14, 1853.

97. Lord Howden to Earl of Clarendon, February 1, 1854, no. 39, FO 72/842, BNA.

98. "Annexation of Cuba—The Prospect," *National Anti-Slavery Standard,* November 18, 1854.

99. Barringer to John Clayton, June 19, 1850, no. 19, roll 36, M31, RG 59, NA; Schmidt-Nowara, *Empire and Antislavery,* 57–58; Kiernan, *Revolution of 1854 in Spanish History;* Esdaile, *Spain in the Liberal Age,* 104–10; Bowen, *Spain and the American Civil War;* Langley, "Slavery, Reform, and American Policy in Cuba"; May, *Southern Dream of a Caribbean Empire.*

100. William H. Robertson to William Marcy, November 27, 1853, roll 26, M899, RG 59, NA.

101. Marques de la Pezuela to Leopolda A. de Cueto, July 10, 1865, legajo 4645, exp. 26, no. 2, Ultramar, Cuba Gobierno, AHN; Pezuela to Conde de San Luis, April 8, 1854, legajo 4645, exp. 45, no. 12, Ultramar, Cuba Gobierno, AHN; Sartorius, *Ever Faithful,* 87–89; Corwin, *Spain and the Abolition of Slavery,* 117–21.

102. Robertson to Marcy, June 21, 1854, roll 27, M899, RG 59, NA.

103. Robertson to Marcy, April 26, 1854, roll 27, M899, RG 59, NA; Horne, *Race to Revolution,* 82–99.

104. Alex M. Clayton to Marcy, December 15, 1853, roll 26, M899, RG 59, NA.

105. "Correspondence," *Provincial Freeman,* June 23, 1855; Horne, *Race to Revolution.*

106. Urban, "Africanization of Cuba Scare."

107. Naish, *Slavery and Silence,* 187.

108. Claiborne, *Life and Correspondence of John A. Quitman,* 2:207–8.

109. Clayton to Marcy, December 15, 1853, roll 26, M899, RG 59, NA; Madán to Franklin Pierce, October 4, 1853, roll 27, M899, RG 59, NA; Robertson to Marcy, April 26, 1854, M899, RG 59, roll 27, NA; Howden to My Lord, May 5, 1854, no. 59, FO 72/840, BNA.

110. Pedro Santacilia to Porfirio Valiente, June 20, 1854, ser. 1, box 1, folder 38, Ramiro Casañas Collection, Cuban Heritage Collection, University of Miami Libraries.

111. As a reminder that politics was complex in Cuba, as in Spain and the United States, Gutiérrez de la Concha had reputedly lost his position for also cracking

down on royal family–favored planters, including Julián Zulueta, who were importing large numbers of slaves and passing bribes to the court. Robertson to Marcy,
December 29, 1853, roll 26, M899, RG 59, NA; "The Cuban Question," *Frederick Douglass' Paper*, February 9, 1855.

112. "Gleanings," *Provincial Freeman*, August 19, 1854.

113. Mercadal, *Castelar*, 35; Esdaile, *Spain in the Liberal Age*, 104–10; Kiernan, *Revolution of 1854 in Spanish History*, 4–7; Fuentes Aragones, *Fin de Antiguo Régimen*,
175–77.

114. "The Ostend Conference," *National Era*, March 15, 1855.

115. Potter, *Impending Crisis*, 175–96; Etchison, *Bleeding Kansas*.

116. Matthew Karp rightly argued that Southern politicians were not always sin-
gle-mindedly focused on annexation but often sought to establish alliances that ce-
mented their commercial power in Cuba and Brazil and supported slavery in those
regions. Yet between 1848 and 1854, the California and Kansas conflicts turned
their attention back to the need to add slave states to reconfigure the nation's internal political structure, a goal that remained paramount for many Southern politicians who saw little future of additional slave states in the U.S. West. Karp, *This
Vast Southern Empire*.

117. Oakes, *Scorpion's Sting*, 107–8, 118–27, 131–40.

118. "The Occasion and Its Duties," *National Era*, April 6, 1854.

119. "To the People of Ohio," *National Era*, June 22, 1854. Gregg Lightfoot calls
Kansas "the American Cuba." Lightfoot, "Manifesting Destiny," 439.

120. "Position and Policy of the Administration," *National Anti-Slavery Standard*,
July 9, 1853.

121. "Address to the People of the United States," *National Era*, June 29, 1854.

122. Howden to Clarendon, March 4, 1855, no. 91, FO 72/865, BNA.

123. "The Present State of Kansas," *National Anti-Slavery Standard*, December
27, 1856.

124. "Speech of Hon. J. R. Giddings of Ohio," *Frederick Douglass' Paper*, January 12, 1855.

125. "The Cuban Conspiracy," *National Anti-Slavery Standard*, February 24, 1855.

126. "Our Foreign Policy," *National Era*, February 3, 1853.

127. On the ways that antislavery and imperialism mutually constructed each
other in the nineteenth-century British Empire, see Huzzey, *Freedom Burning*.
Huzzey is right to point out that antislavery isn't inherently imperialist.

128. "Annexation of Cuba," *National Era*, August 28, 1851.

129. "Territorial Expansion—the Position of the Hon. Gerrit Smith," *National
Era*, July 20, 1854.

130. "Important Correspondence in Relation to Cuba—the True Policy," *National
Era*, January 13, 1853.
Manisha Sinha portrayed a much closer relation between abolitionism and anti-
imperialism. Although many abolitionists (like liberal imperialists elsewhere)
were critics of the practice of empire, many of them also expressed interest in
expansion for liberty, and this tendency was even more pronounced among antislavery politicians. By my lights very few of them were genuinely anti-imperialist,

and those who were found themselves marginalized even within anti-slavery and abolition. Associating anti-slavery with the American goal of expansion was simply irresistible, even for those who saw the dangers; many of course were so deep in that American culture of expansion that they did not see the dangers, at least once the Slave Power was destroyed. All of this was part of the complicated tangle of ideas within a broad abolition and antislavery movement, a tangle that makes the movement so fascinating and so challenging to place in the context of contemporary politics. Sinha, *Slave's Cause*, 338–80.

131. Hammond, "Slavery, Sovereignty, and Empires"; McDaniel, *Problem of Democracy*; Blackburn, *American Crucible*; Davis, *Inhuman Bondage*; Huzzey, *Freedom Burning*; Martinez, *Slave Trade and Origins of International Human Rights Law*; Sarracino, *Inglaterra, sus dos caras*.

132. On antislavery leaders as crusaders, see Howard Temperley's claims about the "eagerness with which, when preaching failed, they [antislavery leaders] used the arm of the state as their instrument." The field should once again reckon with Temperley's notion of the shared impulse to "remake the world in its own image" that shaped antislavery and imperialism. Temperley, "Anti-Slavery as a Form of Cultural Imperialism," 337, 348–49.

133. *National Anti-Slavery Standard*, October 28, 1854.

134. Harrold, *Gamaliel Bailey*, 81–84, 127–28; Brooks, "Stoking the 'Abolition Fire,'" 545–46.

135. "The Coming Revolution," *National Anti-Slavery Standard*, May 5, 1855.

136. "The Rising Cloud," *Liberator*, April 27, 1855.

137. Santacilia to Valiente, June 19, 20, 1854, ser. 1, box 1, folder 38, Ramiro Casañas Collection, Cuban Heritage Collection, University of Miami Libraries; *La Verdad*, August 25, 1855.

138. Michel Gobat's portrayal of William Walker dramatically overturns U.S. presumptions that he was a simple tool of slave owners (an area where he draws upon Albert Z. Carr) and that cut Walker off from Nicaraguan politics. Gobat also noted the "seductive nature of what we now call U.S. liberal imperialism" for Nicaraguans who allied with Walker. Gobat, *Empire by Invitation*, 4, 99–100, 135, 246–47; Gobat, "Invention of Latin America"; Carr, *World and William Walker*, 24, 39, 91, 202.

For a recent example of a common, thinner view of Walker, see Johnson, *River of Dark Dreams*, 366–74.

139. "Walker's Plot Unveiled," *National Anti-Slavery Standard*, November 29, 1856; Scroggs, *Filibusters and Financiers*, 7, 150, 218–30; May, *Manifest Destiny's Underworld*; Gobat, *Empire by Invitation*, 246–47; Stiles, *First Tycoon*, 290.

140. Campbell to Clayton, June 4, 1850, roll 22, M899, RG 59, NA; Campbell to Buchanan, May 17, 1848, M899, RG 59, NA; Tamayo, *Benito Juárez*, 5:387–90.

141. Tamayo, *Benito Juárez*, 2:8–12; Sierra, *Juárez su obra y su tiempo*, 79–83; Prida Santacilia, *Apuntes biográficos*, 23–31; Carrión, "Pedro Santacilia"; *La Verdad*, February 10, March 30, November 20, 1853; March 25, April 10, 25, 1857; Pani, *Serie de admirables acontecimientos*; Kelly, "North American Crisis"; Downs, "Mexicanization of American Politics."

142. "Republican Party Platform of 1856."

143. "1856 Democratic Party Platform."

144. *Letters of Lydia Maria Child*, 84.

145. "Conservatism," *National Era*, August 21, 1856.

146. "Will the Union Be Dissolved?," *National Era*, August 30, 1855.

147. "Inaugural Address, March 4, 1857."

148. "Second Annual Message to Congress on the State of the Union, December 6, 1858."

149. *National Era*, June 24, 1858.

150. "The South Becoming Conservative," *National Anti-Slavery Standard*, December 4, 1858.

151. Valiente to José Mora, February 19, 1857, ser. 1, box 1, folder 48, Ramiro Casañas Collection, Cuban Heritage Collection, University of Miami Libraries.

152. Basler, *Collected Works*, 3:115, 117; May, *Slavery, Race, and Conquest in the Tropics*.

153. "The Issue Its History," *National Era*, February 3, 1859.

154. "Political Intelligence," *National Era*, March 24, 1859.

155. "Democratic Senatorial Caucus," *National Era*, January 20, 1859.

156. "Parties," *Charleston Mercury*, April 1, 1859.

157. Raymond, *Disunion and Slavery*, 36.

158. Eichhorn, "North Atlantic Trade."

159. Lazo, *Writing to Cuba*, 141–54.

160. "The Cuban Scheme," *National Anti-Slavery Standard*, July 14, 1855.

161. "El Pueblo," *National Anti-Slavery Standard*, October 20, 1855.

162. Howden to Clarendon, April 10, 12, 1857, nos. 143, 145, FO 72/915, BNA; Thomas Savage to Marcy, February 9, 1857, no. 12, M899 RG 59, NA; A. K. Blythe to Lewis Cass, May 16, 1857, no. 27, M899, RG 59, NA; *National Era*, April 9, 1857; Tamayo, *Benito Juárez*, 2:398–402; *La Verdad*, March 25, April 25, 1857.

163. Jélomer, *Pedro Santacilia*, 2:318, 339, 435; Rojas, *Repúblicas de aire*, 305–8.

164. "The Acquisition of Cuba," *National Era*, March 10, 1859.

165. "Annexation of Canada," *National Era*, March 31, 1859.

166. "The Acquisition of Cuba—Colonization of Central America," *National Era*, March 24, 1859.

167. "Abolition of Slavery in Cuba," *National Era*, March 10, 1859.

168. "Tract No. 2," *National Era*, July 14, 1859.

169. "The Presidents," *National Era*, March 31, 1859.

170. "The Real Question," *National Era*, October 14, 1858.

171. On British abolitionism in Brazil and the relation of the Civil War's coming to Brazilian history, see Mota, "Imminence of Emancipation," 18–87; Saba, "American Mirror"; and Marques, *United States and the Transatlantic Slave Trade*.

172. Basler, *Collected Works*, 4:154.

173. Ibid., 4:172.

174. Richard Blackett made a powerful case for runaway slaves' resistance and for Northern African American and white abolitionist success in rousing popular opinion against the law. Lincoln was in part out of step with popular opinion, in part fearful of inflaming Northern constitutionalists, in part focused on areas like

foreign policy that he could control as president. Blackett, *Captive's Quest for Freedom*; Basler, *Collected Works*, 4:183; May, *Slavery, Race, and Conquest in the Tropics*.

175. Basler, *Collected Works*, 4:268–69.

176. "The Second American Revolution," *New York Herald*, October 18, 1860.

177. John Crampton to Lord Russell, September 19, 1863, no. 105, FO 185/418, BNA.

178. Basler, *Collected Works*, 4:316–17.

179. Schmidt-Nowara, *Empire and Antislavery*.

180. On the practical and ideological engagements between U.S. and Mexican liberals, the Edward Lee Plumb Papers are a rich source. See, e.g., Edward Plumb to George F. Allen, October 19, 31, 1856, January 1, 31, 1857, all in box 1, folder 1, Edward Lee Plumb Papers, Stanford University Libraries.

181. Notes, ser. 3, W. A. Swanberg Papers, Columbia University Rare Book and Manuscript Library.

182. "Princeton Centennial Celebration," *Liberator*, July 6, 1860.

183. Eller, *We Dream Together*, 114.

184. "Revolution in St. Domingo," *National Anti-Slavery Standard*, April 6, 1861.

185. "On the Recognition of Hayti, and on Haytian Ambassadors," *Liberator*, July 4, 1862.

186. Francisco Serrano to Ministro de la Guerra y de Ultramar, November 26, 1861, legajo 4648, exp. 12, no. 2, AHN.

187. Ferrer, *Insurgent Cuba*, 5; García Mora, "Fuerza de la palabra."

188. "The Christian Inquirer," *National Anti-Slavery Standard*, October 4, 1862.

189. "Emancipation, Its Policy and Security as a War Measure," *Liberator*, October 10, 1862.

CHAPTER THREE

1. López, *José Martí*, 83; Martí, "República española," 5–6, 15.

2. "Special Session Message," July 4, 1861.

3. "Second Annual Message, December 1, 1862."

4. "Transcript of Gettysburg Address."

5. Downs, "Mexicanization of American Politics."

6. On both the general sense of political history—especially of liberal republicanism—being launched from the Americas, not Europe, and the possibilities of writing transnational political history, see Sanders, *Vanguard of the Atlantic World*.

7. "The Christian Inquirer," *National Anti-Slavery Standard*, October 4, 1862.

8. "Emancipation, Its Policy and Security as a War Measure," *Liberator*, October 10, 1862.

9. "Slavery and the Rebellion, One and Inseparable," *National Anti-Slavery Standard*, November 12, 1864.

10. "Emancipation Celebration," *National Anti-Slavery Standard*, July 9, 1864.

11. On the diplomatic history of the Civil War, see Jones, *Blue and Gray Diplomacy*.

12. Pani, "Dreaming of a Mexican Empire"; Kelly, "North American Crisis."

13. Jélomer, *Pedro Santacilia*, 1:614–15.

14. Gabriel García Tassara to Domingo Dulce, May 30, 1865, MSS 20283/2 (1), BNE.

15. On crusades and antislavery, see Temperley, "Anti-Slavery as a Form of Cultural Imperialism."

16. "Appeal to the American People," *National Anti-Slavery Standard*, June 24, 1865.

17. "Wm. Lloyd Garrison, Esq.," *Christian Recorder*, February 24, 1866.

18. "Letter from Richmond," *Christian Recorder*, April 22, 1865.

19. Tassara to Capitán General, September 26, 1865, Ultramar, Cuba Gobierno, 4696/25, no. 2, AHN.

20. Tassara to Capitán General, April 28, 1865, Ultramar, Cuba Gobierno, 4645/44, no. 2, AHN.

21. Eller, *We Dream Together*, 207–8.

22. Tassara to Dulce, May 30, 1865, MSS 20283/2 (1), BNE.

23. Robert Bunch to Lord Russell, June 15, 1865, enclosed in James Murray to Lionel Sackville-West, August 11, 1865, Slave Trade no. 6, FO 185/445, BNA; Schmidt-Nowara, *Empire and Antislavery*, 107.

24. Ferrer, *Insurgent Cuba*, 2, 5; García Mora, "Fuerza de la palabra."

25. Bunch to Lord Russell, June 15, 1865, no. 26, enclosed in Murray to Sackville-West, August 11, 1865, Slave Tradeno. 5, FO 185/445, BNA; Horne, *Race to Revolution*, 100–22; Childs, "Cuba, the Atlantic Crisis of the 1860s."

26. Eller, *We Dream Together*, 209–10, 216, 222.

27. Emilio Castelar to Ambrosio Valiente, 1866, box 1, folder 72, Ramiro Casañas Collection, Cuban Heritage Collection, University of Miami Libraries; Schmidt-Nowara, *Empire and Antislavery*, 7–8, 50, 52, 70–74, 117–18.

28. Corwin, *Spain and the Abolition of Slavery in Cuba*, 173–214.

29. Schmidt-Nowara, *Empire and Antislavery*, 4.

30. Tamayo, *Benito Juárez*, 11:617–18.

31. See, e.g., the disappointments of Chilean diplomat Benjamin Vicuña Mackenna, who traveled to the United States in 1866 to try without success to persuade Secretary of State William Seward to defend American republics against European encroachments. Mackenna, *Diez meses*, 1:187–88.

32. Carta del represente de España en los Estados Unidos, Sr. D. Tacundo Goni, February 15, 1868, Carpeta 8, Ms 20282 (2), BNE.

33. Rugemer, *Problem of Emancipation*, 291–300.

34. Guterl, *American Mediterranean*; Rothman, *Beyond Freedom's Reach*.

35. Tamayo, *Benito Juárez*, 12:858–59.

36. Ibid., 13:924–25.

37. Ibid., 14:134.

38. Cardoso, "Central America."

39. Tamayo, *Benito Juárez*, 15:334–35.

40. "The Inauguration and the Inaugural of President Grant—the New Epoch," *New York Herald*, March 4, 1869.

41. Ferrer, *Insurgent Cuba*, 1–5.

42. Scott, *Slave Emancipation in Cuba*, 45–58; Ferrer, *Insurgent Cuba*, 17.

43. Eller, *We Dream Together*, 231.

44. Ferrer, *Insurgent Cuba*, 25–29.

45. See, e.g., the notes on the back of Leonardo del Monte to Moses Taylor, December 6, 1869, box 305, folder 2, reel 1, Moses Taylor Papers, NYPL. Taylor introduced Edward Plumb to Cuban exile leader Miguel de Aldama in spring 1869 as Plumb prepared to go to Havana as consul general. Taylor to Plumb, May 4, 1869, box 2, folder 13, Edward Lee Plumb Papers, Stanford University Libraries.

46. Domingo Ruiz Caracas to Manuel Quesada, January 20, 1871, vol. 809, Taylor Papers, NYPL; Pérez, *Sugar, Cigars, and Revolution* and "Schism of 1868."

47. José de Armas y Céspedes, "The Cuban Revolution: Notes from the Diary of a Cuban," 1869, and C. Carlos del Castillo, "Position of the United States on the Cuban Question," n.d., box 308, Taylor Papers, NYPL; Poyo, *Exile and Revolution*.

48. "Cuba.—England," *National Anti-Slavery Standard*, May 8, 1869.

49. "President Colored Men's Convention," *Christian Recorder*, January 30, 1869.

50. *National Anti-Slavery Standard*, May 8, 1869.

51. "Cuba—England," *Christian Recorder*, November 14, 1868.

52. Samuel R. Scottron to Castillo, July 21, 1873, box 305, folder 8, Taylor Papers, NYPL; Washington, *Negro in Business*, 150–60.

53. Tamayo, *Benito Juárez*, 14:522–23.

54. Petition, Estevan Centeno, Bernardo Carrilo et al., March 6, 1869, Independencia de Cuba, vol. 2, L-E 1334, SRE.

55. *La Discusión*, May 23, 1869; Pérez, *Cuba*, 83–90; Scott, *Slave Emancipation in Cuba*, 46–64; Ferrer, *Insurgent Cuba*, 17–27; Espinosa Blas and Wingartz Plata, "Juárez y Cuba," 127–29; González Barrios, "Cuba en el entorno militar"; *La Época*, January 25, 1869, 1; Simon, *Papers of Ulysses S. Grant*, 24:248.

56. "Colored Cuban Sympathizers," *National Anti-Slavery Standard*, May 15, 1869.

57. "Thirty-Sixth Anniversary of the American Anti-Slavery Society," *National Anti-Slavery Standard*, May 29, 1869.

58. "Massachusetts Republican Convention—Address by Hon. Charles Sumner," *National Anti-Slavery Standard*, October 2, 1869; Priest, "Thinking about Empire."

59. Plumb to Hamilton Fish, October 2, 1869, box 2, folder 16, Plumb Papers, Stanford University Libraries.

60. Edward Thornton to Lord Stanley, January 10, 1870, ser. 2, box 3, vol. 3, Sir Edward Thornton Correspondence with the British Foreign Office, Yale University Library, Manuscripts and Archives.

61. *Revolución Cuba y Puerto Rico*, May 5, 1869; González Barrios, "Cuba en el entorno militar," 114–15; Espinosa Blas and Wingartz Plata, "Juárez y Cuba," 128–31; Muller, "Cuban Émigrés," 58–61; John A. Dix to John P. Hale, January 21, 1869, box 2, John P. Hale Papers, Dartmouth College Archives; Cardoso, "Central America," 5:220. Thanks to Kate Masur for a transcript of the Hale letter.

62. José María Lafragua to Ramón Céspedes, May 22, 1873, Independencia de Cuba, vol. 2, L-E 1334 (16), SRE.

63. Pedro Santacilia to Hilario Cisneros y Saco, July 11, 1872, no. 2271, C. M. Ponce, BNC.

64. For negotiations in Peru and Chile, see the letters of Ambrosio Valiente in

ser. 1, box 1, folders 13–16, 77, Ramiro Casañas Collection, Cuban Heritage Collection, University of Miami Libraries.

On the role of South Americans in spurring the Cuban revolts, see Dulce to Ministro de Ultramar, May 19, 1866, legajo 54, no. 25, 399, Asuntos Políticos, ANC.

65. Occasionally Prim's admiration for Juárez and Lincoln led contemporaries to class him as a republican, but his fight to preserve a constitutional monarchy in the 1869 constitution revealed that he was what he repeatedly said, a man who recognized the power of republicanism in the Americas (and for this reason was respected by Spanish republicans) but believed in monarchism in Europe. "He is anything but a Republican," Sickles wrote. Daniel Sickles to J. Bancroft Davis, October 16, 1870, Letterpress, vol. 1, Daniel Sickles Papers, NYPL.

66. Dix to Hale, November 16, 1868, box 2, Hale Papers, Dartmouth College Archives.

67. Esdaile, *Spain in the Liberal Age*, 119–40; Piqueras, *Revolución democrática*.

68. Prim, *General McClellan and the Army of the Potomac*.

69. Vichese García, *Emilio Castelar*, 78–81.

70. "Abolition of Slavery in the Spanish Dominions—Interesting Meeting in Madrid," *National Anti-Slavery Standard*, November 21, 1868.

71. Schmidt-Nowara, *Empire and Antislavery*, 127–36, 154–58; Carr, "Liberalism and Reaction"; Brandt, *Toward the New Spain*; Hale, *Transformation of Liberalism*, 37–44; Hennessy, *Federal Republic in Spain*; "Que Vergüenza," *La Iberia*, February 4, 1873; *El Americano*, January 27, 1873.

72. Sanchez del Real, *Emilio Castelar*, 182–83.

73. Ibid., 189–90; Sanchez Andrés, *Castelar y el parlamentarismo decimonónico Español*, 28–38.

74. *Discursos parlamentarios de Don Emilio Castelar*, 1:5.

75. Ibid., 1:96.

76. Towle, *Certain Men of Mark*, 146–47.

77. Surwillo, "Poetic Diplomacy."

78. *National Anti-Slavery Standard*, October 16, 1869.

79. *National Anti-Slavery Standard*, October 17, 1868.

80. Charles O'Leary to Lord Russell, April 17, 1865, enclosed in Edmund Hammond to Sir Frederick Bruce, July 1, 1865, no. 269, FO 115/434, BNA.

81. The romantic aura of Sickles's story and the paucity of his personal papers have led some biographers to emphasize gossip and innuendo in their portrayal of his time in Spain. Edgcumb Pinchon, in particular, described Sickles as a scheming royalist trying to reinstall Queen Isabella, his alleged lover, to the throne. But his actions, his letters, and the interpretation of his behavior by both critical and admiring contemporaries in Spain do not support these claims, which seem to be based on Sickles's own self-aggrandizing talk late in his life. For examples of the (to my view) absurd claims that researcher William Hobart Royce fed to Pinchon, see William Royce to Pinchon, July 16, 26, 1942, box 1, William Hobart Royce Papers, NYPL. Pinchon, *Dan Sickles*.

More recent works have been much more reliable in their treatment of Sickles but still are vague in their handling of his time in Spain and at times overwhelmed by Sickles's extravagant personality. Keneally, *American Scoundrel*; Brandt, *Congressman Who Got Away with Murder*.

82. See Pinchon, *Dan Sickles*; Keneally, *American Scoundrel*; and Brandt, *Congressman Who Got Away with Murder*.

83. Sickles to My Dear General, January 21, 1871, Letterpress, vol. 1, Sickles Papers, NYPL.

84. Sickles to John Hay, May 16, 1871, Letterpress, vol. 1, Sickles Papers, NYPL.

85. Sickles's grandiosity and his constant access to gossip both were fed by his proficiency in Spanish, something most ministers to the country had lacked. When he gave a speech to King Amadeo in Spanish, he noted that it was believed to be the first speech delivered by a U.S. minister in the language since Washington Irving's farewell speech twenty-five years earlier. Sickles to Fish, October 6, 1870, Letterpress, vol. 1, Sickles Papers, NYPL.

86. *La Época*, September 10, 1869.

87. By contrast to my argument (and to the judgment of most observers on the ground), Sickles's secretary John Hay believed that Secretary of State Hamilton Fish had inadvertently killed any chance for a purchase early on by dictating terms. Although Hay began as a cynic about Sickles, he came to respect him. Hay to John Nicolay, January 30, 1870, box 2, Tyler Dennett Collection, LoC.

88. John Milton Hay to Nicolay, October 7, 1869, in Henry Adams and Clara Louise Hay, *Letters of John Hay and Extracts from Diary*, 1:387.

89. Sickles to Joseph Cooper, December 17, 1872, Letterpress, vol. 2, Sickles Papers, NYPL; A. Graham Dunlop to Lord Clarendon, July 15, 1869, no. 77, FO 72/1217, BNA; Ramos Martínez, "Manuel Calvo y Aguirre"; Amores Carredano and Ramos Martínez, "Leadership of Manuel Calvo y Aguirre"; Schmidt-Nowara, *Empire and Antislavery*, 145.

90. A. H. Layard to Granville, March 15, 1871, no. 5, FO 185/522, BNA.

91. Layard to Granville, November 7, 1871, no. 6, FO 185/522, BNA.

92. Sickles to Edmund Sturge, November 19, 1871, Letterpress, vol. 1, Sickles Papers, NYPL.

93. "Correspondence from Havana," *La Discusión*, March 8, 1873.

94. Schmidt-Nowara, *Empire and Antislavery*, 4–6.

95. On meetings at Sickles's house, see Sickles to Fish, January 22, 1871, Letterpress, vol. 1, Sickles Papers, NYPL.

96. *La Discusión*, February 16, 1871.

97. See, e.g., Sickles to Don Cristino Martos, June 13, 1871, Letterpress, vol. 1, Sickles Papers, NYPL, and Sickles to Rafael de la Labra, December 22, 1873, Letterpress, vol. 3, Sickles Papers, NYPL.

98. When British minister A. H. Layard forwarded Sickles's appeals to London and British antislavery groups appealed directly to Spain, Lord Granville urged them to be quiet. Granville to Layard, March 31, 1871, no. 5, FO 185/22, BNA; Granville to Layard, April 10, 1871, no. 7, FO 185/22, BNA. For the impact of Sickles and other U.S. sources in pressing British abolitionists to act, see Cooper et al.

to Granville, July 10, 1871, in Granville to Layard, July 22, 1871, no. 16, FO 185/22, BNA.

99. Sickles to My Dear General, November 9, 1871, Letterpress, vol. 1, Sickles Papers, NYPL.

100. *La Época*, April 22, 1870.

101. Corwin, *Spain and the Abolition of Slavery*, 251.

102. "Discurso pronunciado en contra de la esclavitud," 5.

103. *Discursos parlamentarios: studio notas y comentarios*, 289.

104. Hay to Edward King, January 29 1870, box 2, Dennett Collection, LoC.

105. Hay to Jessie L. Bross, June 20, 1870, box 2, Dennett Collection, LoC.

106. Castelar, *Discursos políticos*, 1:213-14.

107. Sickles to Davis, March 7, 1871, and Sickles to Fish, March 2, 1872, Letterpress, vol. 1, Sickles Papers, NYPL.

108. John Crawford to Stanley, October 30, 1868, no. 18, FO 72/1189, BNA.

109. *Cuban Question and American Policy*, 25.

110. Dunlop to Clarendon, June 3, 1869, no. 56, FO 87/1216, BNA.

111. Hay to Charles Hay, March 27, 1870, box 2, Tyler Dennett Collection, LoC.

112. Ferrer, *Insurgent Cuba*, 43-59.

113. Sickles to Mr. Ryan, September 28, 1872, Letterpress, vol. 2, Sickles Papers, NYPL.

114. *La Discusión*, September 12, 1872.

115. Sickles to Alfred Forbert, October 9, 1872, Letterpress, vol. 2, Sickles Papers, NYPL.

116. Dunlop to Granville, October 16, 1872, enclosed in George Enfield to Layard, November 9, 1872, Slave Trade no. 23, FO 185/540, BNA; see also Dunlop to Granville, December 31, 1871, enclosed in Enfield to Layard, February 2, 1872, no. 10, FO 185/528, BNA.

117. Sickles to James MacHenry, September 30, 1872, Letterpress, vol. 2, Sickles Papers, NYPL.

118. Quoted in Bradford, *Virginius Affair*, 142.

119. Sickles to Cooper, December 17, 1872, Letterpress, vol. 2, Sickles Papers, NYPL.

120. Castelar, *Discursos políticos*, 2:267, 287.

121. Uncharacteristically though probably wisely, he kept "mum" and skipped a massive abolitionist to avoid bad press. Sickles to Fish, January 22, 1873, Letterpress, vol. 2, Sickles Papers, NYPL.

122. *La Iberia*, December 24, 1872

123. *Revista de España*, January 1873, 269.

124. *La Iberia*, February 1, 1873.

125. Sickles to Col. Hoffman, November 13, 1872, Letterpress, vol. 2, Sickles Papers, NYPL.

126. Schmidt-Nowara, *Empire and Antislavery*, 87, 144, 152.

127. "Que Vergúenza," *La Iberia*, February 4, 1873.

128. Layard to Granville, February 13, 1873, no. 76, FO 185/542, BNA.

129. Hammond to Layard, March 26, 1873, no. 82, FO 185/542, BNA.

130. Layard to Granville, February 16, 1873, FO 185/542, BNA.

131. Sickles to Hay, March 2, 1873, Letterpress, vol. 2, Sickles Papers, NYPL; Hennessy, *Federal Republic in Spain*; Schmidt-Nowara, *Empire and Antislavery*, 154–57.

132. *La Discusión*, February 16, 1873; *La Ilustración Española y Americana*, February 24, 1873.

133. *La Iberia*, February 16, 1873.

134. Sickles to Admiral James Alden, February 27, 1873, Letterpress, vol. 2, Sickles Papers, NYPL.

135. Sickles to Hay, March 2, 1873, Letterpress, vol. 2, Sickles Papers, NYPL.

136. *La Discusión*, February 20, 1873.

137. *La Discusión*, February 22, 1873.

138. *La Época*, March 4, 1873.

139. *La Esperanza*, March 19, 1873.

140. *La Discusión*, February 23, 1873.

141. Castelar to Lew Wallace, n.d. [1873], enclosed in Sickles to Wallace, November 4, 1873, Letterpress, vol. 2, NYPL.

142. *La Época*, March 19, 1873.

143. Castelar, *Discursos políticos*, 2:337.

144. *El Imparcial*, May 4, 1873.

145. *La República*, May 5, 1873, 2.

146. "Puerto Rico Emancipation," *Christian Recorder*, April 3, 1873.

147. "Second Inaugural of Ulysses S. Grant."

148. "Spain; Free Cuba," *Christian Recorder*, February 20, 1873.

149. *Slavery in Cuba*, 16.

150. "The Colored Citizens of New York . . . ," *Christian Recorder*, December 21, 1872.

151. Granville to Layard, February 18, 1873, no. 28, FO 185/540, BNA.

152. *Discursos parlamentarios de Don Emilio Castelar*, 1:73.

153. Sickles to Elihu Washburne, March 10, August 5, 1873, vol. 80, E. B. Washburne Papers, LoC.

154. Sickles to Ryan, April 18, 1873, Letterpress, vol. 2, Sickles Papers, NYPL.

155. Sickles to Adam Badeau, June 12, 1873, Letterpress, vol. 2, Sickles Papers, NYPL.

156. Fish to J. C. B. Davis, July 28, 1873, Letterbook 6, box 190, Hamilton Fish Papers, LoC.

157. To capture this situation, David Hannay in 1896 urged English readers to ponder "the interval between the death of Oliver Cromwell and the Restoration of Charles II." Hannay, *Don Emilio Castelar*, 145–46.

158. Castelar, *Discursos políticos*, 2:272.

159. *Der Volksstaat*, October 31, November 2, 5, 1873, in Marx and Engels, *Revolution in Spain*, available at Marx Engels Archive, https://www.marxists.org/archive/marx/works/1873/bakunin/index.htm.

160. Layard to Granville, October 14, 1873, no. 462, FO 185/545, BNA.

161. Sickles to William Chandler, September 10, 1873, Letterpress, vol. 2, Sickles Papers, NYPL.

162. Sickles to Castelar, October 20, 1873, Letterpress, vol. 2, Sickles Papers, NYPL.

163. Castelar to Sickles, n.d. [1873], 463-64, Letterpress, vol. 2, Sickles Papers, NYPL.

164. *La Iberia*, August 19, 1873.

165. "The Cuban Insurrection," *Times* (London), March 25, 1873, copy in box 307, Taylor Papers, NYPL.

166. "La cuestión de Cuba," box 308, Taylor Papers, NYPL.

167. Jélomer, *Pedro Santacilia*, 1:261-62.

168. Sickles to Cooper, September 3, 1873, Letterpress, vol. 2, Sickles Papers, NYPL.

169. "The Sale of Cuba," *Times* (London), April 18, 1873, copy in box 307, Taylor Papers, NYPL.

170. Lord Tenterden to Thornton, February 21, 1874, ser. 1, box 2, vol. 2, Thornton Correspondence, Yale University Library, Manuscripts and Archives.

171. H. August Cowper to Granville, July 13, 1873, enclosed in Tenterden to Hugh McDonnell, August 13, 1873, FO 185/547, BNA.

172. Quoted in Ferrer, *Insurgent Cuba*, 59.

173. Bradford, *Virginius Affair;* Langley, *Cuban Policy of the United States*, 73-76.

174. Thornton to Granville, November 17, 1873, ser. 2, box 4, vol. 4, Thornton Correspondence, Yale University Library, Manuscripts and Archives.

175. Santiago Soler to Castelar, November 29, 1873, no. 2367, Castelar Correspondence, AHN.

176. Thornton to Granville, November 11, 1873, ser. 3, box 6, vol. 6, Thornton Correspondence, Yale University Library, Manuscripts and Archives.

177. *La Época*, November 16, 1873.

178. Simon, *Grant Papers*, 24:248.

179. *La Época*, December 4, 1873.

180. Simon, *Grant Papers*, 24:249-51.

181. Researcher William Royce wrote to Sickles's biographer Edgcumb Pinchon that "it is apparent that on the Spanish cycle of General Sickles' life you will have to exercise your imagination to a generous extent. This you may easily do, with a wealth of romance and incident, and nothing to controvert." William Royce to Edgcumb Pinchon, March 7, 1943, box 1, Royce Papers, NYPL.

Compounding this problem, biographer W. A. Swanberg noted that on Sickles's time in Spain, "I will have to rely heavily on the Pinchon book, since he has access to memoirs I have so far been unable to locate." "Sickles the Incredible," notes on uncataloged manuscript, box 37, W. A. Swanberg Papers, Columbia University Rare Book and Manuscript Library.

182. Washburne to Fish, January 30, 1874, vol. 100, Fish Papers, LoC.

183. Fish to Washburne, February 12, 1874, box 191, Letterbook 9, Fish Papers, LoC.

184. Sickles to James Harlan, January 20, 1874, Letterpress, vol. 3, Sickles Papers, NYPL.

185. Valero Escandell, *Palabra de Emilio Castelar*, 101-13.

186. Tamayo, *Benito Juárez*, 15:1008.

187. Thornton to Tenterden, January 6, 1874, ser. 3, box 6, vol. 6, Thornton Correspondence, Yale University Library, Manuscripts and Archives.

188. *Correspondencia de Emilio Castelar*, 2–3.

189. Ferrer, *Insurgent Cuba*, 60.

190. Simon, *Grant Papers*, 26:391–94.

191. Sexton, "United States, Cuban Rebellion"; Langley, *Cuban Policy of the United States*, 77–79; Fradera, "Moments in a Postponed Abolition." In an interesting view into a continental vision of republican crisis, Henry Hall compared Democrat Samuel Tilden's supporters to "as unscrupulous a set of revolutionists as ever preyed upon poor Mexico" and used their alleged deal-making with Cuban insurgent Miguel de Aldama as evidence. Simon, *Grant Papers*, 26:391–94; Henry Hall to Plumb, box 4, folder 38, Plumb Papers, Stanford University Libraries. See also Downs, "Mexicanization of American Politics."

192. Ferrer, *Insurgent Cuba*, 63–66.

193. *Christian Recorder*, November 8, 1877.

194. Sickles to Badeau, May 8, 1871, Letterpress, vol. 1, Sickles Papers, NYPL.

195. Thornton to Granville, n.d. [December 1874], ser. 2, box 4, vol. 4, Thornton Correspondence, Yale University Library, Manuscripts and Archives.

196. "Thirty-Sixth Anniversary of the American Anti-Slavery Society," *National Anti-Slavery Standard*, May 22, 1869.

197. "Thirty-Sixth Anniversary of the American Anti-Slavery Society," *National Anti-Slavery Standard*, May 29, 1869.

198. On the role of hope in the civil rights movement, see Chappell, *Stone of Hope*.

199. Eric Foner's *Reconstruction* remains the dominant interpretation of the era. See also Downs and Masur, *World the Civil War Made*.

200. Ferrer, *Insurgent Cuba*, 95–100.

201. For an interesting view of the Confederate mythology of the Lost Cause by a contemporary Spanish historian, see González Calleja, "Causas perdidas."

202. Bayly, *Birth of the Modern World*, 161–64; Osterhammel, *Transformation of the World*, 417; Maier, *Leviathan 2.0*, 80–150. For an optimistic answer, see Doyle, *Cause of All Nations*.

AFTERWORD

1. Douglass, *Life and Times*, 611.

2. Ibid.

3. Young, *Around the World with General Grant*, 2:361–62.

4. Du Bois, *Black Reconstruction*, 30.

5. Some legal scholars emphasize the constitutional transformations of the 1930s as the crucial turning point for the creation of a third constitutional order. See Ackerman, *Civil Rights Revolution*, and Ackerman, "Revolution on a Human Scale." For a distinct portrayal of a sharp divergence in the 1930s, see Orren, *Belated Feudalism*.

For responses to the Ackerman thesis, see Leuchtenburg, "When the People

Spoke, What Did They Say?," and Kalman, "Law, Politics, and the New Deal(s)." See also *"AHR* Forum."

6. "Second Annual Message, December 1, 1862."

7. Slezkine poignantly described the "sickness and sorrow" that plagued the 1920s Soviet Bolsheviks—and also Millerites and Xhosa and other millenarians—in his chapter "The Great Disappointment." Slezkine, *House of Government*, 220–21.

8. Prida Santacilia, *Apuntes biográficos*, 49.

9. H. M. Alden to Emilio Castelar, December 4, 1875, no. 2366, Sección: Diversos Títulos y Familias, AHN.

10. Castelar, "Spain: A Democratic Nation," *Forum*, May 1891, 276.

11. Jélomer, *Pedro Santacilia*, 1:285–86.

12. Santacilia to Dolores Sellén, January 20, 1910, CM Santacilia no. 3, BNC; Katz, "Mexico: Restored Republic and Porfiriato"; Alvarez Junco and Pan-Montojo, *Más se perdió en Cuba*.

13. On tragedy in History, see Blight, *American Oracle*, 22–30.

14. "Irving Howe Interviews Gershom Scholem," 55–56; Biale, *Gershom Scholem*.

15. Yeats, *Collected Poems*, 81; Schwartz, *In Dreams Begin Responsibilities*, 1–9.

BIBLIOGRAPHY

ARCHIVAL SOURCES

Cuba
  Archivo Nacional de la República de Cuba, Havana
  Biblioteca Nacional de Cuba José Martí, Havana
Mexico
  Archivo Histórico Genaro Estrada de la Secretaría de Relaciones Exteriores,
    Mexico City
Spain
  Archivo Histórico Nacional, Madrid
  Biblioteca Nacional de España, Madrid
United Kingdom
  National Archives, London
United States
  Center for American History, University of Texas, Austin
  Columbia University Rare Book and Manuscript Library, New York
  Dartmouth College Archives, Hanover, New Hampshire
  Library of Congress, Washington, D.C.
  National Archives at College Park, Maryland
  New-York Historical Society, New York
  New York Public Library, Archives and Manuscript Division
  Stanford University Libraries, Manuscripts Division of the Department of
    Special Collections, California
  University of Miami Libraries, Cuban Heritage Collection, Florida
  Yale University Library, Manuscripts and Archives, New Haven, Connecticut

NEWSPAPERS

El Americano (Paris)
Army and Navy Journal (New York City)
Charleston Daily Mercury
Charleston Mercury
Chicago Tribune
Christian Recorder (Philadelphia)
Columbia (S.C.) Daily Phoenix
Congressional Globe (Washington, D.C.)

La Discusión (Madrid)
Douglass' Monthly (Rochester, N.Y.)
La Época (Madrid)
La Esperanza (Madrid)
Forum (New York City)
Frederick Douglass' Newspaper (Rochester, N.Y.)
Frederick Douglass' Paper (Rochester, N.Y.)
La Iberia (Madrid)
El Imparcial (Madrid)
Journal of the Senate of the United States of America (Washington, D.C.)
The Liberator (Boston)
The Nation (New York City)
National Anti-Slavery Standard (New York City and Philadelphia)
National Era (Washington, D.C.)
New York Herald
New York Times
North Star (Rochester, N.Y.)
Observer (Fayetteville, N.C.)
Provincial Freeman (Windsor, Canada)
La Revolución Cuba y Puerto Rico (New York City)
La Verdad (New York City)

PRIMARY AND SECONDARY SOURCES

Ackerman, Bruce. "Higher Lawmaking." In *Responding to Imperfection: The Theory and Practice of Constitutional Amendment*, edited by Sanford Levinson, 63–88. Princeton, N.J.: Princeton University Press, 1995.

———. "Oliver Wendell Holmes Lectures: The Living Constitution." *Harvard Law Review* 120 (May 2007): 1747–49.

———. "Revolution on a Human Scale." *Yale Law Journal* 108 (1999): 2279–349.

———. *We the People.* 3 vols. Cambridge, Mass.: Harvard University Press, 1991–2014.

Adams, Henry, and Clara Louise Hay, eds. *Letters of John Hay and Extracts from Diary*. Washington, D.C.: N.p., 1908.

Adelman, Jeremy. *Sovereignty and Revolution in the Iberian Atlantic*. Princeton, N.J.: Princeton University Press, 2007.

Agamben, Giorgio. *State of Exception*. Translated by Kevin Attell. Chicago: University of Chicago Press, 2005.

Alvarez Junco, José, and Juan Pan-Montojo, eds. *Más se perdió en Cuba: España, 1898 y la crisis de fin de siglo*. Madrid: Alianza Editorial, 1998.

Amar, Akhil Reed. *America's Unwritten Constitution*. New York: Basic Books, 2012.

"Amending America: Proposed Amendments to the United States Constitution, 1789 to 2014." *National Archives*. https://www.archives.gov/open/dataset-amendments.html.

Ames, Blanche Butler, ed. *Chronicles from the Nineteenth Century: Family Letters of Blanche Butler and Adelbert Ames Married July 21st, 1870.* N.p.: Clinton, Mass., 1907.

Ames, Herman V. *The Proposed Amendments to the Constitution of the United States during the First Century of Its History.* Washington, D.C.: Government Printing Office, 1897.

Amores Carredano, Juan Bosco, and Jon Ander Ramos Martínez. "The Leadership of Manuel Calvo y Aguirre in the Spanish Party and among Basques and Navarrese in Cuba." In *Basques in Cuba*, edited by William A. Douglass and translated by Artiz Branton, 37–50. Reno, Nev.: Center for Basque Studies Press, 2016.

Annual Report of the Secretary of War. Washington, D.C.: Government Printing Office, 1871.

Arendt, Hannah. *On Revolution.* New York: Penguin Press, 1963.

Armitage, David. *Civil Wars: A History in Ideas.* New York: Alfred A. Knopf, 2017.

Armstrong, David. *Revolution and World Order: The Revolutionary State in International Society.* New York: Oxford University Press, 1993.

Aynes, Richard L. "Unintended Consequences of the Fourteenth Amendment and What They Tell Us about Its Interpretation." *Akron Law Review* 39 (2006): 289–321.

Bancroft, Frederic Bancroft, ed. *Speeches, Correspondence and Political Papers of Carl Schurz.* New York: G. P. Putnam's Sons, 1913.

Baptist, Edward E. *The Half Has Never Been Told: Slavery and the Making of American Capitalism.* New York: Basic Books, 2014.

Barcia, Manuel. *West African Warfare in Bahia and Cuba: Soldier Slaves in the Atlantic World, 1807–1844.* New York: Oxford University Press, 2014.

Barnes, Gilbert Hobbes. *The Antislavery Impulse, 1830–1844.* New York: D. Appleton-Century, 1933.

Basler, Roy P., ed. *The Collected Works of Abraham Lincoln.* 9 vols. New Brunswick, N.J.: Rutgers University Press, 1953.

Bayly, C. A. *The Birth of the Modern World, 1780–1914: Global Connections and Comparisons.* Malden, Mass.: Blackwell, 2004.

Beard, Charles A., and Mary Ritter Beard. *The Rise of American Civilization.* 2 vols. New York: Macmillan, 1927.

Beissinger, Mark R. "Structure and Example in Modular Political Phenomena: The Diffusion of Bulldozer/Rose/Orange/Tulip Revolutions." *Perspectives on Politics* 5 (June 2007): 259–76.

Belz, Herman. *Reconstructing the Union: Theory and Policy during the Civil War.* Ithaca, N.Y.: Cornell University Press, 1969.

Bender, Thomas. *Nation among Nations: America's Place in World History.* New York: Hill and Wang, 2006.

Benedict, Michael Les. "Constitutional History and Constitutional Theory: Reflections on Ackerman, Reconstruction, and the Transformation of the American Constitution." *Yale Law Journal* 108 (1999): 2011–38.

———. *The Impeachment and Trial of Andrew Johnson.* New York: W. W. Norton, 1973.

———. *Preserving the Constitution: Essays on Politics and the Constitution in the Reconstruction Era.* New York: Fordham University Press, 2006.

Benton, Lauren. *A Search for Sovereignty: Law and Geography in European Empires, 1400–1900.* New York: Cambridge University Press, 2010.

Bergeron, Paul H. *The Papers of Andrew Johnson.* 16 vols. Knoxville: University of Tennessee Press, 1967–2000.

Bernstein, Richard B., and Jerome Agel, eds. *Amending America: If We Love the Constitution so Much, Why Do We Keep Trying to Change It?* New York: Crown, 1993.

Biale, David. *Gershom Scholem: Kabbalah and Counter-History.* Cambridge, Mass.: Harvard University Press, 1982.

Blackbourn, David, and Geoff Eley. *The Peculiarities of German History: Bourgeois Society and Politics in Nineteenth-Century Germany.* New York: Oxford University Press, 1984.

Blackburn, Robin. *American Crucible: Slavery, Emancipation, and Human Rights.* New York: Verso, 2011.

———. *An Unfinished Revolution: Karl Marx and Abraham Lincoln.* New York: Verso, 2011.

Blackett, Richard J. M. *Building an Antislavery Wall: Black Americans in the Atlantic Abolitionist Movement, 1830–1860.* Baton Rouge: Louisiana State University Press, 1983.

———. *The Captive's Quest for Freedom: Resistance to the 1850 Fugitive Slave Law.* New York: Cambridge University Press, 2017.

———. *Divided Hearts: Britain and the American Civil War.* Baton Rouge: Louisiana State University Press, 2001.

Blackhawk, Ned. *Violence over the Land: Indians and Empires in the Early American West.* Cambridge, Mass.: Harvard University Press, 2009.

Blair, William A. *With Malice toward Some: Treason and Loyalty in the Civil War Era.* Chapel Hill: University of North Carolina Press, 2014.

Blight, David W. *American Oracle: The Civil War in the Civil Rights Era.* Cambridge, Mass.: Harvard University Press, 2011.

———. *Frederick Douglass' Civil War: Keeping Faith in Jubilee.* Baton Rouge: Louisiana State University Press, 1989.

Bond, James E. "The Original Understanding of the Fourteenth Amendment in Illinois, Ohio, and Pennsylvania." *Akron Law Review* 18 (1985): 435–67.

Bonner, Robert E. *Mastering America: Southern Slaveholders and the Crisis of American Nationhood.* New York: Cambridge University Press, 2009.

———. "The Salt Water Civil War: Thassalogical Approaches, Ocean-Centered Opportunities." *Journal of the Civil War Era* 6, no. 2 (June 2016): 243–67.

Bowen, Wayne H. *Spain and the American Civil War.* Columbia: University of Missouri Press, 2011.

Bradford, Richard H. *The Virginius Affair.* Boulder: Colorado Associated University Press, 1980.

Brandt, Joseph A. *Toward the New Spain*. Chicago: University of Chicago Press, 1933.

Brandt, Nat. *The Congressman Who Got Away with Murder*. Syracuse, N.Y.: Syracuse University Press, 1991.

Brinkley, Alan, Laura Kalman, William E. Leuchtenburg, and G. Edward White. "*AHR* Forum: The Debate over the Constitutional Revolution of 1937." *American Historical Review* 110 (October 2005): 1046–115.

Brock, Daryl. "José Agustín Quintero: Cuban Patriot in Confederate Diplomatic Service." In *Confederates in the Confederacy: José Agustín Quintero, Ambrosio José Gonzales, and Loreta Janeta Velazquez*, edited by Phillip Thomas Tucker, 9–142. Jefferson, N.C.: McFarland, 2002.

Brock, Lisa. "Back to the Future: African-Americans and Cuba in Time(s) of Race." *Contributions in Black Studies* 12, no. 3 (1994): 9–32.

Brock, W. R. *An American Crisis: Congress and Reconstruction, 1865–1867*. New York: St. Martin's Press, 1963.

Brooks, Corey M. *Liberty Power: Antislavery Third Parties and the Transformation of American Politics*. Chicago: University of Chicago Press, 2016.

———. "Reconsidering Politics in the Study of American Abolitionists." *Journal of the Civil War Era* 8, no. 2 (June 2018): 291–317.

———. "Stoking the 'Abolition Fire in the Capitol': Liberty Party Lobbying and Antislavery in Congress." *Journal of the Early Republic* 33, no. 3 (Fall 2013): 545–46.

Butler, Leslie. *Critical Americans: Victorian Intellectuals and Transatlantic Liberal Reform*. Chapel Hill: University of North Carolina Press, 2007.

Calhoun, Charles W. *Conceiving a New Republic: The Republican Party and the Southern Question, 1869–1900*. Lawrence: University Press of Kansas, 2006.

Cañizares-Esguerra, Jorge. *Puritan Conquistadors: Iberianizing the Atlantic, 1550–1700*. Stanford, Calif.: Stanford University Press, 2006.

Carbonell, José Manuel. *Pedro Santacilia, su vida y sus versos: Discurso pronunciado en la inauguración del curso académico de 1924–1925 por el presidente de la academia*. Havana: El Siglo XX, 1924.

Cardoso, Ciro F. S. "Central America: The Liberal Era." In *The Cambridge History of Latin America*, edited by Leslie Bethell, 5:195–228. New York: Cambridge University Press, 1986.

Carr, Albert H. Z. *The World and William Walker*. New York: Harper and Row, 1963.

Carr, Raymond. "Liberalism and Reaction, 1833–1931." In *Spain: A History*, edited by Raymond Carr, 205–42. New York: Oxford University Press, 2000.

Carrión, Jorge. "Pedro Santacilia: Intento de biografía política." In *Pedro Santacilia: El hombre y su obra*, edited by Jorge Boris Rosen Jélomer, 1:i–xlvi. Mexico City: Centro de Investigación Científica Jorge L. Tamayo, 1983.

Castelar, Emilio. *Discursos políticos de Emilio Castelar dentro y fuera del Parlamento en los años 1871 a 1873*. Madrid: Angel de San Martin, n.d.

Chaffin, Tom. *Fatal Glory: Narciso López and the First Clandestine U.S. War against Cuba*. Charlottesville: University of Virginia Press, 1996.

Chappell, David L. *A Stone of Hope: Prophetic Religion and the Death of Jim Crow.* Chapel Hill: University of North Carolina Press, 2004.

Childs, Matt D. "Cuba, the Atlantic Crisis of the 1860s, and the Road to Abolition." In *American Civil Wars: The United States, Latin America, Europe, and the Crisis of the 1860s,* edited by Don H. Doyle, 204–21. Chapel Hill: University of North Carolina Press, 2017.

Claiborne, J. F. H., ed. *Life and Correspondence of John A. Quitman.* 2 vols. New York: Harper and Brothers, 1860.

Clavin, Matthew J. *Aiming for Pensacola: Fugitive Slaves on the Atlantic and Southern Frontiers.* Cambridge, Mass.: Harvard University Press, 2015.

———. *Toussaint L'Ouverture and the American Civil War: The Promise and Peril of a Second Haitian Revolution.* Philadelphia: University of Pennsylvania Press, 2010.

Coakley, Robert W. *The Role of Federal Military Forces in Domestic Disorders, 1789–1878.* Washington, D.C.: Center for Military History, 1988.

Cobb, Charles E. *This Nonviolent Stuff'll Get You Killed: How Guns Made the Civil Rights Movement Possible.* New York: Basic Books, 2014.

Correspondencia de Emilio Castelar, 1868–1898. Madrid: Establecimiento Tipográfico, 1908.

Corwin, Arthur F. *Spain and the Abolition of Slavery in Cuba, 1817–1886.* Austin: University of Texas Press, 1967.

Cox, LaWanda C. Fenlason. "Reflections on the Limits of the Possible." In *Freedom, Racism, and Reconstruction: Collected Writings of LaWanda Cox,* edited by Donald G. Nieman, 243–79. Athens: University of Georgia Press, 1997.

Crane, Brinton. *The Anatomy of Revolution.* New York: W. W. Norton, 1938.

Crofts, Daniel F. *Lincoln and the Politics of Slavery: The Other Thirteenth Amendment and the Struggle to Save the Union.* Chapel Hill: University of North Carolina Press, 2016.

The Cuban Question and American Policy in the Light of Common Sense. New York: N.p., 1869.

La cuestión de Cuba. Valparaiso: Imprenta del Mercurio de Ternero y Letelier, 1874.

Dal Lago, Enrico. *The Age of Lincoln and Cavour: Comparative Perspectives on 19th-Century American and Italian Nation-Building.* New York: Palgrave Macmillan, 2015.

———. *American Slavery, Atlantic Slavery, and Beyond: The U.S. "Peculiar Institution" in International Perspective.* New York: Routledge, 2013.

———. "Lincoln, Cavour, and National Unification: American Republicanism and Italian Liberal Nationalism in Comparative Perspective." *Journal of the Civil War Era* 3, no. 1 (March 2013): 85–113.

———. *William Lloyd Garrison and Giuseppe Mazzini.* Baton Rouge: Louisiana State University Press, 2013.

Dana, Richard Henry, Jr. "The 'Grasp of War' Speech, June 21, 1865." In *Speeches in Stirring Times and Letters to a Son,* edited by Richard H. Dana III, 234–72. Boston: Houghton Mifflin, 1910.

Davis, David Brion. *Inhuman Bondage: The Rise and Fall of Slavery in the New World.* New York: Oxford University Press, 2006.

———. *The Problem of Slavery in the Age of Emancipation.* New York: Alfred A. Knopf, 2014.

———. *The Problem of Slavery in the Age of Revolution.* Ithaca, N.Y.: Cornell University Press, 1975.

———. *The Slave Power Conspiracy and the Paranoid Style.* Baton Rouge: Louisiana State University Press, 1969.

Davis, Rodney O., and Douglas L. Wilson, eds. *The Lincoln-Douglas Debates.* Champaign: University of Illinois Press, 2008.

"A Declaration of the Causes which Impel the State of Texas to Secede from the Federal Union." *American Battlefield Trust.* https://www.battlefields.org/learn /primary-sources/declaration-causes-seceding-states#Texas.

"Declaration of the Immediate Causes Which Induce and Justify the Secession of South Carolina from the Federal Union." December 24, 1860. *The Avalon Project.* avalon.law.yale.edu/19th_century/csa_scarsec.asp.

de la Cova, Antonio Rafael. "The Taylor Administration versus Mississippi Sovereignty: The Round Island Expedition of 1849." *Journal of Mississippi History* 62, no. 4 (Winter 2000): 295–327.

de la Guardia, Carmen, and Juan Pan-Montojo. "Reflexiones sobre una historia transnacional." *Studia historica/Historia contemporánea* 16 (1998): 9–31.

DeLay, Brian. *War of a Thousand Deserts: Indian Raids and the U.S.-Mexican War.* New Haven, Conn.: Yale University Press, 2008.

Desan, Suzzanne, Lynn Hunt, and William Max Nelson, eds. *The French Revolution in Global Perspective.* Ithaca, N.Y.: Cornell University Press, 2013.

Diaz, Maria Angela. "Rising Tide of Empire: Gulf Coast Culture and Society during the Era of Expansion, 1845–1860." Ph.D. diss., University of Florida, 2013.

———. "To Conquer the Coast: The Florida Frontier and the Construction of American Imperialism, 1820–1848." *Florida Historical Quarterly* 95, no. 1 (Summer 2016): 1–25.

Discurso pronunciado en contra de la esclavitud por el ciudadano Emilio Castelar en las Asamblea Constituyente, el dia 21 de Junio de 1870. Madrid: Librería Nueva, 1870.

Discursos parlamentarios: Studio notas y comentarios. Madrid: Narcia, 1973.

Discursos parlamentarios de Don Emilio Castelar en la Asamblea Constituyente. 3 vols. Madrid: Cárlos Bailly-Bailliere, 1871.

Douglass, Frederick. *Life and Times of Frederick Douglass, Written by Himself. . . .* Boston: De Wolfe and Fiske, 1892.

Downs, Gregory P. "The Mexicanization of American Politics: The United States' Transnational Path from Civil War to Stability." *American Historical Review* 117, no. 2 (April 2012): 387–409.

———. "Why the Second American Revolution Deserves as Much Attention as the First." July 19, 2017. *Washington Post Made by History.* https://www.washington post.com/news/made-by-history/wp/2017/07/19/why-the-second-american -revolution-deserves-as-much-attention-as-the-first/.

———, and Kate Masur, eds. *The World the Civil War Made.* Chapel Hill: University of North Carolina Press, 2015.

Doyle, Don H., ed. *American Civil Wars: The United States, Latin America, Europe, and the Crisis of the 1860s.* Chapel Hill: University of North Carolina Press, 2017.

———. *The Cause of All Nations: An International History of the American Civil War.* New York: Basic Books, 2014.

———. *Secession as an International Phenomenon: From America's Civil War to Contemporary Separatist Movements.* Athens: University of Georgia Press, 2010.

Drescher, Seymour. *Abolition: A History of Slavery and Antislavery.* New York: Cambridge University Press, 2009.

———. "From Empires of Slavery to Empires of Antislavery." In *Slavery and Antislavery in Spain's Atlantic Empire*, edited by Josep M. Fradera and Christopher Schmidt-Nowara, 291–316. New York: Berghahn Books, 2013.

Droz-Vincent, Philippe. "The Military amidst Uprisings and Transitions in the Arab World." In *New Middle East: Protest and Revolution in the Arab World,* edited by Fawaz A. Gerges, 180–208. New York: Cambridge University Press, 2013.

Du Bois, W. E. Burghardt. *Black Reconstruction: A History of the Part Which Black Folk Played in the Attempt to Reconstruct Democracy in America, 1860–1880.* New York: Harcourt Brace, 1935.

Dudden, Faye. *Fighting Chance: The Struggle over Woman Suffrage and Black Suffrage in Reconstruction America.* New York: Oxford University Press, 2011.

Dudziak, Mary L. *War Time: An Idea, Its History, Its Consequences.* New York: Oxford University Press, 2012.

Dumond, Dwight L. *Antislavery Origins of the Civil War in the United States.* Ann Arbor: University of Michigan Press, 1939.

Dunkerley, James. *Americana: The Americas in the World, around 1850.* New York: Verso, 2000.

DuVal, Kathleen. *Independence Lost: Lives on the Edge of the American Revolution.* New York: Random House, 2015.

Efford, Alison Clark. *German Immigrants, Race, and Citizenship in the Civil War Era.* New York: Cambridge University Press, 2013.

Egerton, Douglas R. "Rethinking Atlantic Historiography in a Post-Colonial Era: The Civil War in Global Perspective." *Journal of the Civil War Era* 1, no. 1 (March 2011): 79–95.

Eichhorn, Niels. "Civil War Trade Statistics." *Niels Eichhorn.* https://nielseichhorn.com/civil-war-history-trade.html.

———. "North-Atlantic Trade in the Mid-Nineteenth Century: A Case for Peace during the American Civil War." *Civil War History* 61, no. 2 (June 2015): 138–72.

———. "'Up Ewig Ungedeelt' or 'A House Divided': Nationalism and Separatism in the Mid-Nineteenth Century Atlantic World." Ph.D. diss, University of Arkansas, 2013.

"1852 Democratic Party Platform." *The American Presidency Project.* https://www.presidency.ucsb.edu/documents/1852-democratic-party-platform.

"1856 Democratic Party Platform." *The American Presidency Project.* https://www.presidency.ucsb.edu/documents/1856-democratic-party-platform.

Eisenstadt, Shmuel N. *The Great Revolutions and the Civilizations of Modernity.* New York: Brill, 2005.

Eliot, T. S. *Four Quartets.* New York: Harcourt, 1943.

Eller, Anne. "Dominican Civil War, Slavery, and Spanish Annexation, 1844–1865." In *American Civil Wars: The United States, Latin America, Europe, and the Crisis of the 1860s,* edited by Don H. Doyle, 147–66. Chapel Hill: University of North Carolina Press, 2017.

———. *We Dream Together: Dominican Independence, Haiti, and the Fight for Caribbean Freedom.* Durham, N.C.: Duke University Press, 2016.

Emberton, Carole. *Beyond Redemption: Race, Violence, and the American South after the Civil War.* Chicago: University of Chicago Press, 2013.

Epps, Garrett. *Democracy Reborn: The Fourteenth Amendment and the Fight for Equal Rights in Post–Civil War America.* New York: Henry Holt, 2013.

Esdaile, Charles J. *Spain in the Liberal Age: From Constitution to Civil War, 1808–1939.* Malden, Mass.: Blackwell, 2000.

Espinosa Blas, Margarita, and Oscar Wingartz Plata. "Juárez y Cuba: Una interpretación histórica." In *Benito Juárez en América Latina y el Caribe,* edited by Adalberto Santana and Sergio Guerra Vilaboy, 127–39. Mexico City: Universidad Nacional Autónoma de México, 2006.

Etchison, Nicole. *Bleeding Kansas: Contested Liberty in the Civil War Era.* Lawrence: University Press of Kansas, 2004.

Ex parte Merryman. 17 F. Cas. 144 (C.C.D. Md. 1861). *Teaching American History.* teachingamericanhistory.org/library/document/ex-parte-merryman/.

Eyal, Yonatan. *The Young America Movement and the Transformation of the Democratic Party, 1828–1861.* New York: Cambridge University Press, 2007.

Fehrenbacher, Don E. *The Slaveholding Republic: An Account of the United States Government's Relation to Slavery.* Completed and edited by Ward M. McAfee. New York: Oxford University Press, 2001.

Feimster, Crystal. "'What If I Am a Woman': Black Women's Campaigns for Sexual Justice and Citizenship." In *The World the Civil War Made,* edited by Gregory P. Downs and Kate Masur, 249–68. Chapel Hill: University of North Carolina Press, 2015.

Fernández-Armesto, Felipe. *The Americas: A Hemispheric History.* New York, 2005.

Ferrer, Ada. *Freedom's Mirror: Cuba and Haiti in the Age of Revolution.* New York: Cambridge University Press, 2014.

———. *Insurgent Cuba: Race, Nation, and Revolution, 1868–1898.* Chapel Hill: University of North Carolina Press, 1999.

Fick, Carolyn. "From Slave Colony to Black Nation: Haiti's Revolutionary Inversion." *New Countries: Capitalism, Revolutions, and Nations in the Americas, 1750–1870,* edited by John Tutino, 138–74. Durham, N.C.: Duke University Press, 2016.

Field, Kendra. "'No Such Thing as Stand Still': Migration and Geopolitics in African American History." *Journal of American History* 102, no. 3 (December 2015): 693–718.

Finch, Aisha K. *Rethinking Slave Rebellion in Cuba: La Escalera and the Insurgencies of 1841–1844*. Chapel Hill: University of North Carolina Press, 2015.

Finkelman, Paul. *Millard Fillmore*. New York: Henry Holt, 2011.

———. *Slavery and the Founders: Race and Liberty in the Age of Jefferson*. Armonk, N.Y.: M. E. Sharpe, 1996.

Fitz, Caitlin. *Our Sister Republics: The United States in an Age of American Revolutions*. New York: W. W. Norton/Liveright, 2016.

Fleche, Andre M. *The Revolution of 1861: The American Civil War in the Age of Nationalist Conflict*. Chapel Hill: University of North Carolina Press, 2012.

Fletcher, George P. *Our Secret Constitution: How Lincoln Redefined American Democracy*. New York: Oxford University Press, 2000.

Foner, Eric. *Free Labor, Free Soil, Free Men: The Ideology of the Republican Party before the Civil War*. New York: Oxford University Press, 1970.

———. *Reconstruction: America's Unfinished Revolution*. New York: Harper and Row, 1988.

———. *The Second Founding: How the Civil War and Reconstruction Remade the Constitution*. New York: Norton, 2019.

Foran, John. *Taking Power: On the Origins of Third World Revolutions*. New York: Cambridge University Press, 2009.

Foster, Gaines M. "What's Not in a Name: The Naming of the Civil War." *Journal of the Civil War Era* 8, no. 3 (September 2018): 416–54.

Fradera, Josep Maria. *Colonias para después de un Imperio*. Barcelona: Bellaterra, 2005.

———. *The Imperial Nation: Citizens and Subjects in the British, French, Spanish, and American Empires*. Translated by Ruth MacKay. Princeton, N.J.: Princeton University Press, 2018.

———. "Moments in a Postponed Abolition." In *Slavery and Antislavery in Spain's Atlantic Empire*, edited by Fradera and Christopher Schmidt-Nowara, 256–90. New York: Berghahn Books, 2013.

Franco, José Luciano. *Revoluciones y conflictos internacionales en el Caribe, 1789–1854*. Havana: Academia de ciencias, 1965.

Freehling, William W. *The Road to Disunion*. Vol. 2: *Secessionists Triumphant, 1854–1861*. New York: Oxford University Press, 2008.

Friedman, Barry. "The History of the Countermajoritarian Difficulty, Part II: Reconstruction's Political Court." *Georgetown Law Journal* 91, no. 1 (November 2002): 153–260.

Fuentes Aragones, Juan Francisco. *Historia de España: El fin de Antiguo Régimen, política y sociedad*. Madrid: Sintesis, 2007.

Gaffield, Julia. *Haitian Connections in the Atlantic World: Recognition after Revolution*. Chapel Hill: University of North Carolina Press, 2015.

Gallagher, Gary W. *The Union War*. Cambridge, Mass.: Harvard University Press, 2012.

Gannon, Kevin M. "The Civil War as a Settler-Colonial Revolution." January 18, 2016. *Age of Revolutions*. https://ageofrevolutions.com/2016/01/18/the-civil-war-as-a-settler-colonial-revolution/.

García Mercadal, José. *Emilio Castelar: Discursos y ensayos.* Madrid: Aguilar, 1964.

García Mora, Luis Miguel. "La fuerza de la palabra: El autonomismo en Cuba en el ultimo tercio del siglo XIX." *Revista de Indias* 61, no. 223 (2001): 715–48.

Gemme, Paola. *Domesticating Foreign Struggles: The Italian Risorgimento and Antebellum American Identity.* Athens: University of Georgia Press, 2005.

"General Orders No. 100: The Lieber Code." *The Avalon Project.* avalon.law.yale.edu/19th_century/lieber.asp.

Gerstle, Gary. *Liberty and Coercion: The Paradox of American Government from the Founding to the Present.* Princeton, N.J.: Princeton University Press, 2015.

Gillette, William. *Retreat from Reconstruction, 1869–1879.* Baton Rouge: Louisiana State University Press, 1982.

Gobat, Michel. *Empire by Invitation: William Walker and Manifest Destiny in Central America.* Cambridge, Mass.: Harvard University Press, 2018.

———. "The Invention of Latin America: A Transnational History of Anti-Imperialism, Democracy and Race." *American Historical Review* 118, no. 5 (December 2013): 1345–73.

Goldman, Robert. *A Free Ballot and a Fair Count: The Department of Justice and the Enforcement of Voting Rights in the South, 1877–1893.* New York: Fordham University Press, 2001.

Goldstone, Jack A. "Analyzing Revolutions and Rebellions: A Reply to the Critics." In *Debating Revolutions*, edited by Nikki R. Keddie, 178–99. New York: NYU Press, 1994.

———. "Rethinking Revolutions: Integrating Origins, Processes, and Outcomes." *Comparative Studies of South Asia, Africa and the Middle East* 29, no. 1 (2009): 18–32.

———. *Revolution and Rebellion in the Early Modern World.* Berkeley: University of California Press, 1991.

———. "Toward a Fourth Generation of Revolutionary Theory." *Annual Review of Political Science* 4 (2001): 139–87.

———, ed. *The Encyclopedia of Political Revolutions.* New York: Routledge, 1998.

González Barrios, René. "Cuba en el entorno militar de Benito Juárez." In *Benito Juárez en América Latina y El Caribe*, edited by Adalberto Santana and Sergio Guerra Vilaboy, 113–25. Mexico City: Universidad Nacional Autónoma de México, 2006.

González Calleja, Eduardo. "Causas perdidas y estrategias de supervivencia simbólica: La 'Lost Cause' Confederada como pretexto." In *Construyendo memorias: Relatos históricos para Euskadi después del terrorismo*, edited by José María Ortiz de Orruño et al., 113–50. Madrid: Los Libros de la Catarata, 2013.

———. *Una cuestión de honor: La polémica sobre la anexión de Santo Domingo vista desde España, 1861–1865.* Santo Domingo, Dominican Republic: Fundación García Arévalo, 2005.

González-Ripoll, María Dolores, and Luis Miguel García Mora. *El Caribe en el periodo independiente y de las nacionalidades.* Morelia, Mexico: Universidad Michoacana de San Nicolás Hidalgo, 1997.

González-Ripoll, María Dolores, Consuelo Naranjo, Ada Ferrer, Gloria García, and Josef Opatrný. *El rumor de Haití en Cuba: Temor, raza, y rebeldía, 1789–1844*. Madrid: CSIC, 2004.

Goodwin, Jeffrey. "Why We Were Surprised (Again) by the Arab Spring." *Swiss Political Science Review* 17, no. 4 (2011): 452–56.

Graden, Dale T. *Disease, Resistance and Lies: The Demise of the Transatlantic Slave Trade to Brazil and Cuba*. Baton Rouge: Louisiana State University Press, 2014.

Grant, Ulysses S. *Personal Memoirs of U. S. Grant*. 2 vols. New York: C. L. Webster, 1885.

Greeley, Horace. *The American Conflict: A History of the Great Rebellion in the United States of America, 1860–65*. . . . 2 vols. Hartford, Conn.: O. D. Case, 1866.

Greenberg, Amy S. *Manifest Manhood and the Antebellum American Empire*. New York: Cambridge University Press, 2005.

———. *A Wicked War: Polk, Clay, Lincoln, and the 1846 U.S. Invasion of Mexico*. New York: Alfred A. Knopf, 2012.

Gruesz, Kristen Silva. *Ambassadors of Culture: The Transamerican Origin of Latino Writing*. Princeton, N.J.: Princeton University Press, 2002.

Guardino, Peter F. *The Dead March: A History of the Mexican-American War*. Cambridge, Mass.: Harvard University Press, 2017.

Guelzo, Allen C. "The History of Reconstruction's Third Phase." February 4, 2018. *History News Network*. https://historynewsnetwork.org/article/168010.

———. *Reconstruction: A Concise History*. New York: Oxford University Press, 2018.

———. "United States Civil War." In *Encyclopedia of Political Revolutions*, edited by Jack A. Goldstone, 499–500. New York: Routledge, 1998.

Guterl, Matthew Pratt. *American Mediterranean: Southern Slaveholders in the Age of Emancipation*. Cambridge, Mass.: Harvard University Press, 2013.

Guyatt, Nicholas. *Bind Us Apart: How Enlightened Americans Invented Racial Segregation*. New York: Oxford University Press, 2016.

Hahn, Steven. *A Nation under Our Feet: Black Political Struggles in the South from Slavery to the Great Migration*. Cambridge, Mass.: Harvard University Press, 2003.

———. *A Nation without Borders: The United States and Its World in an Age of Civil Wars, 1830–1910*. New York: Viking, 2016.

Hale, Charles A. *The Transformation of Liberalism in Late Nineteenth-Century Mexico*. Princeton, N.J.: Princeton University Press, 1989.

Hale, Henry E. "Regime Change Cascades: What We Have Learned from the 1848 Revolutions to the 2011 Arab Uprisings." *Annual Review of Political Science* 16 (2013): 331–53.

Halstead, Murat. *The War Claims of the South: The New Southern Confederacy, with the Democratic Party as Its Claim Agency* . . . . Cincinnati, Ohio: Robert Clarke, 1876.

Hamilton, Alexander. "Federalist No. 84." May 28, 1788. *The Avalon Project*. avalon.law.yale.edu/18th_century/fed84.asp.

Hamilton, J. G. de Roulhac. *Reconstruction in North Carolina*. New York: Columbia University, 1914.

———, ed. *Correspondence of Jonathan Worth.* 2 vols. Raleigh, N.C.: Edwards and
    Broughton, 1909.
Hammond, John Craig. "Slavery, Sovereignty, and Empires: North American Bor-
    derlands and the American Civil War, 1660–1860." *Journal of the Civil War Era* 4,
    no. 2 (June 2014): 264–98.
Hannay, David. *Don Emilio Castelar.* London: Bliss, Sands, and Foster, 1896.
Harris, William C. *Presidential Reconstruction in Mississippi.* Baton Rouge:
    Louisiana State University Press, 1968.
Harrold, Stanley. *Border War: Fighting over Slavery before the Civil War.* Chapel
    Hill: University of North Carolina Press, 2010.
———. *Gamaliel Bailey and Antislavery Union.* Kent, Ohio: Kent State University
    Press, 1986.
Hart, Gideon M. "Military Commissions and the Lieber Code: Toward a New
    Understanding of the Jurisdictional Foundations of Military Commissions."
    Military Law Review 203 (Spring 2010): 1–77.
Hawgood, J. A. "Liberalism and Constitutional Development." In *New Cambridge
    Modern History*, Vol. 10: *The Zenith of European Power, 1830–1870*, edited by
    J. P. T. Bury, 185–212. New York: Cambridge University Press, 2008.
Hennessy, C. A. M. *The Federal Republic in Spain: Pi y Margall and the Federal
    Republican Movement, 1868–74.* New York: Oxford University Press, 1962.
Hobsbawm, Eric. *The Age of Capital, 1848–1875.* New York: Vintage Books, 1975.
———. *The Age of Empire, 1875–1914.* New York: Pantheon, 1987.
———. *The Age of Revolution, 1789–1848.* New York: New American Library, 1962.
Hogue, James K. *Uncivil War: Five New Orleans Street Battles and the Rise and Fall
    of Radical Reconstruction.* Baton Rouge: Louisiana State University Press, 2006.
Holland, Catherine A. *The Body Politic: Foundings, Citizenship, and Difference in
    the American Political Imagination.* New York: Routledge, 2001.
Holt, Michael F. *The Rise and Fall of the American Whig Party: Jacksonian Politics
    and the Onset of the Civil War.* New York: Oxford University Press, 1999.
Horne, Gerald. *Confronting Black Jacobins: The U.S., the Haitian Revolution, and
    the Origins of the Dominican Republic.* New York: NYU Press, 2015.
———. *Race to Revolution: The U.S. and Cuba during Slavery and Jim Crow.* New
    York: Monthly Review Press, 2014.
Hudson, Linda S. *Mistress of Manifest Destiny: A Biography of Jane McManus
    Storm Cazneau, 1807–1878.* Austin: Texas State Historical Association, 2001.
Huebner, Timothy S. *Liberty and Union: The Civil War Era and American Consti-
    tutionalism.* Lawrence: University Press of Kansas, 2016.
Hunt, Alfred N. *Haiti's Influence on Antebellum America: Slumbering Volcano in the
    Caribbean.* Baton Rouge: Louisiana State University Press, 1988.
Huston, James. "The Meaning of the Events Leading to the Civil War." *Reviews in
    American History* 34, no. 3 (September 2006): 324–31.
Huzzey, Richard. *Freedom Burning: Anti-Slavery and Empire in Victorian Britain.*
    Ithaca, N.Y.: Cornell University Press, 2012.
Hyman, Harold M. *A More Perfect Union: The Impact of the Civil War and Recon-
    struction on the Constitution.* New York: Alfred A. Knopf, 1973.

Ibarra Martínez, Francisco. "Pedro Santacilia y Palacios." In *Pedro Santacilia: El hombre y su obra,* edited by Jorge Boris Rosen Jélomer, 1:xlvi–1. Mexico City: Centro de Investigación Científica Jorge L. Tamayo, 1983.

"Inaugural Address, March 4, 1857." *The American Presidency Project.* https://www.presidency.ucsb.edu/documents/republican-party-platform-1856.

"Inaugural Address, March 4, 1861." *The American Presidency Project.* https://www.presidency.ucsb.edu/documents/inaugural-address-34.

"Inaugural Address of Franklin Pierce, Friday, March 4, 1853." *The Avalon Project.* avalon.law.yale.edu/19th_century/pierce.asp.

"Irving Howe Interviews Gershom Scholem: 'The Only Thing in My Life I Have Never Doubted Is the Existence of God.'" *Present Tense* 8, no. 1 (Autumn 1980): 53–57.

Janney, Caroline E. *Remembering the Civil War: Reunion and the Limits of Reconciliation.* Chapel Hill: University of North Carolina Press, 2013.

"Jefferson Davis' First Inaugural Address." *The Papers of Jefferson Davis.* https://jeffersondavis.rice.edu/archives/documents/jefferson-davis-first-inaugural-address.

Johnson, Walter. *River of Dark Dreams: Slavery and Empire in the Cotton Kingdom.* Cambridge, Mass.: Harvard University Press, 2013.

Jones, Catherine A. *Intimate Reconstructions: Children in Postemancipation Virginia.* Charlottesville: University of Virginia Press, 2015.

Jones, Howard. *Blue and Gray Diplomacy: A History of Union and Confederate Foreign Relations.* Chapel Hill: University of North Carolina Press, 2010.

Jones, Jacqueline. *Goddess of Anarchy: The Life and Times of Lucy Parsons, American Radical.* New York: Basic Books, 2017.

Kaczorowski, Robert J. "Revolutionary Constitutionalism in the Era of the Civil War and Reconstruction." *New York University Law Review* 61 (November 1986): 863–940.

———. "'To Begin the Nation Anew': Congress, Citizenship, and Civil Rights after the Civil War." *American Historical Review* 92, no. 1 (February 1987): 45–68.

Kalman, Laura. "Law, Politics, and the New Deal(s)." *Yale Law Journal* 108 (1999): 2165–213.

Karp, Matthew. *This Vast Southern Empire: Slaveholders at the Helm of American Foreign Policy.* Cambridge, Mass.: Harvard University Press, 2016.

Katz, Friedrich. "Mexico: Restored Republic and Porfiriato." In *The Cambridge History of Latin America*, edited by Leslie Bethell, 5:3–78. New York: Cambridge University Press, 1986.

Katz, Mark N. *Revolutions and Revolutionary Waves.* New York: Palgrave, 1997.

Kaye, Anthony E. "The Second Slavery: Modernity in the Nineteenth-Century South and the Atlantic World." *Journal of Southern History* 75, no. 3 (August 2009): 627–50.

Kelman, Ari. *A Misplaced Massacre: Struggling over the Memory of Sand Creek.* Cambridge, Mass.: Harvard University Press, 2013.

Kelly, Patrick J. "The North American Crisis of the 1860s." *Journal of the Civil War Era* 2, no. 3 (September 2012): 337–68.

Keneally, Thomas. *American Scoundrel: The Life of the Notorious Civil War General Dan Sickles*. New York: Doubleday/Talese, 2002.

Kenny, Gale L. *Contentious Liberties: American Abolitionists in Post-Emancipation Jamaica, 1834–1866*. Athens: University of Georgia Press, 2010.

Kiernan, V. G. *The Revolution of 1854 in Spanish History*. Oxford: Clarendon Press, 1966.

Kimmel, Michael S. *Revolution: A Sociological Interpretation.* Philadelphia: Temple University Press, 1990.

Knight, Franklin W. *Slave Society in Cuba during the Nineteenth Century*. Madison: University of Wisconsin Press, 1970.

Kornblith, Gary J. "Rethinking the Coming of the Civil War: A Counterfactual Exercise." *Journal of American History* 90, no. 1 (June 2003): 76–105.

Kurzman, Charles. "Can Understanding Undermine Explanation? The Confused Experience of Revolution." *Philosophy of the Social Sciences* 34, no. 3 (September 2004): 328–51.

———. *The Unthinkable Revolution in Iran*. Cambridge, Mass.: Harvard University Press, 2004.

Kyvig, David E. *Explicit and Authentic Acts: Amending the U.S. Constitution, 1776–1995*. Lawrence: University Press of Kansas, 1996.

Landers, Jane G. *Atlantic Creoles in the Age of Revolutions*. Cambridge, Mass.: Harvard University Press, 2010.

Langley, Lester D. *The Cuban Policy of the United States: A Brief History*. New York: John Wiley and Sons, 1968.

———. "Slavery, Reform, and American Policy in Cuba, 1823–1878." *Revista de Historia de América* 65/66 (1968): 71–84.

———. *Struggle for the American Mediterranean: United States–European Rivalry in the Gulf-Caribbean, 1776–1904*. Athens: University of Georgia Press, 1982.

Lawson, George. "Negotiated Revolutions." *Review of International Studies* 31, no. 3 (July 2005): 473–93.

Lazo, Rodrigo. *Writing to Cuba: Filibustering and Cuban Exiles in the United States*. Chapel Hill: University of North Carolina Press, 2005.

Leroy, Justin. "Empire and the Afterlife of Slavery: Black Anti-Imperialisms of the Long Nineteenth Century." Ph.D. diss., New York University, 2014.

Letters of Lydia Maria Child with a Biographical Introduction by John G. Whittier and Appendix by Wendell Phillips. Boston: Houghton, Mifflin, 1884.

Leuchtenburg, William E. "When the People Spoke, What Did They Say?" *Yale Law Journal* 108 (1999): 2077–114.

Levine, Bruce. *The Fall of the House of Dixie: The Civil War and the Social Revolution That Transformed the South*. New York: Random House, 2013.

———. "The Second American Revolution." August 17, 2015. *Jacobin*. https://www.jacobinmag.com/2015/08/second-american-revolution-civil-war-charleston-emancipation-lincoln-union.

Levine, Robert S. *Martin R. Delany: A Documentary Reader*. Chapel Hill: University of North Carolina Press, 2003.

Levinson, Sanford. "Accounting for Constitutional Change (Or, How Many Times

Has the United States Constitution Been Amended? (A) <26; (B) 26; (C) >26; (D) All of the Above)." In *Responding to Imperfection*, edited by Sanford Levinson, 13–36. Princeton, N.J.: Princeton University Press, 1995.

———. "The Ten Year War: What If Lincoln Had Not Exited after Four Years?" *Tulsa Law Review* 51, no. 2 (Spring 2016): 313–38.

Lim, Elvin T. *The Lovers' Quarrel: The Two Foundings and American Political Development.* New York: Oxford University Press, 2014.

Litwack, Leon F. *Been in the Storm so Long: The Aftermath of Slavery.* New York: Alfred A. Knopf, 1979.

Lightfoot, Gregg Thomas. "Manifesting Destiny on Cuban Shores: Narciso López, Cuban Annexationism and the Path of American Empire, 1800–1859." Ph.D. diss., Cornell University, 2015.

López, Alfred J. *José Martí: A Revolutionary Life.* Austin: University of Texas Press, 2014.

López Mesa, Enrique Ernesto. *La comunidad cubana de New York: Siglo XIX.* Havana: Centro de Estudios Martianos, 2002.

Magliocca, Gerard N. *American Founding Son: John Bingham and the Invention of the Fourteenth Amendment.* New York: NYU Press, 2013.

Maier, Charles S. *Leviathan 2.0: Inventing Modern Statehood.* Cambridge, Mass.: Harvard University Press, 2014.

Maizlish, Stephen E. *A Strife of Tongues: The Compromise of 1850 and the Ideological Foundations of the American Civil War.* Charlottesville: University of Virginia Press, 2018.

Malia, Martin. *History's Locomotives: Revolutions and the Making of the Modern World.* New Haven, Conn.: Yale University Press, 2006.

Maltz, Earl M. *Civil Rights, the Constitution, and Congress, 1863–1869.* Lawrence: University Press of Kansas, 1990.

———. "Reconstruction without Revolution: Republican Civil Rights Theory in the Era of the Fourteenth Amendment." *Houston Law Review* 24 (March 1967): 221–79.

Marques, Leonardo. *The United States and the Transatlantic Slave Trade to the Americas, 1776–1867.* New Haven, Conn.: Yale University Press, 2016.

Marquese, Rafael. "The Civil War in the United States and the Crisis of Slavery in Brazil." In *American Civil Wars: The United States, Latin America, Europe, and the Crisis of the 1860s*, edited by Don H. Doyle, 222–46. Chapel Hill: University of North Carolina Press, 2017.

———, Tâmis Parron, and Marcía Berbel. *Slavery and Politics: Brazil and Cuba, 1790–1850.* Translated by Leonardo Marques. Albuquerque: University of New Mexico Press, 2016.

Martí, José. *La república española ante la revolución cubana.* Madrid: Cárlos Bailly-Bailliere, 1873.

Martinez, Jennifer. *The Slave Trade and Origins of International Human Rights Law.* New York: Oxford University Press, 2011.

Martínez-Fernández, Luis. *Torn between Empires: Economy, Society, and Patterns*

of Political Thought in the Hispanic Caribbean, 1840–1878. Athens: University of
Georgia Press, 1994.

Marx, Karl, and Friedrich Engels. *Revolution in Spain*. London: Lawrence and
Wishart, 1939. Available online at https://www.marxists.org/archive/marx
/works/1873/bakunin/index.htm.

Mathisen, Erik. *The Loyal Republic: Traitors, Slaves and the Remaking of Citizenship in Civil War America*. Chapel Hill: University of North Carolina Press,
2018.

———. "The Second Slavery, Capitalism, and Emancipation in Civil War America." *Journal of the Civil War Era* 8, no. 4 (December 2018): 677–99.

May, Robert E. *John A. Quitman: Old South Crusader*. Baton Rouge: Louisiana
State University Press, 1985.

———. "Lobbyists for Commercial Empire: Jane Cazneau, William Cazneau,
and U.S. Caribbean Policy, 1846–1878." *Pacific Historical Review* 48, no. 3
(August 1979): 383–412.

———. *Manifest Destiny's Underworld: Filibustering in Antebellum America*.
Chapel Hill: University of North Carolina Press, 2002.

———. *Slavery, Race, and Conquest in the Tropics*. New York: Cambridge University Press, 2013.

———. *The Southern Dream of a Caribbean Empire: 1854–1861*. Baton Rouge:
Louisiana University Press, 1973.

McAdam, Doug, Sidney Tarrow, and Charles Tilly. *The Dynamics of Contention*.
New York: Cambridge University Press, 2001.

McDaniel, W. Caleb. "The Bonds and Boundaries of Antislavery." *Journal of the
Civil War Era* 4, no. 1 (March 2014): 84–105.

———. "New Light on a Lincoln Quote." April 2, 2011. https://wcm1.web.rice.edu
/new-light-on-lincoln-quote.html.

———. *The Problem of Democracy in the Age of Slavery: Garrisonian Abolitionists
and Transatlantic Reform*. Baton Rouge: Louisiana State University Press, 2015.

McDaniel, W. Caleb, and Bethany L. Johnson. "New Approaches to Internationalizing the History of the Civil War Era: An Introduction." *Journal of the Civil War
Era* 2, no. 2 (June 2012): 145–50.

McPherson, Edward. *A Handbook of Politics for 1868*. Washington, D.C.: Philip
and Solomons, 1868.

———. *The Political History of the United States of America, During the Great
Rebellion, From November 6, 1860, to July 4, 1864; . . . .* Washington, D.C.: Philip
and Solomons, 1864.

———. *The Political History of the United States of America during the Period of
Reconstruction, (From April 15, 1865 to July 15, 1870,) . . . .* Washington, D.C.:
Philip and Solomon, 1871.

McPherson, James M. *Abraham Lincoln and the Second American Revolution*.
New York: Oxford University Press, 1991.

———. *Battle Cry of Freedom*. New York: Oxford University Press, 1988.

"Message Proposing Constitutional Amendments." July 18, 1868. *Miller Center*.

https://millercenter.org/the-presidency/presidential-speeches/july-18-1868
-message-proposing-constitutional-amendments.

Messer-Kruse, Timothy. *The Yankee International: Marxism and the American Reform Tradition, 1848–1876.* Chapel Hill: University of North Carolina Press, 1998.

Mirabal, Nancy Raquel. *Suspect Freedoms: The Racial and Sexual Politics of Cubanidad in New York, 1823–1937.* New York: NYU Press, 2017.

Montgomery, Cora. *The King of Rivers with a Chart of Our Slave and Free Soil Territory.* New York: Charles Wood, 1850.

Moore, Barrington, Jr. *Social Origins of Dictatorship and Democracy: Lord and Peasant in the Making of the Modern World.* Boston: Beacon Press, 1966.

Morrison, Michael A. *Slavery and the American West: The Eclipse of Manifest Destiny and the Coming of the Civil War.* Chapel Hill: University of North Carolina Press, 1997.

Mota, Isadoura Moura. "On the Imminence of Emancipation: Black Geopolitical Literacy and Anglo-American Abolitionism in Nineteenth-Century Brazil." Ph.D. diss., Brown University, 2017.

Muller, Dalia Antonia. *Cuban Émigrés and Independence in the Nineteenth-Century Gulf World.* Chapel Hill: University of North Carolina Press, 2017.

———. "Cuban Émigrés, Mexican Politics and the 'Cuban Question,' 1895–1899." Ph.D. diss., University of California, Berkeley, 2007.

Murphy, Joseph T. "The British Example: West Indian Emancipation, the Freedom Principle, and the Rise of Antislavery Politics in the United States, 1833–1843." *Journal of the Civil War Era* 8, no. 4 (December 2018): 621–46.

Naish, Paul D. *Slavery and Silence: Latin America and the U.S. Slave Debate.* Philadelphia: University of Pennsylvania Press, 2017.

Naranjo Orovio, Consuelo. *La nación soñado: Cuba, Puerto Rico y Filipinas ante el 98.* Madrid: Doce Calles, 1996.

Neely, Mark E., Jr. *The Fate of Liberty: Abraham Lincoln and Civil Liberties.* New York: Oxford University Press, 1991.

Nelson, William E. *The Fourteenth Amendment: From Political Principle to Judicial Doctrine.* Cambridge, Mass.: Harvard University Press, 1988.

Nevins, Allan. *The War for the Union: War Becomes Revolution, 1862–1863.* New York: Konecky and Konecky, 1960.

Niven, John. *The Salmon P. Chase Papers.* 5 vols. Kent, Ohio: Kent State University Press, 1993–98.

Oakes, James. *Freedom National: The Destruction of Slavery in the United States.* New York: W. W. Norton, 2012.

———. *The Scorpion's Sting: Antislavery and the Coming of the Civil War.* New York: W. W. Norton, 2014.

Official Proceedings of the Democratic National Convention, Held in 1860, at Charleston and Baltimore. Cleveland, Ohio: Nevins' Print, 1860.

Opatrný, Josef. *U.S. Expansionism and Cuban Annexationism in the 1850s.* Lewiston, N.Y.: Edwin Mellen Press, 1993.

Orren, Karen. *Belated Feudalism: Labor, the Law, and Liberal Development in the United States.* New York: Cambridge University Press, 1991.

Osterhammel, Jürgen. *The Transformation of the World: A Global History of the Nineteenth Century.* Translated by Patrick Camiller. Princeton, N.J.: Princeton University Press, 2014.

Painter, Nell Irvin. *Exodusters: Black Migration to Kansas after Reconstruction.* New York: Alfred A. Knopf, 1976.

Paludin, Phillip S. *A Covenant with Death: The Constitution, Law, and Equality in the Civil War Era.* Urbana: University of Illinois Press, 1975.

Pani, Erika. "Dreaming of a Mexican Empire: The Political Projects of the 'Imperialistas.'" *Hispanic American Historical Review* 82, no. 1 (2002): 1–32.

———. *El Segundo Imperio: Pasados de usos múltiples.* Mexico City: CIDE, 2004.

———. *Una series de admirables acontecimientos: México y el mundo en la época de la Reforma, 1848–1867.* Mexico City: Educación y cultura, 2013.

Paquette, Gabriel. *Imperial Portugal in the Age of Atlantic Revolutions: The Luso-Brazilian World, c. 1770–1850.* New York: Cambridge University Press, 2013.

Paquette, Robert L. *Sugar Is Made with Blood: The Conspiracy of La Escalera and the Conflict between Empires over Slavery in Cuba.* Middletown, Conn.: Wesleyan University Press, 1990.

Parker, Noel. *Revolutions and History: An Essay in Interpretation.* Malden, Mass.: Blackwell, 1999.

Parrish, William Earl, ed. *The Civil War: A Second American Revolution?* New York: Holt, Rinehart, and Winston, 1970.

Patel, David, and Valerie Bunce. "Turning Points and the Cross-National Diffusion of Popular Protest." *Comparative Democratization* 10, no. 1 (2012): 10–13.

Pérez, Lisandro. "The Schism of 1868 and the Growth of Cuban New York." *Camino Real*, no. 10 (2015): 61–76.

———. *Sugar, Cigars, and Revolution: The Making of Cuban New York.* New York: New York University Press, 2018.

Pérez, Louis A., Jr. *Cuba: Between Reform and Revolution.* New York: Oxford University Press, 1988.

———. "We Are the World: Internationalizing the National, Nationalizing the International." *Journal of American History* 89 (2002): 558–66.

Pinchon, Edgcumb. *Dan Sickles, Hero of Gettysburg and "Yankee King of Spain."* Garden City, N.J.: Doubleday, Doran, 1945.

Pincus, Steve. *1688: The First Modern Revolution.* New Haven, Conn.: Yale University Press, 2009.

Piqueras, José A. *La revolución democrática: Cuestión social, colonialismo, y grupos de presión.* Madrid: Ediciones de la Revista de Trabajo y Seguridad Social, 1992.

Plummer, Brenda Gayle. *Haiti and the United States: The Psychological Moment.* Athens: University of Georgia Press, 1992.

Pomeroy, Earl S. "Lincoln, the Thirteenth Amendment, and the Admission of Nevada." In *Lincoln Looks West: From the Mississippi to the Pacific*, edited by

Richard W. Etulain, 113–20. Carbondale: Southern Illinois University Press, 2010.

Porter, Horace. *Campaigning with Grant.* New York: Century, 1897.

Potter, David. *The Impending Crisis, 1848–1861.* Completed and edited by Don E. Fehrenbacher. New York: Harper and Row, 1976.

Poyo, Gerald E. "The Evolution of Cuban Separatist Thought in the Emigré Communities of the United States, 1848–1895." *Hispanic American Historical Review* 66, no. 3 (August 1986): 485–507.

———. *Exile and Revolution: José D. Poyo, Key West, and Cuban Independence.* Gainesville: University of Florida Press, 2014.

———. *"With All and for the Good of All": The Emergency of Popular Nationalism in the Cuban Communities of the United States, 1848–1898.* Durham, N.C.: Duke University Press, 1989.

"Presidential Proclamations—Establishment of the Reconstruction Era National Monument." January 12, 2017. https://obamawhitehouse.archives.gov/the-press -office/2017/01/12/presidential-proclamations-establishment-reconstruction -era-national.

Prida Santacilia, Pablo. *Apuntes biográficos de Pedro Santacilia.* Mexico City: Secretaría de Educación Pública, 1966.

Priest, Andrew. "Thinking about Empire: The Administration of U. S. Grant, Spanish Colonialism and the Ten Years' War in Cuba." *Journal of American Studies* 48 (2014): 541–58.

Prim y Prats, Juan. *General McClellan and the Army of the Potomac.* New York: John Bradburn, 1864.

Quigley, David. *Second Founding: New York City, Reconstruction, and the Making of American Democracy.* New York: Farrar, Straus and Giroux, 2004.

Rael, Patrick. *Eighty-Eight Years: The Long Death of Slavery in the United States, 1777–1865.* Athens: University of Georgia Press, 2015.

Ramos Martínez, Jon Ander. "Manuel Calvo y Aguirre, una eminencia en la sombra." *Guregandik* 4 (2008): 210–77.

Randall, James G. *Constitutional Problems under Lincoln.* New York: D. Appleton, 1926.

Ransom, Roger L. "The Economics of Civil War." August 24, 2001. *EH.net.* https:// eh.net/encyclopedia/the-economics-of-the-civil-war/.

———. "Fact and Counterfact: The 'Second American Revolution' Revisited." *Civil War History* 45 (1999): 28–60.

———, and Richard Sutch. "Conflicting Visions: The American Civil War as a Revolutionary Event." *Research in Economic History* 20 (2001): 249–301.

Raymond, Henry J. *Disunion and Slavery. A Series of Letters to Hon. W. L. Yancey, of Alabama.* New York: N.p., 1861.

Reid-Vazquez, Michele. *The Year of the Lash: Free People of Color in Cuba and the Nineteenth-Century Atlantic World.* Athens: University of Georgia Press, 2011.

Report of the Joint Committee on Reconstruction at the First Session, Thirty-Ninth Congress. Washington, D.C.: Government Printing Office, 1866.

"Republican Party Platform of 1856." *The American Presidency Project.* https://www.presidency.ucsb.edu/documents/republican-party-platform-1856.

Reséndez, Andrés. *The Other Slavery: The Uncovered Story of Indian Enslavement in America.* Boston: Houghton Mifflin, 2016.

Richards, Leonard L. *The California Gold Rush and the Coming of the Civil War.* New York: Alfred A. Knopf, 2007.

———. *The Slave Power: The Free North and Southern Domination, 1780–1860.* Baton Rouge: Louisiana State University Press, 2000.

Roberts, Alaina E. "Chickasaw Freedpeople at the Crossroads of Reconstruction." Ph.D. diss., Indiana University, 2017.

Roberts, Timothy Mason. *Distant Revolutions: 1848 and the Challenge to American Exceptionalism.* Charlottesville: University of Virginia Press, 2009.

Rojas, Rafael. *Las repúblicas de aire: Utopía y desencanto en la revolución de Hispanoamérica.* Mexico City: Taurus, 2009.

Rosen, Jeffrey, and Tom Donnelly. "America's Unfinished Second Founding." October 19, 2015. *Atlantic.* https://www.theatlantic.com/politics/archive/2015/10/americas-unfinished-second-founding/411079/.

Rosen Jélomer, Jorge Boris, ed. *Pedro Santacilia: El hombre y su obra.* 2 vols. Mexico City: Centro de Investigación Científica Jorge L. Tamayo, 1983.

Rossiter, Clinton L. *Constitutional Dictatorship: Crisis Governance in the Modern Democracies.* Princeton, N.J.: Princeton University Press, 1948.

Rothera, Evan. "Civil Wars and Reconstruction in America: The United States, Mexico, and Argentina, 1860–1880." Ph.D. diss., Pennsylvania State University, 2017.

Rothman, Adam. *Beyond Freedom's Reach: A Kidnapping in the Twilight of Slavery.* Cambridge, Mass.: Harvard University Press, 2015.

Rugemer, Edward Bartlett. *The Problem of Emancipation: The Caribbean Roots of the Civil War.* Baton Rouge: Louisiana State University Press, 2008.

———. "Slave Rebels and Abolitionists: The Black Atlantic and the Coming of the Civil War." *Journal of the Civil War Era* 2, no. 2 (June 2012): 179–202.

Saba, Roberto. "American Mirror: The United States and the Empire of Brazil in the Age of Emancipation." Ph.D. diss., University of Pennsylvania, 2017.

Sabato, Hilda. "Arms and Republican Politics in Spanish America: The Critical 1860s." In *American Civil Wars: The United States, Latin America, Europe, and the Crisis of the 1860s,* edited by Don H. Doyle, 185–203. Chapel Hill: University of North Carolina Press, 2017.

Sampson, Robert D. *John L. O'Sullivan and His Times.* Kent, Ohio: Kent State University Press, 2003.

Sánchez, Romy. "Quitter la très fidele: Exilés et bannis au temps de séparatisme cubain (1834–1879)." Ph.D. diss., Université de Paris, Panthéon-Sorbonne, 2016.

Sánchez Andrés, Agustín, ed. *Castelar y el parlamentarismo decimonónico español: Discursos políticos.* Madrid: Comunidad de Madrid, 1999.

Sánchez del Real, Andrés. *Emilio Castelar: Su vida, su carácter, sus costumbres, sus obras, sus discursos, su influencia, en la idea democrática.* Barcelona: Administración, 1873.

Sanders, James E. *The Vanguard of the Atlantic World: Creating Modernity, Nation, and Democracy in Nineteenth-Century Latin America.* Durham, N.C.: Duke University Press, 2014.

Santacilia, Pedro. *El arpa del proscripto.* New York: J. Durand, 1864.

Sarracino, Rodolfo. *Inglaterra, sus dos caras en la lucha cubana por la abolición.* Havana: Editorial Letras Cubanas, 1989.

Sartorius, David. *Ever Faithful: Race, Loyalty, and the Ends of Empire in Spanish Cuba.* Durham, N.C.: Duke University Press, 2013.

Schmidt-Nowara, Christopher. *Empire and Antislavery: Spain, Cuba, and Puerto Rico, 1833–1874.* Pittsburgh: University of Pittsburgh Press, 1999.

———. "'La España Ultramarina': Colonialism and Nation-Building in Nineteenth-Century Spain." *European History Quarterly* 4, no. 22 (2004): 191–214.

———. "From Aggression to Crisis: The Spanish Empire in the 1860s." In *American Civil Wars: The United States, Latin America, Europe, and the Crisis of the 1860s,* edited by Don H. Doyle, 125–46. Chapel Hill: University of North Carolina Press, 2017.

———. *Slavery, Freedom, and Abolition in Latin America and the Atlantic World.* Albuquerque: University of New Mexico Press, 2011.

Schmitt, Carl. *Political Theology: Four Chapters on the Concept of Sovereignty.* Translated by George Schwab. Cambridge, Mass.: MIT Press, 1985.

Schneider, Elena A. *The Occupation of Havana: War, Trade, and Slavery in the Atlantic World.* Chapel Hill: Omohundro Institute/University of North Carolina Press, 2018.

Schoen, Brian. "The Civil War in Europe." In *The Cambridge History of the American Civil War,* Vol. 2: *Affairs of the State,* edited by Aaron Sheehan-Dean. New York: Cambridge University Press, 2019.

———. *The Fragile Fabric of Union: Cotton, Federal Politics, and the Global Origins of the Civil War.* Baltimore: Johns Hopkins University Press, 2011.

Schwartz, Delmore. *In Dreams Begin Responsibilities and Other Stories.* 3rd ed. New York: New Directions, 1978.

Scott, Julius. *The Common Wind: Afro-American Currents in the Age of Haitian Revolution.* New York: Verso, 2018.

Scott, Rebecca J. *Degrees of Freedom: Louisiana and Cuba after Slavery.* Cambridge, Mass.: Harvard University Press, 2005.

———. *Slave Emancipation in Cuba: The Transition to Free Labor in Cuba, 1860–1899.* Pittsburgh: University of Pittsburgh Press, 2000.

———, and Jean M. Hébrard. *Freedom Papers: An Atlantic Odyssey in the Age of Emancipation.* Cambridge, Mass.: Harvard University Press, 2012.

Scroggs, William O. *Filibusters and Financiers: The Story of William Walker and His Associates.* New York: Macmillan, 1916.

"Second Annual Message, December 1, 1862." *The American Presidency Project.* https://www.presidency.ucsb.edu/documents/second-annual-message-9.

"Second Inaugural of Ulysses S. Grant." March 4, 1873. *The Avalon Project.* avalon
.law.yale.edu/19th_century/grant2.asp.

Sefton, James E. *The United States Army and Reconstruction, 1865–1877.* Baton
Rouge: Louisiana State University Press, 1967.

Senate Document 112-9, 112th Cong., 2nd sess. Washington, D.C.: Government
Printing Office, 2012.

Senate Resolution 198. June 10, 2015. Congressional Record Online. https://www
.congress.gov/congressional-record/2015/6/10/senate-section/article/S4033-1.

Sewell, Richard H. *Ballots for Freedom: Antislavery Politics in the United States,
1837–1860.* New York: Oxford University Press, 1976.

Sexton, Jay. *The Monroe Doctrine: Empire and Nation in Nineteenth-Century
America.* New York: Hill and Wang, 2011.

———. "Steam Transport, Sovereignty, and Empire in North America, circa 1850–
1885." *Journal of the Civil War Era* 7, no. 4 (December 2017): 620–47.

———. "Toward a Synthesis of Foreign Relations in the Civil War Era, 1848–1877."
American Nineteenth Century History 5 (Fall 2004): 50–73.

———. "The United States, the Cuban Rebellion, and the Multilateral Initiative of
1875." *Diplomatic History* 30, no. 3 (June 2006): 335–65.

*The Sherman Letters: Correspondence between General and Senator Sherman from
1837 to 1891.* New York: Charles Scribner's Sons, 1894.

Sierra, Justo. *Juárez su obra y su tiempo, estudio histórico.* Mexico City: J. Bassescá,
1905.

Simon, John Y., et al., eds. *The Papers of Ulysses S. Grant.* 31 vols. Carbondale:
Southern Illinois University Press, 1967–2012.

Simpson, Brooks D. *Let Us Have Peace: Ulysses S. Grant and the Politics of War
and Reconstruction, 1861–1868.* Chapel Hill: University of North Carolina Press,
1991.

———. *The Reconstruction Presidents.* Lawrence: University Press of Kansas, 2009.

Skocpol, Theda. *States and Social Revolutions: A Comparative Analysis of France,
Russia, and China.* New York: Cambridge University Press, 1979.

Silber, Nina. *The Romance of Reunion: Northerners and the South, 1865–1900.*
Chapel Hill: University of North Carolina Press, 1993.

Sinha, Manisha. *The Slave's Cause: A History of Abolition.* New Haven, Conn.:
Yale University Press, 2016.

*Slavery in Cuba: A Report of the Proceedings of the Meeting, Held at the Cooper
Institute.* New York: Powers, MacGowan and Sleeper, 1872.

Slezkine, Yuri. *The House of Government: A Saga of the Russian Revolution.* Princeton, N.J.: Princeton University Press, 2017.

Slotkin, Richard. *The Long Road to Antietam: How the Civil War Became a Revolution.* New York: Liveright, 2012.

Smith, Adam I. P. *The Stormy Present: Conservatism and the Problem of Slavery in
Northern Politics, 1846–1865.* Chapel Hill: University of North Carolina Press,
2017.

Smith, Stacey L. *Freedom's Frontier: California and the Struggle over Unfree Labor,*

Emancipation, and Reconstruction. Chapel Hill: University of North Carolina Press, 2013.

Sohrabi, Nader. "Global Waves, Local Actors: What the Young Turks Knew about Other Revolutions and Why It Mattered." *Comparative Studies in Society and History* 44, no. 1 (January 2002): 45–79.

———. "Historicizing Revolutions: Constitutional Revolutions in the Ottoman Empire, Iran, and Russia, 1905–1908." *American Journal of Sociology* 100, no. 6 (May 1995): 1383–447.

"Special Session Message." July 4, 1861. *The American Presidency Project*. https://www.presidency.ucsb.edu/documents/special-session-message-5.

Sperber, Jonathan. *The European Revolutions, 1848–1851*. New York: Cambridge University Press, 1994.

Stanley, Amy Dru. *From Bondage to Contract: Wage Labor, Marriage, and the Market in the Era of Slave Emancipation*. New York: Cambridge University Press, 1998.

Steiner, Bernard C. *The Life of Reverdy Johnson*. Baltimore: Norman, Remington, 1914.

Stephens, Alexander H. "Corner Stone Speech." March 21, 1861, Savannah, Ga. *Teaching American History*. teachingamericanhistory.org/library/document/cornerstone-speech/.

Stiles, T. J. *The First Tycoon: The Epic Life of Cornelius Vanderbilt*. New York: Vintage, 2009.

Summers, Mark Wahlgren. *The Ordeal of the Reunion: A New History of Reconstruction*. Chapel Hill: University of North Carolina Press, 2014.

Surwillo, Lisa. "Poetic Diplomacy: Carolina Coronado and the American Civil War." *Comparative American Studies: An International Journal* 5, no. 4 (2007): 409–22.

"Symposium: Moments of Change: Transformation in American Constitutionalism." *Yale Law Journal* 108 (1999): 1917–2349.

Tamayo, Jorge L., ed. *Benito Juárez: Documentos, discursos y correspondencia*. 15 vols. Mexico City: Secretaria del Patrimonio Nacional, 1964–70.

Tarragó, Rafael E., ed. *Experiencias políticas de los cubanos en la Cuba española, 1512–1898*. Barcelona: Puvill Libros, 1995.

Taylor, Amy Murrell. *Embattled Freedom: Journeys through the Civil War's Slave Refugee Camps*. Chapel Hill: University of North Carolina Press, 2018.

Taylor, Richard. *Destruction and Reconstruction: Personal Experiences of the Late War*. New York: D. Appleton, 1879.

Temperley, Howard. "Anti-Slavery as a Form of Cultural Imperialism." In *Anti-Slavery, Religion, and Reform: Essays in Memory of Roger Anstey*, edited by Christine Bolt and Seymour Drescher, 335–50. Folkestone, U.K.: William Dawson and Sons, 1980.

Thomas, Brook. *Civic Myths: A Law-and-Literature Approach to Citizenship*. Chapel Hill: University of North Carolina Press, 2007.

———. *The Literature of Reconstruction: Not in Plain Black and White*. Baltimore: Johns Hopkins University Press, 2017.

Thomas, Kenneth R. *The Constitution of the United States of America, Analysis and Interpretation: Analysis of Cases Decided by the Supreme Court of the United States to June 28, 2012.* Washington, D.C.: Government Printing Office, 2013.

Tilly, Charles. *European Revolutions, 1492–1992.* Cambridge, Mass.: Blackwell, 1993.

Tomich, Dale W., ed. *New Frontiers of Slavery.* Albany: SUNY Press, 2016.

———, and Michael Zeuske. "The Second Slavery: Mass Slavery, World Economy and Comparative Microhistories." *Review: A Journal of the Fernand Braudel Center* 31, no. 3 (2008): 91–100.

Tutino, John. "The Americas in the Rise of Industrial Capitalism." In *New Countries: Capitalism, Revolutions, and Nations in the Americas, 1750–1870*, edited by John Tutino, 25–70. Durham, N.C.: Duke University Press, 2016.

———. "Introduction: Revolutions, Nations, and a New Industrial World." In *New Countries: Capitalism, Revolutions, and Nations in the Americas, 1750–1870*, edited by John Tutino, 1–24. Durham, N.C.: Duke University Press, 2016.

Towers, Frank. "Partisans, New History, and Modernization: The Historiography of the Civil War's Causes, 1861–2011." *Journal of the Civil War Era* 1, no. 2 (June 2011): 237–64.

Towle, George Makepeace. *Certain Men of Mark: Studies of Living Celebrities.* Boston: Roberts Brothers, 1880.

Trans-Atlantic Slave Trade Database. http://www.slavevoyages.org/assessment /estimates.

"Transcript of Gettysburg Address (1863)." https://www.ourdocuments.gov/doc .php?flash=false&doc=36&page=transcript.

"Transcript of President Abraham Lincoln's Second Inaugural." April 10, 1865. https://www.ourdocuments.gov/doc.php?flash=false&doc=38&page=transcript.

Trelease, Allen W. *White Terror: The Ku Klux Klan Conspiracy and Southern Reconstruction.* New York: Harper and Row, 1971.

Trimberger, Ellen Kay. *Revolution from Above: Military Bureaucrats and Development in Japan, Turkey, Egypt and Peru.* New Brunswick, N.J.: Transaction Books, 1978.

Trouillot, Michel-Rolph. *Silencing the Past: Power and the Production of History.* Boston: Beacon Press, 1995.

Turner, Henry McNeal Turner. "Fifteenth Amendment: A Speech on the Benefits Accruing from the Ratification of the Fifteenth Amendment and Its Incorporation into the United States Constitution. Delivered at the Celebration Held in Macon, Ga., April 19, 1870." *Digital Public Library of America.* http://dp.la/item /23419a844e5c48fb5efb5606402o0bb0e.

Tyrrell, Ian. *Transnational Nation: United States History in Global Perspective since 1789.* New York: Palgrave Macmillan, 2007.

Tyson, Timothy B. *Radio Free Dixie: Robert F. Williams and the Roots of Black Power.* Chapel Hill: University of North Carolina Press, 1999.

Urban, C. Stanley. "The Africanization of Cuba Scare, 1853–1855." *Hispanic American Historical Review* 37, no. 1 (February 1957): 29–45.

Valelly, Richard M. *The Two Reconstructions: The Struggle for Black Enfranchisement.* Chicago: University of Chicago Press, 2004.

Valero Escandell, José Ramón, ed. *La palabra de Emilio Castelar.* Alicante, Spain: Universidad de Alicante, 1984.

Varon, Elizabeth R. *Armies of Deliverance: A New History of the Civil War.* New York: Oxford University Press, 2019.

Venegas Delgado, Hernán M. *La Gran Colombia: México y la independencia de las Antillas Hispanas.* Mexico City: Plaza y Valdés, 2010.

"Veto Message on Admitting Nebraska into the Union." January 29, 1867. *Miller Center.* https://millercenter.org/the-presidency/presidential-speeches/january -29-1867-veto-message-admitting-nebraska-union.

"Veto Message on Legislation Amending the Judiciary." March 25, 1868. *Miller Center.* https://millercenter.org/the-presidency/presidential-speeches/march -25-1868-veto-message-legislation-amending-judiciary.

Vichese García, Jorge. *Emilio Castelar: La patria y la república.* Madrid: Biblioteca Nueva, 2001.

Vicuña Mackenna, Benjamin. *Diez meses de misión a los Estados Unidos de Norte America como ajente confidencial de Chile por B. Vicuña Mackenna.* Santiago: Imprenta de la Libertad, 1867.

Volck, Adalbert J. "The Knight of the Rueful Countenance." *A. Lincoln at 200,* Newberry Library and Chicago History Museum. https://publications.newberry .org/lincoln/items/show/190.

Vorenberg, Michael. "The 1866 Civil Rights Act and the Beginning of Military Reconstruction." In *The Greatest and the Grandest Act: The Civil Rights Act of 1866 from Reconstruction to Today,* edited by Christian G. Samito, 60–88. Carbondale: Southern Illinois University Press, 2018.

———. *Final Freedom: The Civil War, the Abolition of Slavery, and the Thirteenth Amendment.* New York: Cambridge University Press.

Wakelyn, Jon L. *Southern Pamphlets on Secession, November 1860–April 1861.* Chapel Hill: University of North Carolina Press, 1996.

Waldstreicher, David. *Slavery's Constitution: From Revolution to Ratification.* New York: Hill and Wang, 2009.

Walt, Stephen M. *Revolution and War.* Ithaca, N.Y.: Cornell University Press, 1996.

Walzer, Michael. *The Revolution of the Saints: A Study in the Origins of Radical Politics.* Cambridge, Mass.: Harvard University Press, 1965.

Wang, Xi. *The Trial of Democracy: Black Suffrage and Northern Republicans, 1860–1910.* Athens: University of Georgia Press, 1996.

The War of the Rebellion: A Compilation of the Official Records of the Union and Confederate Armies. 70 vols. Washington, D.C.: Government Printing Office, 1881–1901.

Washington, Booker T. *The Negro in Business.* Coshocton, Ohio: Vail, 1907.

Way, Lucan. "The Real Causes of the Color Revolutions." *Journal of Democracy* 19, no. 3 (July 2008): 55–69.

Welles, Gideon. *Diary of Gideon Welles, Secretary of the Navy under Lincoln and Johnson.* 3 vols. Boston: Houghton Mifflin, 1911.

Weyland, Kurt. "The Diffusion of Revolution: '1848' in Europe and Latin America." *International Organization* 63, no. 3 (Summer 2009): 391–423.

"Whig Party Platform of 1852." *The American Presidency Project*. https://www.presidency.ucsb.edu/documents/whig-party-platform-1852.

White, G. Edward. "Recovering the Legal History of the Confederacy." *Washington and Lee Legal Review* 68, no. 2 (2011): 467–556.

Wiecek, William M. *The Sources of Anti-Slavery Constitutionalism in America, 1760–1848*. Ithaca, N.Y.: Cornell University Press, 1977.

Wilentz, Sean. *No Property in Man: Slavery and Antislavery at the Nation's Founding*. Cambridge, Mass.: Harvard University Press, 2018.

Williams, Kidada. *They Left Great Marks on Me: African American Testimonies of Racial Violence from Emancipation to World War I*. New York: NYU Press, 2012.

———. "The Wounds that Cried Out: Reckoning with African Americans' Testimonies of Trauma and Suffering from Nightriding." In *The World the Civil War Made*, edited by Gregory P. Downs and Kate Masur, 159–82. Chapel Hill: University of North Carolina Press, 2015.

Williams, Lou Falkner. *The Great South Carolina Ku Klux Klan Trials, 1871–1872*. Athens: University of Georgia Press, 2004.

Wilson, Woodrow. "The Reconstruction of the Southern States." *Atlantic Monthly*, January 1901.

Witt, John Fabian. *Lincoln's Code*: *The Laws of War in American History*. New York: Free Press, 2012.

Yeats, William Butler. *The Collected Poems of W. B. Yeats.* Edited by Richard J. Finneran. London: Woodworth Editions, 1994.

Young, John Russell. *Around the World with General Grant: A Narrative of the Visit of General U.S. Grant, Ex-president of the United States, to Various Countries in Europe, Asia, and Africa, in 1877, 1878, 1879. . . .* 2 vols. New York: Subscription Book Department, 1879.

Zaforteza, Carlos Alfaro. "The *Moderado* Party and the Introduction of Steam Power in the Spanish Navy, 1844–1854." *War in History* 13, no. 4 (November 2006): 441–67.

Zimmerman, Andrew, ed. *The Civil War in the United States: Karl Marx and Friedrich Engels.* New York: International Publishers, 2016.

———. "From the Rhine to the Mississippi: Property, Democracy, and Socialism in the American Civil War." *Journal of the Civil War Era* 5, no. 1 (March 2015): 3–37.

———. "From the Second American Revolution to the First International and Back Again." In *The World the Civil War Made*, edited by Gregory P. Downs and Kate Masur, 304–36. Chapel Hill: University of North Carolina Press, 2015.

INDEX